# AMERICA?

## DATE DUE

# WHO'S RUNNING AMERICA?

## the

### carter

### years

## Second Edition

**THOMAS R. DYE**
*Florida State University*

PRENTICE-HALL, INC., ENGLEWOOD CLIFFS, NEW JERSEY 07632

*Library of Congress Cataloging in Publication Data*

DYE, THOMAS R. (date).
  Who's Running America?

    Includes bibliographical references and index.
    1. Elite (Social sciences)—United States.
I. Title.
HN90.E4D93  1978       301.44'92'0973       78-18936
ISBN 0-13-958462-5

© 1979, 1976 by Prentice-Hall, Inc., Englewood Cliffs, N.J. 07632

Printed in the United States of America

10  9  8  7  6  5  4  3  2

PRENTICE-HALL INTERNATIONAL, INC., *London*
PRENTICE-HALL OF AUSTRALIA PTY. LIMITED, Sydney
PRENTICE-HALL OF CANADA, LTD., *Toronto*
PRENTICE-HALL OF INDIA PRIVATE LIMITED, *New Delhi*
PRENTICE-HALL OF JAPAN, INC., *Tokyo*
PRENTICE-HALL OF SOUTHEAST PTE. LTD., *Singapore*
WHITEHALL BOOKS LIMITED, *Wellington, New Zealand*

# contents

# preface

*Who's Running America? The Carter Years* was *not* supported by any grant or contract from any institution, public or private. It grew out of a graduate seminar at the Florida State University on "Research on Power and Elites" in the spring of 1972. Biographical data for over 5000 members of various institutional elites was painstakingly collected and coded by students. John W. Pickering, now Assistant Professor of Political Science at Memphis State University, made the most important contributions, and his Ph.D. dissertation, "The Concentration of Power and Authority in the American Political System," deserves independent reading by serious students of American elites. Others making significant contributions were Eugene R. DeClercq, now Assistant Professor of Political Science at George Washington University, and G. Edward Weston, Assistant Professor of Journalism at the University of Florida.

Two articles based on the same data collected for this work were published in social science journals in the early seventies:

Thomas R. Dye, Eugene R. DeClercq, and John W. Pickering, "Concentration, Specialization, and Interlocking among Institutional Elites," *Social Science Quarterly* (June 1973), pp. 8–28.

Thomas R. Dye and John W. Pickering, "Governmental and Corporate Elites: Convergence and Specialization," *Journal of Politics* (November 1974), pp. 900–925.

We are grateful to the editors of these journals, Charles Bonjean and Donald Strong, for their assistance and encouragement. We are also indebted to a number of commentators who wrote us before and after publication of these articles, including scholars G. William Domhoff, Suzanne Keller, John Walton, Robert Lineberry, and Victor Reinemer of the staff of the Senate Committee on Government Affairs.

The absence of any sources of support, and the magnitude of the data collection involved, slowed work on the volume and produced several problems that may disturb some readers. The most serious problem is the time lag between original data collection, which was based on 1972 sources, and the publication date of this volume, 1979. The Second Edition updates much of our data to 1977, but the statistical analysis and tables presented in Part III are still based upon our original data collection. We do not believe these time lags affect any major findings (although we note in Chapter 7 the recent addition of a small number of women and blacks to top institutional positions); but there will be some discrepancies between our reported data and institutional leadership today.

The First Edition of this book was published in 1976 and described national leadership in the Nixon-Ford years. The First Edition was subtitled, "Institutional Leadership in the United States." Our concern is still with the top institutional leadership in the nation, both public and private.

The Second Edition of this volume—"The Carter Years"—reflects the changes in national leadership which occurred with the election of Jimmy Carter to the presidency and the advent of a new Democratic administration. The year 1977 brought many "new faces" into power in Washington, not only in the executive branch, but in Congress as well.

Jimmy Carter, virtually unknown to the general public in early 1976 eked out a narrow victory over President Gerald Ford in November 1976 and brought a new cabinet into office in January 1977. We will contend Carter was *not* unknown to the "Establishment"; that his selection as Democratic nominee was in part a result of considered judgment by the Establishment that a new, trustworthy face was desirable after the Vietnam and Watergate years; and that his cabinet is reflective of traditional, established liberal leadership. Leadership in Congress also changed in 1977: Robert Byrd replaced Mike Mansfield as Senate Majority Leader; Thomas P. "Tip" O'Neil replaced Carl Albert as Speaker of the House; Howard Baker replaced Hugh Scott as Senate Minority Leader; and so on. But again, we will contend that the new faces represented only a superficial change; that the new congressional leadership was chosen from among "established" leaders on Capitol hill; and that no significant changes in national policy can be expected. Finally, we shall note some changes in the leadership of industry, banking, utilities, the mass media, the foundations, the universities, and the civic organizations over the past few years. But these changes are minimal. Indeed, most of the individuals named in the First Edition are still running these nongovernmental sectors of American society. And even when the names change, the social backgrounds, values and attitudes, modes of inter- action, and basic policy directions do not change.

This volume is divided into three parts. Part I, Power in American Society, sets forth our questions for research, defines terms and concepts, and explains our method of identifying the nation's institutional elite. Part II, Institutional Leadership in America, describes concentration of power in industry, finance, insurance, utilities, government, the news media, the law, foundations, civic and cultural organizations, and uni- versities. It also describes the type of persons who occupy top institu- tional leadership positions in these various sectors of society: it "names names" and, in so doing, makes use of brief biographical sketches. These sketches are designed to give us a general introduction to the character- istics of elites: the schools they attend, their early careers, their record of achievement, and the multiple positions of leadership that they oc- cupy. These sketches are derived from a wide variety of sources—*Who's Who in America, Current Biography, Forbes, Fortune, Congressional Quarterly,* and individual articles and books collected by myself and my students over several years.[1] The sketches in Part II are designed to pave the way for more systematic analysis of biographical data, which follows in Part III.

Part III, The Structure of Institutional Elites, is a systematic in- vestigation of such factors as interlocking and specialization among elites, overlapping elite membership, recruitment paths, socioeconomic back- grounds, previous experience, racial and sexual bias, club membership and life styles, attitudes and opinions, competition and consensus, fac- tionalism, and patterns of interaction in policymaking. Part III relies heavily on computerized biographical files which we compiled at Florida State University over an extended time period on several thousand top institutional elites. What is suggested in a general way about character- istics of America's elites in Part II is subject to more careful systematic analysis in Part III.

The decision to "name names" was carefully considered. We know that occupants of top institutional positions change over time, and that some of our information would be out of date by the time of publication.

---

[1] *Who's Who in America,* published biannually by Marquis Who's Who, Inc., Chicago; *Current Biography,* published monthly and annually by H. L. Wilson Co., New York; *Forbes,* published biweekly by Malcom S. Forbes, New York; *Fortune,* published monthly by Time-Life, Inc., New York; *Congressional Quarterly Weekly Report,* published weekly by Congressional Quarterly, Inc., Washington.

And with thousands of names, some mistakes are inevitable. But the biographical sketches provide "flesh and bones" to the statistical analysis—they "personalize" the numbers and percentages in our research. The men who run America *are* real people, and we know of no better way to impress our readers with this fact.

# WHO'S RUNNING AMERICA?

# POWER
# IN
# AMERICAN SOCIETY

part I

# men
# at the top

▶▶▶▶▶▶▶▶▶▶▶▶▶▶▶▶▶▶▶▶▶▶▶▶▶▶▶▶▶▶▶▶▶▶▶▶▶▶▶▶▶▶▶▶▶▶▶▶▶▶▶▶▶▶▶▶▶▶▶▶▶▶

# 1

Great power in America is concentrated in a tiny handful of men. A few thousand individuals out of 215 million Americans decide about war and peace, wages and prices, consumption and investment, employment and production, law and justice, taxes and benefits, education and learning, health and welfare, advertising and communication, life and leisure. In all societies—primitive and advanced, totalitarian and democratic, capitalist and socialist—only a few men exercise great power. This is true whether such power is exercised in the name of "the people" or not.

*Who's Running America?* is about men at the top of the institutional structure in America—who they are, how much power they wield, how they came to power, and what they do with it. In a modern, complex industrial society, power is concentrated in large institutions—corporations, banks, utilities, insurance companies, broadcasting networks, the White House, Congress and the Washington bureaucracy, the military establishment, the prestigious law firms, the foundations, and the universities. The men at the top of these institutions are the objects of our study in this book.

We want to ask such questions as: Who occupies the top positions of authority in America? How concentrated or dispersed is power in this nation? How do these institutional leaders attain their positions? What are their backgrounds, attitudes, and goals? What relationships exist among and between these men of power? How much cohesion or competition characterizes their relationships? Do they agree or disagree on crucial issues confronting the nation? How do they go about making important decisions or undertaking new programs or policies?

An *elite* is the few that have power in society; the *masses* are the many who do not. We shall call our men of power "elites" because they possess formal authority over large institutions which shape the lives of all Americans.

America is by no means unique in its concentration of great power in the hands of a few. The universality of elites is a prominent theme in the works of scholars throughout the ages. The Italian sociologist Vilfredo Pareto put it succinctly: "Every people is governed by an elite, by a chosen element of the population." [1]

Traditional social theorizing about elites views them as essential, functional components of social organization. The necessity of elites derives from the general need for *order* in society. Whenever human beings find themselves living together, they establish a set of ordered relationships so that they can know how others around them will behave. Without ordered behavior, the concept of society itself would be impossible. Among these ordered relationships is the expectation that a few people will make decisions on behalf of the group. Even in primitive societies, someone has to decide when the hunt will begin, how it will proceed, and what will be done with the catch.

Nearly two centuries ago Alexander Hamilton defended the existence of the elite by writing, "All communities divide themselves into the few and the many. The first are the rich and well-born, the other the masses of people. The voice of the people has been said to be the voice of God; and however generally this maxim has been quoted and believed, it is not true in fact. The people are turbulent and changing, they seldom judge or determine right." [2] The Italian political scientist Gaetano Mosca agreed, saying that the elite, "always the less numerous, performs all of the political functions, monopolizes power, and enjoys the advantages that power brings, whereas the second, the more numerous class, is directed and controlled by the first, in a manner that is now more or less legal, now more or less arbitrary and violent." [3] Contemporary social scientists have echoed the same theme. Sociologist Robert Lynd writes:

> It is the necessity in each society—if it is to be a society, not a rabble—to order the relations of men and their institutional ways of achieving needed ends. . . . Organized power exists—always and everywhere, in societies large or small, primitive or modern—because it performs the necessary function

[1] V. Pareto, *Mind and Society* (New York: Harcourt, Brace, and Co., 1935), p. 246.
[2] A. Hamilton, *Records of the Federal Convention of 1797.*
[3] G. Mosca, *The Ruling Class* (New York: McGraw-Hill Book Co., 1939), p. 50.

of establishing and maintaining the version of order by which a given society in a given time and place lives.[4]

Political scientists Harold Lasswell and Daniel Lerner are even more explicit: "The discovery that in all large-scale societies the decisions at any given time are typically in the hands of a small number of people, confirms a basic fact: Government is always government by the few, whether in the name of the few, the one, or the many." [5]

Elitism is *not* a result of inadequate education of the masses, or of poverty, or of a "military-industrial complex," or of capitalist control of the mass media, or of any special problem in society. The necessity for leadership in social organizations applies universally. Robert Michels, who as a student was active in socialist politics in Europe in the early 1900s, concluded reluctantly that elitism was *not* a product of capitalism. *All* large organizations—political parties, labor unions, governments— are oligarchies, even radical *socialist* parties. In Michels' words, "He who says organization says oligarchy." Michels explains his famous "iron law of oligarchy" as a characteristic of *any* social system.[6]

Thus, the elitist character of American society is not a product of political conspiracy, capitalist exploitation, or any specific malfunction of democracy. *All* societies are elitist. There cannot be large institutions without great power being concentrated within the hands of the few at the summit of these institutions—the men at the top.

## THE INSTITUTIONAL BASIS OF POWER

Power is not an attribute of individuals but of social organizations. Accordingly, although power may be most evident in its exercise, its true essence is the potential for control in society that accompanies certain roles in the social system. This notion reflects Max Weber's classic formulation of the definition of power:

> In general, we understand by "power" the *chance* of a man or of a number of men to realize their own will in a communal act even against the resistance of others who are participating in the action.[7]

4 Robert Lynd, "Power in American Society," in *Problems of Power in American Society,* ed. Arthur Kornhauser (Detroit: Wayne State University Press, 1957), pp. 3–4.

5 Harold Lasswell and Daniel Lerner, *The Comparative Study of Elites* (Stanford: Stanford University Press, 1952), p. 7.

6 Robert Michels, *Political Parties: A Sociological Study of the Oligarchical Tendencies of Modern Democracy* (1915) (New York: Free Press, 1962), p. 70.

7 In Hans Gerth and C. Wright Mills, eds., *From Max Weber* (New York: Oxford University Press, 1946), p. 180.

"Chance" in this context means the opportunity or capacity for effecting one's will. Viewed in this fashion, power is not so much the *act* of control as the *potential to act*—the social *expectation* that such control is possible and legitimate—that defines power.

Power is simply the capacity or potential of persons in certain roles to make decisions that affect the conduct of others in the social system. Sociologist Robert O. Schultze puts it in these words:

> . . . a few have emphasized that *act as such* rather than the *potential to act* is the crucial aspect of power. It seems far more sociologically sound to accept a Weberian definition which stresses the potential to act. Power may thus be conceived as an inherently group-linked property, an attribute of social statuses rather than of individual persons. . . . Accordingly, power will denote the *capacity* or *potential* of persons *in certain statuses* to set conditions, make decisions, and/or take actions which are determinative for the existence of others within a given social system.[8]

Thus, elites are people who occupy power roles in society. In a modern, complex society, these roles are institutionalized; the elite are the individuals who occupy positions of authority in large institutions. Authority is the expected and legitimate capacity to direct, manage, and guide programs, policies, and activities of the major institutions of society.

It is true, of course, that not all power is institutionalized. Power can be exercised in transitory and informal groups and in interpersonal interactions. Power is exercised, for example, when a mugger stops a pedestrian on the street and forces him to give up his wallet, or when a political assassin murders a President. But great power is found only in institutional roles. C. Wright Mills, a socialist critic of the structure of power in American society, observed:

> No one . . . can be truly powerful unless he has access to the command of major institutions, for it is over these institutional means of power that the truly powerful are, in the first instance, powerful.[9]

Adolf A. Berle, who spent a lifetime studying private property and the American corporation, was equally impressed with the institutional basis of power:

> Power is invariably organized and transmitted through institutions.

[8] Robert O. Schultze, "The Bifurcation of Power in a Satellite City," in *Community Political Systems*, ed. Morris Janowitz (Glencoe: Free Press, 1961), p. 20.
[9] C. Wright Mills, *The Power Elite* (New York: Oxford University Press, 1956), p. 9.

Top power holders must work through existing institutions, perhaps extending or modifying them, or must at once create new institutions. There is no other way of exercising power—unless it is limited to the range of the power holder's fist or his gun.[10]

Individuals do not become powerful simply because they have particular qualities, valuable skills, burning ambitions, or sparkling personalities. These assets may be helpful in gaining positions of power, but it is the position itself that gives an individual control over the activities of other individuals. This relationship between power and institutional authority in modern society is described by Mills:

> If we took the one hundred most powerful men in America, the one hundred wealthiest, and the one hundred most celebrated away from the institutional positions they now occupy, away from their resources of men and women and money, away from the media of mass communication . . . then they would be powerless and poor and uncelebrated. For power is not of a man. Wealth does not center in the person of the wealthy. Celebrity is not inherent in any personality. To be clelebrated, to be wealthy, to have power, requires access to major institutions, for the institutional positions men occupy determine in large part their chances to have and to hold these valued experiences.[11]

Power, then, is an attribute of *roles* in a social system, not an attribute of individuals. People are powerful when they occupy positions of authority and control in social organizations. Once they occupy these positions, their power is felt as a result not only in their actions but in their failures to act as well. Both have great impact on the behaviors of others. Elites "are in positions to make decisions having major consequences. Whether they do or do not make such decisions is less important than the fact that they do occupy such pivotal positions: their failure to act, their failure to make a decision, is itself an act that is often of greater consequence than the decisions they do make." [12]

Political scientists Peter Bachrach and Morton S. Baratz have argued persuasively that individuals in top institutional positions exercise power whether they act overtly to influence particular decisions or not.[13] They contend that when the social, economic, and political values of elite groups or, more importantly, the structure of the institutions themselves, limit the scope of decision making to only those issues which do not threaten top elites, then power is being exercised. Bachrach and

---

[10] Adolf A. Berle, *Power* (New York: Harcourt, Brace and World, 1967), p. 92.

[11] Mills, *The Power Elite*, p. 9.

[12] *Ibid.*, p. 4.

[13] Peter Bachrach and Morton S. Baratz, "Decisions and Non-Decisions," *American Political Science Review*, 57 (September 1963), 632–642.

Baratz refer to this phenomenon as *"non*–decision making." A has power over B when he succeeds in suppressing issues that might in their resolution be detrimental to A's preferences. In short, the institutional structure of our society (and the people at the top of that sructure) encourages the development of some kinds of public issues, but prevents other kinds of issues from ever being considered by the American public. Such "non–decision making" provides still another reason for studying institutional leadership.

## POWER AS DECISION MAKING: AN ALTERNATIVE VIEW

It is our contention, then, that great power is institutionalized—that it derives from roles in social organizations and that individuals who occupy top institutional positions possess power whether they act directly to influence particular decisions or not. But these views—often labeled as "elitist"—are not universally shared among social scientists. We are aware that our institutional approach to power conflicts with the approach of many scholars who believe that power can only be viewed in a decision-making context.

This alternative approach to power—often labeled as "pluralist" —defines power as *active participation in decision making.* Persons are said to have power *only* when they participate directly in particular decisions. Pluralist scholars would object to our presumption that people who occupy institutional positions and who have formal authority over economic, governmental, or social affairs necessarily have power. Pluralists differentiate between the "potential" for power (which is generally associated with top institutional positions) and "actual" power (which assumes active participation in decision making). Political scientist Robert A. Dahl writes:

> Suppose a set of individuals in a political system has the following property: there is a high probability that if they agree on a key political alternative, and if they all act in some specified way, then that alternative will be chosen. We may say of such a group that it has a high *potential* for control. . . . But a *potential* for control is not, except in a peculiarly Hobbesian world, equivalent to *actual* control.[14]

Pluralists contend that the potential for power is not power itself. Power occurs in individual interactions: "A has power over B to the

---

[14] Robert A. Dahl, "Critique of the Ruling Elite Model," *American Political Science Review*, 52 (June 1958), 66. [Italics mine.]

extent that he can get B to do something that B would not otherwise do." [15] We should not simply assume that power attaches to high office. Top institutional officeholders may or may not exercise power—their "power" depends upon their active participation in particular decisions. They may choose not to participate in certain decisions; their influence may be limited to specific kinds of decisions; they may be constrained by formal and informal checks on their discretion; they may be forced to respond to the demands of individuals or groups within or outside the institutions they lead; they may have little real discretion in their choice among alternative courses of action.

Pluralists would argue that research into institutional leadership can describe at best only the *potential* for control that exists within American society. They would insist that research on national leadership proceed by careful examination of a series of important national decisions—that the individuals who took an active part in these decisions be identified and a full account of their decision-making behavior be obtained. Political scientist Nelson Polsby, a former student of Robert A. Dahl at Yale, reflects the interests of pluralists in observing specific decisions:

> How can one tell, after all, whether or not an actor is powerful unless some sequence of events, competently observed, attests to his power? If these events take place, then the power of the actor is not "potential" but actual. If these events do not occur, then what grounds have we to suppose that the actor is powerful?[16]

And, indeed, much of the best research and writing in political science has proceeded by studying specific cases in the uses of power.

Pluralism, of course, is more than a definition of power and a method of study—it is an integrated body of theory that seeks to reaffirm the fundamental democratic character of American society. Pluralism arose in response to criticisms of the American political system to the effect that individual participation in a large, complex, bureaucratic society was increasingly difficult. Traditional notions of democracy had stressed individual participation of all citizens in the decisions that shape their own lives. But it was clear to scholars of all persuasions that relatively few individuals in America have any *direct* impact on national decision making.

Pluralism developed as an ideology designed to reconcile the *ideals* of democracy with the *realities* of a large-scale, industrial, technocratic

---

[15] Robert A. Dahl, "The Concept of Power," *Behavioral Science,* 2 (1957), 202.
[16] Nelson Polsby, *Community Power and Political Theory* (New Haven: Yale University Press, 1963), p. 60.

society. Jack L. Walker writes that the "principal aim" of the pluralists "has been to make the theory of democracy more realistic, to bring it into closer correspondence with empirical reality. They are convinced that the classical theory does not account for 'much of the real machinery' by which the system operates." [17]

Pluralists recognize that an elite few, rather than the masses, rule America and that "it is difficult—nay impossible—to see how it could be otherwise in large political systems." [18] However, they reassert the essentially democratic character of America by arguing that:

1. While individuals do not participate directly in decision making, they can join organized *groups* and make their influence felt through group participation.
2. Competition between leadership groups helps protect the individual—that is, countervailing centers of power check each other and guard against abuse of power.
3. Individuals can choose between competing groups in elections.
4. Leadership groups are not closed; new groups can be formed and gain access to the political system.
5. The existence of multiple leadership groups in society gives rise to a "polyarchy." Leaders who exercise power over some kinds of decisions do not necessarily exercise power over other kinds of decisions.
6. Public policy may not be majority preference, but it is the rough equilibrium of group influence and therefore a reasonable approximation of society's preferences.

We are committed in this volume to the study of the institutional structure of American society, for the reasons cited earlier. It is *not* our purpose to assert the superiority of our approach to power in America over the approaches recommended by others. We do *not* intend to debate the merits of "pluralism" or "elitism" as political philosophies. Abstract arguments over conceptualizations, definitions, and method of study already abound in the literature on power. Rather, working within an *institutional* paradigm, we intend to present systematic evidence about the concentration of resources in the nation's largest institutions, to find out who occupies top positions in these institutions, to explore interlocking and convergence among these top position-holders, to learn how they rose to their positions, to investigate the extent of their consensus or disagreement over the major issues confronting the nation, to explore the extent of competition and factionalism among various segments of

---

[17] Jack L. Walker, "A Critique of the Elitist Theory of Democracy," *American Political Science Review*, 60 (June 1966), 286.

[18] Robert A. Dahl, "Power, Pluralism and Democracy," paper delivered at the Annual Meeting of the American Political Science Association, 1966, p. 3.

the nation's institutional leadership, and to learn how institutional leadership interacts in national policy making.

We hope to avoid elaborate theorizing about power, pluralism, and elitism. We propose to present what we believe to be interesting data on national institutional elites and to permit our readers to relate it to their own theory or theories of power.

## IDENTIFYING POSITIONS OF POWER

A great deal has been said about "the power elite," "the ruling class," "the liberal establishment," "the military-industrial complex," "the rich and the super-rich," and so on. But even though many of these notions are interesting and insightful, we never really encounter a systematic definition of precisely *who* these people are, how we can identify them, how they came to power, and what they do with their power.

Admittedly, the systematic study of power and elites is a frustrating task. Political scientists Herbert Kaufman and Victor Jones once observed:

> There is an elusiveness about power that endows it with an almost ghostly quality. It seems to be all around us, yet this is "sensed" with some sixth means of reception rather than with the five ordinary senses. We "know" what it is, yet we encounter endless difficulties in trying to define it. We can "tell" whether one person or group is more powerful than another, yet we cannot measure power. It is as abstract as time yet as real as a firing squad.[19]

We agree that power is elusive and that elites are not easy to identify, particularly in a society like ours. Scholars have encountered great difficulty in finding a specific working definition of a national elite—a definition that can be used to actually identify men of power. But this is the necessary starting place for any serious inquiry into power in America.

So our first task is to develop an operational *definition* of a national elite. We must formulate a definition that is consistent with our theoretical notions about the institutional basis of power that enables us to identify, by name and position, those individuals who possess great power in America.

Our "men at the top" will be individuals who occupy *the top positions in the institutional structure of American society*. These are

[19] Herbert Kaufman and Victor Jones, "The Mystery of Power," *Public Administration Review*, 14 (Summer 1954), 205.

the individuals who possess the formal authority to direct, manage, and guide programs, policies, and activities of the major corporate, governmental, legal, educational, civic, and cultural institutions in the nation. Our definition of a national elite, then, is consistent with the notion that great power in America resides in large institutions.

For purposes of analysis in this book, we have divided society into three sectors—corporate, governmental, and public interest.

In the *corporate sector,* our operational definition of the elite is *those individuals who occupy formal positions of authority in institutions that control over half of the nation's total corporate assets.* The corporate sector includes industrial corporations; utilities, transportation, and communications; banking; and insurance. Our procedure in identifying the largest corporations was to rank corporations by the size of their assets, and then to cumulate these assets, moving from the top of the rankings down, until roughly 50 percent of the nation's total assets in each field were included. (See Tables 2–1, 2–2, 2–3, and 2–4 in the next chapter.) Then we identified by name the presidents and directors of these corporations. This procedure produced a list of 3,572 names of individuals at the top of the corporate world in 1970.

In the *governmental sector,* the operational definition of the elite is *those individuals who occupy formal positions of authority in the major civilian and military bureaucracies of the national government.* Positions of authority in the governmental sector were defined as the President and Vice-President; secretaries, under secretaries, and assistant secretaries of all executive departments; White House presidential advisers and ambassadors-at-large; congressional committee chairpersons and ranking minority committee members in the House and Senate; House and Senate majority and minority party leaders and whips; Supreme Court Justices; members of the Federal Reserve Board and the Council of Economic Advisers. This group totaled 227 in 1970. The military bureaucracy—because of its special theoretical interest and prominence in traditional elite literature—is included in the governmental sector. (The military is also treated separately where appropriate.) Positions of authority in the military include both civilian offices and top military commands: secretaries, under secretaries, and assistant secretaries of the Departments of the Army, Navy, Air Force; all four-star generals and admirals in the Army, Navy, Air Force, and Marine Corps, including the chairman of the Joint Chiefs of Staff; the chiefs of staff and vice-chiefs of staff of the Army and Air Force, the chief and vice-chief of Naval Operations, and the commanding officers of the major military commands. In 1970 there were 18 Army generals, 13 Air Force generals, nine admirals, and two Marine generals, in addition to civilian officials, for a total of 59 positions.

In the *public interest sector,* our definition of the elite is *those individuals who occupy formal positions of authority in the mass media, the prestigious law firms, the major philanthropic foundations, the leading universities, and the recognized national civic and cultural organizations.* The identification of these institutions involves some subjective judgments. These judgments can be defended, but we recognize that other judgments could be made. In the *mass media* we include the three television networks: CBS, NBC, and ABC; The *New York Times*; Time, Inc.; *Washington Post-Newsweek*; Associated Press and United Press International wire services; and ten newspaper chains which account for one-third of the nation's daily newspaper circulation. There are 213 presidents and directors of these institutions. Because of the rapidly growing influence of the mass media in America's elite structure, we have devoted a special chapter to "the newsmakers." Other public interest elites are considered together under the general heading of The Civic Establishment. In *education*, the 12 colleges and universities identified in our study do not control any significant proportion of *all* higher education resources in the nation. However, they do control 50 percent of all *private endowment funds* in higher education (this was the formal basis of their selection), and they are consistently ranked among the most "prestigious" private colleges and universities. Their presidents and trustees numbered 656 in 1970. Our selection of foundations was based on *The Foundation Directory's* data on the nation's top 12 foundations which control 38.6 percent of all foundation assets. Since the *Directory* does not identify foundations by size of assets beyond these 12 leading institutions, our study will relate to the 121 directors of these top foundations. Identifying top positions in the field of *law* is an even more subjective task. Our definition of positions of authority includes the 176 senior partners of 28 top New York and Washington law firms. Top positions in *civic and cultural affairs* can be identified only by qualitative evaluation of the prestige and influence of various well-known organizations. We have identified 12 leading organizations, including the Brookings Institution, Council on Foreign Relations, and the Committee on Economic Development, among civic associations; and the Metropolitan Museum of Art, the Metropolitan Opera, the Lincoln Center for the Performing Arts, and the Smithsonian Institution among cultural institutions. In 1970 these 12 organizations were legally governed by 392 individuals.

Any effort to operationalize a concept as broad as a national institutional elite is bound to generate discussion over the inclusion or exclusion of specific sectors, institutions, or positions. (Why law, but not medicine? Why not religious institutions, or labor unions? Why not Governors or Mayors of big cities?) *Systematic* research on national elites is still in the exploratory stage, and there are no explicit guidelines. Our choices involve many subjective judgments. But let us see what we can learn about concentration, specialization, and interlocking using the definitions above; perhaps other researchers can improve upon our attempt to operationalize this elusive notion of a national institutional elite. In the analysis to follow, we will present findings for our aggregate corporate, governmental, and public interest elites, and for specific sectors of these elites. Clearly, findings for specific sectors will be free of whatever bias might exist in the aggregate elite, as a result of our inclusion or exclusion of specific sectors.

## DIMENSIONS OF AMERICA'S ELITE: THE TOP FIVE THOUSAND

Our definition of a national institutional elite results in the identification of 5,416 elite positions:

| | |
|---|---:|
| Corporate Sector | |
| Industrial corporations | 1534 |
| Utilities, communications, transportation | 476 |
| Banking | 1200 |
| Insurance | 362 |
| Total | 3572 |
| Governmental Sector | |
| U.S. Government | 227 |
| Legislative, executive, judicial, military | 59 |
| Total | 286 |
| Public Interest Sector | |
| Mass media | 213 |
| Education | 656 |
| Foundation | 121 |
| Law | 176 |
| Civic and cultural | 392 |
| Total | 1558 |
| Total | 5416 |

These top positions, taken collectively, control half of the nation's industrial assets; half of all assets in communication, transportation, and utilities; half of all banking assets, two-thirds of all insurance assets. They control the television networks, the influential news agencies, and the major newspaper chains. They control nearly 40 percent of all the assets of private foundations and half of all private university endowments. They direct the nation's largest and best known New York and Washington law firms. They direct the nation's major civic and cultural organizations. They occupy key federal governmental positions in the executive, legislative, and judicial branches. And they occupy all the top command positions in the Army, Navy, Air Force, and Marines.

These aggregate figures—roughly 5000 positions—are themselves important indicators of the concentration of authority and control in American society. Of course, these figures are the direct product of our specific definition of top institutional positions. Yet these aggregate statistics provide us, for the first time, with an explicit definition and quantitative estimate of the size of the national elite in America.

## SOME QUESTIONS FOR RESEARCH

Our definition of America's institutional elite provides a starting place for exploring some of the central questions confronting students of power. How concentrated are institutional resources in America? How much concentration exists in industry and finance, in government, in the mass media, in education, in the foundations, and in civic and cultural affairs? Who are the people at the top of the nation's institutional structure? How did they get there? Did they inherit their positions or work their way up through the ranks of the institutional hierarchy? What are their general attitudes, beliefs, and goals? What do they think about their own power? Do elites in America generally agree about major national goals and the general directions of foreign and domestic policy, and limit their disagreements to the *means* of achieving their goals and the details of policy implementation? Or do leaders disagree over fundamental *ends* and values and the future character of American society?

Are institutional elites in America "interlocked" or "specialized"? That is, is there convergence at the "top" of the institutional structure in America, with the same group of people dominating decision making in industry, finance, education, government, the mass media, foundations, and civic and cultural affairs? Or is there a separate elite in each sector of society with little or no overlap in authority? Are there opportunities to rise to the top of the leadership structure for individuals from both sexes, all classes, races, religions, and ethnic groups, through multiple career paths in different sectors of society? Or are opportunities to acquire key leadership roles generally limited to white, Anglo-Saxon, Protestant, upper- and upper-middle-class males whose careers are based primarily in industry and finance? Is the nation's institutional leadership recruited primarily from private "name" prep schools and "Ivy League" universities? Do leaders join the same clubs, intermarry, and enjoy the same life styles? Or is there diversity in educational backgrounds, social ties, club memberships, and life styles among the elite?

How much competition and conflict takes place among America's institutional elite? Are there clear-cut factions within the nation's leadership struggling for preeminence and power, and if so, what are the underlying sources of this factionalism? Do different segments of the nation's institutional elite accommodate each other in a system of bargaining, negotiation, and compromising based on a widely shared consensus of values?

How do institutional elites make national policy? Are there established institutions and procedures for elite interaction, communication, and consensus building on national policy questions? Or are such questions decided in a relatively unstructured process of competition, bargaining, and compromise among a large number of diverse individuals and interest groups? Do the "proximate policy makers"—the President, Congress, courts—respond to mass opinion, or do they respond primarily to initiatives originating from elite organizations, foundations, and civic associations?

These are the questions that we will tackle in the pages to follow. In Part II, Institutional Leadership in America, we will describe the concentration of power in a limited number of institutions in various sectors of society. We will also describe in general terms the type of individuals who occupy top positions in these institutions; we will provide a number of brief biographical sketches suggestive of the characteristics of these elites—who they are and how they got there. These sketches are designed to "personalize" the statistical analysis that follows. In Part III, The Structure of Institutional Elites, we will examine the questions posed above in a more systematic fashion, employing computerized data files on our top five thousand elites.

# INSTITUTIONAL
# LEADERSHIP
# IN
# AMERICA

part II

# the corporate
# directors

▶▶▶▶▶▶▶▶▶▶▶▶▶▶▶▶▶▶▶▶▶▶▶▶▶▶▶▶▶▶▶▶▶▶▶▶▶▶▶▶▶▶▶▶▶▶▶▶▶▶▶▶▶▶▶▶▶▶▶▶

# 2

A great deal of power is organized into large economic institutions—
industrial corporations, banks, utilities, and investment firms. Control
of economic resources provides a continuous and important base of power
in any society. Economic organizations decide what will be produced,
how it will be produced, how much will be produced, how much it will
cost, how many people will be employed, who will be employed and
what their wages will be. They determine how goods and services will be
distributed, what technology will be developed, what profits will be
made and how they will be distributed, how much money will be available for loans, what interest rates will be charged, and many similarly
important questions.

Obviously, these decisions affect our lives as much as, or perhaps
even more than, those typically made by governments. We cannot draw
inferences about a "national power structure" from studies of governmental decision making alone. Studies of power in society must include
economic power.

## THE CONCENTRATION OF ECONOMIC POWER

Economic power in America is highly concentrated. Indeed, only about
3500 individuals—two one-thousandths of 1 percent of the population—
exercise formal authority over half of the nation's industrial assets,
nearly half of all banking assets, half of all assets in communications,
transportation and utilities, and two-thirds of all insurance assets. These
individuals are the presidents and directors of the largest corporations

in these fields. The reason for this concentration of power in the hands of so few people is found in the concentration of industrial and financial assets in a small number of giant corporations. The following statistics can only suggest the scale and concentration of modern corporate enterprise in America.

There are more than 200,000 *industrial corporations* in the United States with total assets in 1970 of $884 billion. But the 100 corporations listed in Table 2-1 control 54.9 percent ($495 billion) of all industrial

**TABLE 2-1    Largest Industrial Corporations, by Size of Assets, 1976**

| Rank | Name | Assets (billions of dollars) | Cumulative* Percent |
|------|------|------|------|
| 1 | Exxon | 36.3 | 4.1 |
| 2 | General Motors | 24.4 | 6.9 |
| 3 | Mobil | 18.8 | 8.9 |
| 4 | Texaco | 18.2 | 11.0 |
| 5 | IBM | 17.7 | 13.0 |
| 6 | Ford | 15.8 | 14.8 |
| 7 | Standard Oil of California | 13.8 | 16.4 |
| 8 | Gulf Oil | 13.4 | 19.9 |
| 9 | General Electric | 12.0 | 19.3 |
| 10 | Standard Oil (Indiana) | 11.2 | 20.6 |
| 11 | International Telephone & Telegraph | 11.1 | 21.8 |
| 12 | U.S. Steel | 9.2 | 22.7 |
| 13 | Atlantic Richfield | 8.8 | 23.7 |
| 14 | Shell Oil | 7.8 | 24.6 |
| 15 | Tenneco | 7.2 | 25.4 |
| 16 | Chrysler | 7.1 | 26.2 |
| 17 | E. I. DuPont de Nemours | 7.0 | 27.0 |
| 18 | Dow Chemical | 6.8 | 27.8 |
| 19 | Union Carbide | 6.6 | 28.5 |
| 20 | Standard Oil (Ohio) | 6.3 | 29.3 |
| 21 | Continental Oil | 6.0 | 30.0 |
| 22 | Eastman Kodak | 5.5 | 30.6 |
| 23 | Westinghouse Electric | 5.3 | 31.2 |
| 24 | Western Electric | 5.2 | 31.8 |
| 25 | Phillips Petroleum | 5.1 | 32.4 |
| 26 | Bethlehem Steel | 4.9 | 32.9 |
| 27 | Sun Oil | 4.8 | 33.4 |
| 28 | Xerox | 4.6 | 33.9 |
| 29 | Goodyear Tire & Rubber | 4.3 | 34.4 |
| 30 | R. J. Reynolds Industries | 4.3 | 35.0 |
| 31 | Union Oil of California | 4.2 | 35.5 |
| 32 | Procter & Gamble | 4.1 | 36.0 |
| 33 | Monsanto | 3.9 | 36.4 |
| 34 | Occidental Petroleum | 3.9 | 36.3 |
| 35 | Caterpillar Tractor | 3.9 | 37.2 |
| 36 | RCA | 3.8 | 37.6 |
| 37 | Weyerhauser | 3.7 | 38.0 |

TABLE 2–1    (cont.)

| Rank | Name | Assets (billions of dollars) | Cumulative* Percent |
|------|------|------|------|
| 38 | International Paper | 3.6 | 38.4 |
| 39 | Getty Oil | 3.6 | 38.8 |
| 40 | Cities Service | 3.6 | 39.3 |
| 41 | Philip Morris | 3.6 | 39.8 |
| 42 | International Harvester | 3.6 | 40.2 |
| 43 | Aluminum Co. of America | 3.6 | 40.6 |
| 44 | Gulf & Western Industries | 3.5 | 41.0 |
| 45 | Minnesota Mining & Manufacturing | 3.3 | 41.3 |
| 46 | Firestone Tire & Rubber | 3.3 | 41.6 |
| 47 | Marathon Oil | 3.0 | 41.9 |
| 48 | Deere | 2.9 | 42.2 |
| 49 | Rockwell International | 2.9 | 42.5 |
| 50 | Armco Steel | 2.8 | 42.9 |
| 51 | Amax | 2.8 | 43.2 |
| 52 | National Steel | 2.8 | 43.5 |
| 53 | Amerada Hess | 2.8 | 43.8 |
| 54 | W. R. Grace | 2.7 | 44.1 |
| 55 | United Technologies | 2.6 | 44.5 |
| 56 | Georgia Pacific | 2.6 | 44.8 |
| 57 | Sperry Rand | 2.6 | 45.1 |
| 58 | Burroughs | 2.5 | 45.4 |
| 59 | American Brands | 2.4 | 45.7 |
| 60 | Allied Chemical | 2.4 | 46.0 |
| 61 | IC Industries | 2.3 | 46.3 |
| 62 | Reynolds Metal | 2.3 | 46.6 |
| 63 | Republic Steel | 2.3 | 46.8 |
| 64 | NCR | 2.3 | 47.1 |
| 65 | Kennecott Copper | 2.3 | 47.3 |
| 66 | Honeywell | 2.2 | 47.5 |
| 67 | Owens-Illinois | 2.2 | 47.7 |
| 68 | Continental Group | 2.2 | 48.0 |
| 69 | Kaiser Aluminum | 2.2 | 48.2 |
| 70 | Champion International | 2.2 | 48.5 |
| 71 | Pfizer | 2.2 | 48.8 |
| 72 | LTV | 2.2 | 49.0 |
| 73 | McDonnell Douglas | 2.2 | 49.3 |
| 74 | Ashland Oil | 2.1 | 49.5 |
| 75 | Inland Steel | 2.1 | 49.7 |
| 76 | Litton Industries | 2.0 | 49.9 |
| 77 | PPG Industries | 2.0 | 50.1 |
| 78 | General Foods | 2.0 | 50.3 |
| 79 | American Cyanamid | 2.0 | 50.5 |
| 80 | Anaconda | 2.0 | 50.7 |
| 81 | American Can | 1.9 | 50.9 |
| 82 | Warner-Lambert | 1.9 | 51.2 |
| 83 | FMC | 1.9 | 51.5 |
| 84 | Boeing | 1.9 | 51.7 |
| 85 | Celanese | 1.9 | 51.9 |
| 86 | Coca Cola | 1.9 | 52.1 |
| 87 | TRW | 1.9 | 52.4 |
| 88 | Signal Companies | 1.9 | 52.6 |
| 89 | Beatrice Foods | 1.8 | 52.8 |

**TABLE 2–1    (cont.)**

| Rank | Name | Assets (billions of dollars) | Cumulative* Percent |
|------|------|------|------|
| 90  | Control Data | 1.8 | 52.9 |
| 91  | Kraft | 1.8 | 53.1 |
| 92  | Penzoil | 1.8 | 53.3 |
| 93  | Borden | 1.8 | 53.5 |
| 94  | Merck | 1.8 | 53.7 |
| 95  | Colgate-Palmolive | 1.8 | 53.9 |
| 96  | Phelps Dodge | 1.8 | 54.1 |
| 97  | Lykes | 1.7 | 54.3 |
| 98  | Esmark | 1.7 | 54.5 |
| 99  | Ingersoll-Rand | 1.7 | 54.7 |
| 100 | Burlington Industries | 1.7 | 54.9 |

Total Industrial Assets= 883.9 billion dollars
Total Number of Corporations = 204,259

* In this table, and Tables 2–2, 2–3 and 2–4, cumulative percent refers to the total percentage of the nation's assets in, for example, industrial enterprise at a specific ranking. Thus, the first ten corporations (through Standard Oil of Indiana) account for 20.6 percent of the nation's industrial assets.

assets. The five largest industrial corporations—Exxon (formerly Standard Oil of New Jersey), General Motors, Mobil, Texaco, and IBM—control 13 percent of all industrial assets themselves.

The concentration of resources among a relatively few industrial corporations is increasing over time. In a 25-year period the proportion of all industrial assets controlled by the top 100 corporations grew as follows:

| 1950 | 1955 | 1960 | 1965 | 1970 | 1976 |
|------|------|------|------|------|------|
| 39.8% | 44.3% | 46.4% | 46.5% | 52.3% | 54.9% |

Concentration in *transportation, communications, and utilities* is even greater than in industry. Twenty corporations (see Table 2–2), out of 67,000 in these fields, control 50 percent of the nation's assets in airlines and railroads, communications, and electricity and gas. This sector of the nation's economy is dominated by the American Telephone and Telegraph Company (AT&T)—by total assets the single largest corporation in the U.S.

The financial world is equally concentrated. The 50 largest banks (see Table 2–3), out of 13,500 *banks* serving the nation, control 65.6 per-

**TABLE 2-2   Largest Transportation, Utilities, and Communication Corporations, by Size of Assets, 1976**

| Rank | Name | Assets (billions of dollars) | Cumulative Percent |
|------|------|------|------|
| 1 | American Telephone & Telegraph | 86.7 | 23.3 |
| 2 | General Telephone & Electronics | 13.6 | 27.0 |
| 3 | Southern Company | 8.0 | 29.2 |
| 4 | Pacific Gas & Electric | 7.4 | 31.2 |
| 5 | American Electric Power | 6.9 | 33.0 |
| 6 | Consolidated Edison | 6.6 | 34.8 |
| 7 | Commonwealth Edison | 5.9 | 36.4 |
| 8 | Southern California Edison | 4.9 | 37.7 |
| 9 | Public Service Electric & Gas | 4.7 | 39.0 |
| 10 | Virginia Electric & Power | 4.3 | 40.1 |
| 11 | Philadelphia Electric | 4.2 | 41.2 |
| 12 | Middle South Utilities | 4.1 | 42.4 |
| 13 | Duke Power | 4.0 | 43.4 |
| 14 | General Public Utilities | 3.9 | 44.5 |
| 15 | Southern Pacific | 3.9 | 45.5 |
| 16 | Texas Utilities | 3.9 | 46.6 |
| 17 | Florida Power & Light | 3.9 | 47.6 |
| 18 | Detroit Edison | 3.8 | 48.7 |
| 19 | Consumers Power | 3.8 | 49.7 |
| 20 | Union Pacific | 3.7 | 50.7 |
| 21 | Burlington Northern | 3.4 | 51.6 |
| 22 | Columbia Gas System | 3.2 | 52.5 |
| 23 | Chessie System | 3.0 | 53.3 |
| 24 | Santa Fe Industries | 3.0 | 54.1 |
| 25 | Texas Eastern Corp. | 2.9 | 54.8 |
| 26 | Northeast Utilities | 2.9 | 55.6 |
| 27 | UAL | 2.9 | 56.4 |
| 28 | Niagara Mohawk Paper | 2.8 | 57.2 |
| 29 | Seaboard Coastline Industries | 2.8 | 57.9 |
| 30 | United Telecommunications | 2.7 | 58.6 |
| 31 | Norfolk & Western Railway | 2.7 | 59.4 |
| 32 | Pennsylvania Power & Light | 2.7 | 60.1 |
| 33 | El Paso | 2.6 | 61.0 |

cent of all banking assets. Three banks (BankAmerica, Citicorp, and Chase Manhattan) control 18 percent of all banking assets themselves. In the *insurance* field, 18 companies (see Table 2–4) out of 1,790 control two-thirds of all insurance assets. Two companies (Prudential and Metropolitan) control over one-quarter of all insurance assets.

Control over the resources of these corporations rests in their presidents and directors and the holders of what are called "control blocks" of stock. Corporate power does not rest in the hands of the masses of

**TABLE 2–3    Largest Commercial Banks, by Size of Assets, 1976**

| Rank | Name | Assets (billions of dollars) | Cumulative Percent |
|------|------|------|------|
| 1 | BankAmerica Corp. | 73.9 | 7.3 |
| 2 | Citicorp | 64.3 | 13.7 |
| 3 | Chase Manhattan Corp. | 45.6 | 18.2 |
| 4 | Manufacturers Hanover Corp. | 31.5 | 21.3 |
| 5 | J. P. Morgan & Co. | 28.8 | 24.2 |
| 6 | Chemical New York Corp. | 26.6 | 26.8 |
| 7 | Bankers Trust New York | 22.2 | 29.0 |
| 8 | Continental Illinois | 22.0 | 31.2 |
| 9 | First Chicago Corp. | 19.8 | 33.1 |
| 10 | Western Bancorp | 19.7 | 35.1 |
| 11 | Security Pacific Corp. | 16.4 | 36.7 |
| 12 | Wells Fargo & Co. | 13.0 | 38.0 |
| 13 | Crocker National Corp. | 10.8 | 39.0 |
| 14 | Marine Midland Banks, Inc. | 10.7 | 40.1 |
| 15 | Charter New York Corp. | 10.2 | 41.1 |
| 16 | Mellon National Corp. | 9.3 | 42.0 |
| 17 | First National Boston Corp. | 8.5 | 42.9 |
| 18 | Northwest Bancorp | 8.3 | 43.7 |
| 19 | First Bank System, Inc. | 7.8 | 44.5 |
| 20 | National Detroit Corp. | 7.5 | 45.2 |
| 21 | First Pennsylvania Corp. | 7.2 | 45.9 |
| 22 | First International Bancshares, Inc. | 7.2 | 46.6 |
| 23 | Republic of Texas Corp. | 6.5 | 47.3 |
| 24 | Seafirst Corp. | 5.3 | 47.8 |
| 25 | First City Bancorp. of Texas | 5.2 | 48.3 |
| 26 | Bank of New York Co. | 5.2 | 48.8 |
| 27 | Texas Commerce Bancshares, Inc. | 5.2 | 49.3 |
| 28 | Harris Bankcorp | 4.9 | 49.8 |
| 29 | NCNB Corp. | 4.4 | 50.3 |
| 30 | CleveTrust Corp. | 4.3 | 50.7 |
| 31 | Philadelphia National Corp. | 4.3 | 51.1 |
| 32 | Union Bancorp. | 4.2 | 51.4 |
| 33 | First Wisconsin Corp. | 4.0 | 51.9 |
| 34 | Nortrust Corp. | 3.8 | 52.3 |
| 35 | Michigan National Corp. | 3.7 | 52.7 |
| 36 | BancOhio Corp. | 3.6 | 53.0 |
| 37 | Wachovia Corp. | 3.6 | 53.4 |
| 38 | Girard Co. | 3.5 | 53.7 |
| 39 | Southeast Banking Corp. | 3.4 | 54.1 |
| 40 | Detroitbank Corp. | 3.4 | 54.4 |
| 41 | Pittsburgh National Corp. | 3.4 | 54.7 |
| 42 | Valley National Bank of Arizona | 3.3 | 55.0 |
| 43 | U.S. Bancorp | 3.3 | 55.4 |
| 44 | Citizens & Southern National Bank | 3.1 | 55.7 |
| 45 | Mercantile Bancorp | 3.1 | 56.0 |
| 46 | Manufacturers National Corp. | 3.1 | 56.3 |
| 47 | Fidelcor | 3.1 | 56.6 |
| 48 | National Bank of North America | 3.0 | 59.6 |
| 49 | Rainier Bancorp | 3.0 | 62.6 |
| 50 | BanCal Tri-State Corp | 3.0 | 65.6 |

Total Banking Assets = 1,010.8 billion dollars
Total Number of Banks = 14,659

**TABLE 2–4   Largest Insurance Companies, by Size of Assets, 1976**

| Rank | Name | Assets (billions of dollars) | Cumulative Percent |
|------|------|------|------|
| 1 | Prudential | 43.7 | 13.6 |
| 2 | Metropolitan | 37.5 | 25.3 |
| 3 | Equitable Life Assurance | 22.4 | 32.2 |
| 4 | New York Life | 14.8 | 36.8 |
| 5 | John Hancock Mutual | 14.0 | 41.2 |
| 6 | Aetna Life | 12.0 | 44.9 |
| 7 | Connecticut General Life | 8.8 | 47.6 |
| 8 | Northwestern Mutual | 8.5 | 50.3 |
| 9 | Travelers | 8.4 | 52.9 |
| 10 | Massachusetts Mutual | 6.4 | 54.9 |
| 11 | Mutual of New York | 5.4 | 56.6 |
| 12 | Teachers Insurance & Annuity | 5.1 | 58.1 |
| 13 | New England Mutual | 5.0 | 59.7 |
| 14 | Bankers Life | 4.1 | 61.0 |
| 15 | Connecticut Mutual | 4.0 | 62.5 |
| 16 | Mutual Benefit | 3.8 | 63.7 |
| 17 | Lincoln National Life | 3.5 | 64.8 |
| 18 | Penn Mutual | 3.0 | 65.7 |

Total Insurance Company Assets = 321.6 billion dollars
Total Number of Companies = 1,750

corporate employees, or even in the hands of the millions of middle- and upper-class Americans who own corporate stock. A. A. Berle, Jr., a corporation lawyer and corporate director who has written extensively on the modern corporation, states,

> The control system in today's corporations, when it does not lie solely in the directors as in the American Telephone and Telegraph Company, lies in a combination of the directors of a so-called control block [of stock] plus the directors themselves. For practical purposes, therefore, the control or power element in most large corporations rests in its group of directors, and it is autonomous—or autonomous if taken together with a control block. . . . This is a self-perpetuating oligarchy.[1]

The power of stockholders over corporations is a legal fiction. Stockholders are seldom able to replace management. When confronted with mismanagement, stockholders simply sell their stock rather than try to challenge the powers of management. Berle describes this situation as follows:

[1] A. A. Berle, Jr., *Economic Power and a Free Society* (New York: Fund for the Republic, 1958), p. 10.

Management control is a phrase meaning merely that no large concentrated stockholding exists which maintains a close working relationship with the management or is capable of challenging it, so that the board of directors may regularly expect a majority, composed of small and scattered holdings, to follow their lead. Thus, they need not consult with anyone when making up their slate of directors, and may simply request their stockholders to sign and send in a ceremonial proxy. They select their own successors. . . . Nominal power still resides in the stockholders; actual power in the board of directors.[2]

## THE MULTINATIONALS: WORLDWIDE BIG BUSINESS

The concentration of industrial power in a relatively few large institutions is not an exclusively American phenomenon. On the contrary, since World War II the growth of world trade, increasing overseas investments, and international corporate mergers have combined to create giant multinational corporations whose operations span the globe. The trend toward corporate concentration of resources is worldwide. Moreover, it is not only large American corporations which have expanded their markets throughout the world, invested in overseas plants and banks, and merged with foreign countries. Large European and Japanese firms are not far behind in the quest for world business. Just as American companies have greatly expanded investments abroad, so too have foreign companies sharply increased their business in the United States. The result is the emergence of truly supranational corporations, which not only trade worldwide but which also build and operate plants in many nations.

The 50 largest industrial corporations in the world are listed in Table 2–5 by their total sales figures for 1976. Ranked at top of the list are the two largest American firms—Exxon and General Motors—followed by the British-Dutch giant, Royal Dutch Shell. In all, 26 of the 50 largest industrial corporations in the world are headquartered *outside* the United States. Indeed the percentage of total sales of the 50 largest multinationals going to American companies has been steadily declining over time.[3]

Thus, critics of American capitalism are incorrect if they charge or imply that corporate multinationalism is strictly an American invention. A careful review of the list also reveals that oil companies are disproportionately represented among the multinationals. The reason is simple: Most of the world's oil is used by nonproducers of oil. This

---

[2] A. A. Berle, Jr., *Power Without Property* (New York: Harcourt, Brace & World, 1959), p. 73.

[3] See *Fortune,* August 1976, p. 243.

**TABLE 2–5    The Multinationals**

| Rank | Company | Headquarters |
|------|---------|--------------|
| 1 | Exxon | New York |
| 2 | General Motors | Detroit |
| 3 | Royal Dutch/Shell Group | London/The Hague |
| 4 | Texaco | New York |
| 5 | Ford Motor | Dearborn, Mich. |
| 6 | Mobil Oil | New York |
| 7 | National Iranian Oil | Teheran |
| 8 | British Petroleum | London |
| 9 | Standard Oil of California | San Francisco |
| 10 | Unilever | London |
| 11 | International Business Machines | Armonk, N.Y. |
| 12 | Gulf Oil | Pittsburgh |
| 13 | General Electric | Fairfield, Conn. |
| 14 | Chrysler | Highland Park, Mich. |
| 15 | International Tel. & Tel. | New York |
| 16 | Philips' Gloeilampenfabrieken | Eindhoven (Netherlands) |
| 17 | Standard Oil (Ind.) | Chicago |
| 18 | Cie Française des Pétroles | Paris |
| 19 | Nippon Steel | Tokyo |
| 20 | August Thyssen-Hütte | Duisburg (Germany) |
| 21 | Hoechst | Frankfurt on Main |
| 22 | ENI | Rome |
| 23 | Daimier-Benz | Stuttgart |
| 24 | U.S. Steel | Pittsburgh |
| 25 | BASF | Ludwigshafen on Rhine |
| 26 | Shell Oil | Houston |
| 27 | Renault | Boulogne-Billancourt (France) |
| 28 | Siemens | Munich |
| 29 | Volkswagenwerke | Wolfsburg (Germany) |
| 30 | Atlantic Richfield | Los Angeles |
| 31 | Continental Oil | Stamford, Conn. |
| 32 | Bayer | Leverkusen (Germany) |
| 33 | E. I. du Pont de Nemours | Wilmington, Del. |
| 34 | Toyota Motor | Toyota-City (Japan) |
| 35 | ELF-Aquitaine | Paris |
| 36 | Nestlé | Vevey (Switzerland) |
| 37 | ICI (Imperial Chemical Industries) | London |
| 38 | Petrobás (Petróleo Brasileiro) | Rio de Janeiro |
| 39 | Western Electric | New York |
| 40 | British-American Tobacco | London |
| 41 | Procter & Gamble | Cincinnati |
| 42 | Hitachi | Tokyo |
| 43 | Westinghouse Electric | Pittsburgh |
| 44 | Mitsubishi Heavy Industries | Tokyo |
| 45 | Union Carbide | New York |
| 46 | Tenneco | Houston |
| 47 | Nissan Motor | Tokyo |
| 48 | Goodyear Tire & Rubber | Akron, Ohio |
| 49 | Montedison | Milan |
| 50 | British Steel | London |

means that multinationalism in the oil industry is essential in getting the oil from producers to users. Sixteen of the world's largest industrial corporations are oil companies. But international corporate mergers and overseas plant investments by *non-oil* companies have also contributed to multinational concentrations of corporate power. For example, General Motors builds Opels in Germany, Vauxhalls in Great Britain, and Frigidaire products in ten countries. Volkswagenwerke not only sells imports in the United States, but now builds autos in Pennsylvania. Not only are industrial corporations involved in this worldwide network of corporate enterprise, but large international banks are equally involved. Multinational corporations have access to the world's largest banks including (1) Banque Nationale de Paris, (2) Dai-Ichi Kangyo Bank (Japan), (3) Deutsche Bank, (4) Société Generale (France), (5) Crédit Lyonnaise (France), (6) Barclays Bank (Britain), (7) Fuji Bank (Japan), (8) Sumitomo Bank (Japan), (9) Bank of Tokyo, and (10) Mitsubishi Bank (Japan). These are the ten largest foreign commercial banks.

While a great deal has been written about the "dangers" of multinationalism in subverting the national interest, in most cases the opposite is true. The multinational corporation is in a very exposed position vis-á-vis its investments overseas. These investments may be confiscated by revolutionary governments without notice; subject to discriminating taxes, duties, or quotas; or forced to be sold or transferred to new foreign owners. The multinational corporation is at the mercy of the host government. Multinationals must conform to the conflicting laws of many nations. On the other hand, the legal maze in which multinationals operate leaves cracks in which clever managers can walk; shifting resources or profits to the lowest tax countries in which they operate, avoiding antitrust laws with international mergers, obscuring corporate reporting through foreign subsidiaries, shifting cash revenues from one currency to another, and so on.

## THE CORPORATE DIRECTORS

Who are the men at the top of the nation's corporate structure? Let us begin with some brief sketches of a few selected corporate leaders. Later in this volume we will examine recruitment patterns, interlocking and specialization, social backgrounds, attitudes and opinions, cohesion and competition, and patterns of interaction. But let us first get a general notion of *who the men at the top are*.

*David Rockefeller*. Chairman of the board of the Chase Manhattan Bank. Youngest of five sons of John D. Rockefeller, Jr.; heir of the Standard Oil Co. (Exxon) fortune; grandson of John D. Rockfeller, Sr., who founded the company that made the Rockefeller family one of the richest in the world. Attended Lincoln School in New York, Harvard, The London School of Economics, and the University of Chicago (Ph.D. degree in economics). Also a member of the board of directors of the B. F. Goodrich Co., Rockefeller Bros., Inc., Equitable Life Insurance Co. He is a trustee of Rockefeller Institute of Medical Research, Museum of Modern Art, Rockefeller Center, and Harvard College. He is also chairman of the Council on Foreign Relations.

*Richard King Mellon.* Chairman of the board of Mellon National Bank and Trust Co.; a director of Aluminum Co. of America (Alcoa), General Motors Corp., Gulf Oil Corp., Koppers Co., Pennsylvania Co., and the Penn Central Railroad (before its bankruptcy). Attended Culver Military Academy and Princeton. Only son of Richard Beatly Mellon and grandson of Thomas Mellon, who established a fortune in Alcoa and Gulf Oil and banking. Uncle, Andrew Mellon, was Secretary of the Treasury under Presidents Harding, Coolidge, and Hoover. Mellon started as a messenger in father's bank; after the death of his father, accepted 34 directorships of major corporations as "head of the Mellon clan." Personally responsible for Pittsburgh's urban renaissance, principal creator of the "Golden Triangle" of that city. A trustee of Carnegie-Mellon University, Mellon Institute, and University of Pittsburgh. Personal wealth exceeds one-half billion dollars.

*Amory Houghton.* Former chairman of the board, Citicorp, and former ambassador to France. Attended St. Paul's School and Harvard. Descendant of four generations of owners of Corning Glass Works. Father was ambassador to Germany under President Harding and ambassador to Great Britain under President Coolidge. Sometimes confused with his counsin, Arthur Amory Houghton, who served as chairman of the board of Corning Glass (also a director of New York Life Insurance, United States Steel Corp., J. Pierpont Morgan Library, New York Philharmonic, Lincoln Center for Performing Arts, Metropolitan Museum of Art, and the New York Public Library). Served as president of Corning Glass before World War II, then switched to banking—first as a director and later chairman of the board of the nation's second largest bank. Devoted a great deal of attention to the Boy Scouts of America (served as national president). He is a director of Metropolitan Life Insurance and Dow Corning Corp.; trustee of the University of Rochester, Brookings Institution, St. Paul's School, and Harvard University. Both he and his cousin Arthur are centimillionaires.

*Henry Ford II.* Chairman and chief executive of the Ford Motor Co. Eldest son of Edsel Bryan Ford (president of the company from 1918 to his death in 1943); grandson of Henry Ford, founder of the company. Attended Hotchkiss School and Yale University. Started in the automobile industry at age 25 as vice-president of Ford Motors; took over the presidency one year later. He was a director of General Foods Corp., and a trustee of the Ford Foundation. He was chairman of the National Alliance of Businessmen, and the National Center for Voluntary Action. He is personally responsible for Detroit's new downtown "Renaissance Center." Brother, Benson Ford, is also a director of Ford Motor Co. and the Ford Foundation, and serves as a director of the American Safety Council and United

Community Funds of America. Another brother, William Clay Ford, is president of the Detroit Lions Professional football club and a director of the Girl Scouts of America and the Henry Ford Hospital. All of the Fords rank at the top of the nation's individual wealth-holders.

*Ellmore C. Patterson.* Chairman of the board of Morgan Guaranty Trust Co. Attended Lake Forest Academy and University of Chicago. Married to Ann Hude Choate, daughter of a prominent investment banker who was associate of J. P. Morgan & Co. Became vice-president of Morgan Guaranty Trust in 1951; executive vice-president in 1959, president in 1969, and chairman of the board in 1971. Also a director of Canadian Life Assurance Co., International Nickel, the Atcheson, Topeka & Santa Fe Railroad, and Standard Brands, Inc. Member of the New York State Banking Board; trustee of the Alfred P. Sloan Foundation, Sloan-Kettering Cancer Institute, Carnegie Endowment for International Peace, University of Chicago, and Council on Foreign Relations.

*Albert L. Williams.* Chairman of the board, IBM. Attended public schools and spent two years at Berkeley College. Spent six years as an accountant for state of Pennsylvania before becoming a salesman for IBM in 1936. Rose to the position of controller in 1942, treasurer in 1947, executive vice-president in 1954, and president in 1961. A director of General Motors Corp., Mobil Oil, Citicorp, Eli Lilly and Co., and General Foods. Also a trustee of the Alfred P. Sloan Foundation.

*Clifton C. Garvin.* Chairman of the board, Exxon Corporation, the world's largest industrial corporation. He attended public schools and received a B.S. in chemical engineering from Virginia Polytechnic Institute. He began work as an engineer for Standard Oil Co. (now Exxon) in Baton Rouge, Louisiana, in 1947. He climbed the executive ranks of Standard Oil and its subsidiaries for 28 years, becoming chairman of the board in 1975. He is also a director of Citicorp and a member of the National Petroleum Council. He is a trustee of the Committee on Economic Development, the Egyptian–U.S. Business Council, Sloan-Kettering Institute for Cancer Research, Alfred P. Sloan Foundation, and the Council on Foreign Relations.

*John D. DeButts.* Chairman of the board of American Telephone and Telegraph (AT&T), the world's largest corporation. He attended public schools and received an engineering degree from the Virginia Military Institute. After failing an eye test, he was denied a military commission; so he began work as a telephone traffic controller for the Chesapeake and Potomac Telephone Co., a subsidiary of AT&T. He became chairman of the board in 1972. He is also a director of Citicorp, U.S. Steel, and Kraftco. He is a trustee of the Duke Endowment Foundation, United Way of America, Duke University, Loyola University of Chicago, the Tax Foundation, and the National Conference of Christians and Jews.

*Alden W. Clausen.* Chairman of the board, BankAmerica, the nation's largest commercial bank. He received a public school education and a B.A. from tiny Carthage College before obtaining a law degree from the University of Minnesota. He immediately started with BankAmerica in San Francisco under its founder and long-term president, A. P. Gianini. He worked his way up to vice-president, senior vice-president, and executive vice-president, to president and chairman of the board in 1970. He is a director of the Federal Reserve Bank of San Francisco. He is chairman of the San Francisco Bay Area Council, United Way of the Bay Area, Japan-U.S. Advisory Council. He is a trustee of the San Francisco Opera, the Stanford Research Institute, and the Harvard Business School.

It is clear from these sketches that some individuals gain corporate power through inheritance, while others come up through the ranks of corporate management. Men such as Rockefeller, Ford, Mellon, and Houghton largely inherited their position and power. Others, such as Garvin, DeButts, and Clausen, rose to power through the ranks of management. In fact, we will see that a surprising percentage of top corporate leaders achieved their power that way.

## THE MANAGERS: CLIMBING THE CORPORATE LADDER

The top echelons of American corporate life are occupied primarily by men who have climbed the corporate ladder from relatively obscure and powerless bottom rungs. It is our rough estimate that only 10 percent of the 3500 presidents and directors of the top 100 corporations are heirs of wealthy families. The rest—the "managers"—owe their rise to power not to family connections, but to their own success in organizational life. Of course, these managers are overwhelmingly upper-middle-class and upper-class in social origin, and most attended Ivy League colleges and universities. (The social origin and background of top elites is discussed in Chapter 7.) The rise of the manager is a recent phenomenon. As recently as 1950, we estimate that 30 percent of the top corporate elite were heirs of wealthy families, compared to our figure of 10 percent for 1976. How can we explain the rise to power of the corporate manager?

Today the requirements of technology and planning have greatly increased the need in industry for specialized talent and skill in organization. Capital is something that a corporation can now supply to itself. There is little need for the old-style "tycoon." Thus, there has been a shift in power in the American economy from capital to organized intelligence, and we can reasonably expect that this shift will be reflected in the deployment of power in society at large. This is reflected in the decline of individual and family controlled large corporations and an increase in the percentage of large corporations controlled by management (see Table 2–6).

Individual capitalists are no longer essential to the accumulation of capital for investment. Approximately *three fifths* of industrial capital now comes from retained earnings of corporations rather than from the investments of individual capitalists. Another *one-fifth* of industrial cap-

**TABLE 2–6** Increase in Management Control of the 200 Largest Industrial Corporations and the Decline in Family Ownership

|  | 1929 | | 1963 | |
| --- | --- | --- | --- | --- |
|  | Number of Corpora- tions | Percent of 200 Largest | Number of Corpora- tions | Percent of 200 Largest |
| Individual or family: | | | | |
| Private ownership | 12 | 6 | 0 | 0 |
| Majority ownership | 10 | 5 | 5 * | 2.5 |
| Minority control | 47 | 23.5 | 18 | 9 |
| Control by legal device | 41 | 20.5 | 8 | 4 |
| Management control | 88 | 44 | 169 | 84.5 |
| Receivership | 2 | 1 | 0 | 0 |

* A&P, Duke, Power, Kaiser Industries, Sun Oil, TWA.

Source: Derived from figures supplied by Robert J. Larner, "Ownership and Control in the 200 Largest Nonfinancial Corporations, 1929 and 1963," *American Economic Review*, 66 (September 1966), 777–787.

ital is borrowed, chiefly from banks. Even though the remaining *one-fifth* of the capital funds of industry comes from "outside" investments, the bulk of these funds are from large insurance companies, mutual funds, and pension trusts, rather than from individual investors. Indeed the individual investor who buys stock in corporations provides only about 5 percent of total industrial capital. Thus, private investors are no longer in a position of dominance in American capital formation.

American capital is primarily administered and expended by managers of large corporations and financial institutions. Stockholders are supposed to have ultimate power over management, but as we have noted, individual stockholders seldom have any control over the activities of the corporations they own. Usually "management slates" for the board of directors are approved as a matter of course by stockholders. Occasionally banks and financial institutions and pension trust or mutual fund managers will get together to replace a management-selected board of directors. But more often than not, banks and trust funds sell their stock in corporations whose management they distrust rather than use the voting power of their stock to replace management. This policy of non-action by institutional investors means that the directors and management of corporations are becoming increasingly self-appointed and unchallengeable—in effect achieving absolute power within the corporation.

Most of the capital in America is owned not by individuals but by corporations, banks, insurance companies, mutual funds, investment companies, and pension trusts. Adolf A. Berle writes:

Of the capital flowing into non-agricultural industry, 60 percent is internally generated through profits and depreciation funds (within corporations). Another 10 or 15 percent is handled through the investment staffs of insurance companies and pension trusts. Another 20 percent is borrowed from banks. Perhaps 5 percent represents individuals who have saved and chosen the application of their savings. This is the system. . . . The capital system is not in many aspects an open market system. It is an administered system.[4]

Liberal economist John Kenneth Galbraith summarizes the changes in America's economic elite:

Seventy years ago the corporation was the instrument of its owners and a projection of their personalities. The names of these principals—Carnegie, Rockefeller, Harriman, Mellon, Guggenheim, Ford—were well known across the land. They are still known, but for the art galleries and philanthropic foundations they established and their descendants who are in politics. The men who now head the great corporations are unknown. Not for a generation did people outside Detroit in the automobile industry know the name of the current head of General Motors. In the manner of all men, he must produce identification when paying by check. So with Ford, Standard Oil, and General Dynamics. The men who now run the large corporations own no appreciable share of the enterprise. They are selected not by the stockholders but, in the common case, by a board of directors which narcissistically they selected themselves.[5]

How do you climb the corporate ladder? It is not easy, and most who begin the climb fall by the wayside at some point in their career before reaching the top. Howard Morgens, president of Procter & Gamble, is a successful manager. He climbed his organization to succeed its president, Neil McElroy (who left to be Secretary of Defense), and headed the corporation for over 15 years. In an interview with this executive, *Forbes* magazine described the qualities of a corporate career riser:

Just to be in the running, a career riser must discipline himself carefully. He must become a seasoned decision-maker. He must cultivate an aura of success and sustain his upward momentum on the executive ladder. He must be loyal to a fault, tolerably bright, fairly creative, politically agile, always tough, sometimes flexible, unfailingly sociable and, in the minds of his company's directors, seem superior to a dozen men who are almost as good. He must also be lucky.[6]

Over time, the organization man accepts the goals of the organization as his own, and the procedures of the bureaucracy as a way of life:

[4] Berle, *Power Without Property,* p. 45.

[5] John Kenneth Galbraith, *The New Industrial State* (Boston: Houghton Mifflin, 1967), p. 323.

[6] "Proud to Be An Organization Man," *Forbes,* May 15, 1972, p. 241.

In staying, however, the career riser must accept the necessarily bureaucratic ways and the shared beliefs of a huge organization. He must be willing to follow prescribed procedures and behavioral norms. He must do things the P&G way or the IBM way or the General Motors way. Moreover, he must find it in himself to believe in the essential goodness of the company, in its traditions and in his co-employees. He must be willing to accept a good deal on faith. He must, in short, conform.[7]

Today, more than ever before, getting to the top requires the skills of a "technocrat"—knowledge of bureaucratic organization, technical skills and information, extensive formal education (including postgraduate degrees), and proven ability to work within legal constraints and governmental regulations. Very few sons (and no daughters) are taking over the presidencies of large corporations owned by their families. Only 9 percent of the nation's 500 largest corporations in 1976 were headed by men whose families had previously run the corporation.[8] Top corporate management is drawn from the ranks of upper-middle-class, well educated, white, male management, financial, and legal experts.

Perhaps the most significant change over the years has been the rising number of top corporate and governmental executives who have acquired graduate degrees. Today over half of the corporate presidents of the 500 largest corporations have advanced degrees—including M.B.A.'s. (Masters of Business Administration), law degrees, and Ph.D's. Less than 3 percent are not college educated.

An increasing number of top corporate leaders are coming out of finance and law, as opposed to production, operations, advertising, sales, engineering, or research. Lawyers and accountants now head two out of every five large corporations.[9] This is further evidence that finance, taxation, and governmental regulation are the chief problems confronting large corporations. The problems of production, sales, engineering, and transportation have faded in relationship to the pressing problems of money and power. Indeed, a *Fortune* survey of the chief executives of the 500 largest corporations in America in 1976 produced the following listing of "most important problems faced by their companies": government (28.1 percent); inflation (11.7 percent); financing (7.9 percent); employee relations (7.8 percent); rapid change (5.5 percent); profit levels (5.0 percent).[10]

But the "managers" who head the nation's largest corporations are

[7] *Ibid.*

[8] Charles G. Burch, "A Group Profile of the Fortune 500 Chief Executives," *Fortune*, May 1976, p. 174.

[9] *Ibid.*, p. 176.

[10] *Ibid.*, p. 177.

not merely paid administrators. On the contrary, the vast majority of corporate presidents, and other top management personnel, own substantial shareholdings of their company's stock. According to *Fortune* magazine, 30 percent of the presidents of the 500 largest companies personally own $1 million or more in their own company's stock. Fully 45 percent own over one-half million dollars worth; 75 percent own at least $100,000 worth; and only 10 percent owned none at all. So the "managers" have a personal stake in their company's growth and profitability—a stake which extends beyond their jobs to their personal investments as well.

Getting to the top by climbing the ladder of the giant corporation is not only difficult, it is also risky. The percentage chances of any one individual making it to the top are infinitesimal.

> Yet hundreds of thousands of executives willingly devote entire careers to working their way up through these giant corporations. On the lower rungs of the ladder, when they are in their 20's, all of them dream of reaching the top. As they advance into their 30's, and receive more responsibility and more money, the dream flowers brightly. Some time in their 40's and 50's, however, most realize they aren't going to make it. They are sorely disappointed, but it's too late to change. Comfortable and secure, they stay. Then each year there are perhaps a dozen or so— the lucky men who go all the way.[11]

It might be instructive to sketch briefly the career of one of "the lucky men" who went "all the way."

### JOHN D. DEBUTTS: UP THE ORGANIZATION

The chairman of the board of the world's largest corporation, American Telephone and Telegraph (AT&T), is John D. DeButts. DeButts spent 36 years in 22 managerial posts, slowly climbing the organization ladder to the top. Today he controls $80 billion in assets and nearly one million employees, more than any other private enterprise in the world. He heads AT&T itself, 23 subsidiary telephone companies, Western Electric Corporation (which manufactures telephone equipment), and Bell Laboratories.

DeButts attended public schools in Greensboro, North Carolina, and aspired to no more than a career in the military. His father was a middle management railroad executive. DeButts attended Virginia Military Institute and graduated with a degree in electrical engineering in 1936. He graduated a Cadet Captain and valedictorian of his class. How-

---

[11] "Proud to Be An Organization Man," p. 244.

ever, he failed an eye examination and was rejected for a military commission. He started as a traffic trainee with the Chesapeake and Potomac Telephone Co., an AT&T subsidiary. He rose through the ranks to become vice-president of Chesapeake and Potomac Telephone and then president of Illinois Bell Telephone. His big break came in 1949 when he was transferred to AT&T headquarters in New York. At the same time the Justice Department had filed an antitrust suit seeking to divorce Western Electric from AT&T and separate many of the Bell subsidiaries. Management wanted to prove in court that the Bell system had to remain under single management to ensure compatible equipment and smooth transferring of calls throughout the country. DeButts was told to gather proof and draft a paper defending AT&T against antitrust suits. DeButts complied and the resulting paper won the case for AT&T in 1956.

DeButts is not a lawyer but his expertise in defending AT&T from antitrust action became the key to his eventual climb to the top. DeButts undertook to learn personally every aspect of the job from telephone installation to cable repair to switchboard operations. He became assistant vice-president of AT&T in 1955, and the company's chief lobbyist in Washington in 1957. He became president of Illinois Bell in 1962 and formed a close acquaintanceship with Mayor Richard J. Daley while organizing civic programs in Chicago. DeButts was brought back to the New York headquarters as executive vice-president and later vice-chairman of the board. He succeeded H. I. Romnes to the chairmanship of AT&T in 1972.

DeButts is an unabashed defender of AT&T's monopoly position in the telephone business. He believes it provides the most efficient service at the lowest cost. He has continued to resist efforts by the Justice Department to sever ties with Western Electric, AT&T's manufacturing arm which supplies all telephone equipment. DeButts introduced the "Ma Bell" bill in Congress which would exempt AT&T from all provisions of the antitrust laws. He disarmingly calls it the "Consumer Communication Reform Act." So far the bill has failed to get very far in the legislative process, but it is a tribute to DeButts' audacity that he should seek to exclude his company from antitrust laws governing all other corporations.

## THE INHERITORS: STARTING AT THE TOP

Unquestionably, the Rockefellers, Fords, duPonts, Mellons, and other families still exercise great power over America's corporate resources. For example, the Mellon family's personal control of Alcoa is legendary:

When Gulf executives speak reverently of "The Board," they are normally referring to a single man, diffident Richard King Mellon, senior member of one of the world's richest families. The only Mellon on Gulf's board, Dick Mellon looks after his family's two billion, 32 percent interest in Gulf—though he rarely is concerned with the day-to-day operations.[12]

The Ford family maintains control of Ford Motor Company, and of course the Rockefellers continue their dominant interest in Chase Manhattan Bank, Citicorp, Standard Oil (Exxon), Equitable Life Assurance Society, Eastern Airlines, and other key banks and industries. The duPonts continue to control E. I. duPont de Nemours Corporation through their family holding company, Christiana Securities.

Research on family holdings in large corporations is not easy. Table 2–7 lists major family holdings of large corporations as revealed by Securities and Exchange Commission's *Official Summary of Security Transactions and Holdings*. Each month the SEC reports stock transactions by officers and directors of corporations, and by stockholders owning 10 percent or more of any corporation. Ferdinand Lundberg painstakingly studied monthly reports for five years in the 1960s to obtain this list.[13] We have updated it from *Fortune* magazine and other sources.

Many members of the corporate elite "start at the top." *Fortune* suggests that 150 of the largest 500 industrial corporations are controlled by one or more members of a single family. True, most of these individual or family controlled corporations are ranked *below* the top 100. But if indeed 30 percent of American industrial corporations are controlled by individuals or family groups, then the claimed disappearance of the traditional American capitalist may have been exaggerated. *Fortune* concludes:

After more than two generations during which ownership has been increasingly divorced from control, it is frequently assumed that all large U.S. corporations are owned by everybody and nobody, and are run and ruled by bland organization men. The individual entrepreneur or family that holds onto the controlling interest and actively manages the affairs of a big company is regarded as a rare anachronism. But a close look at the 500 largest industrial corporations does not substantiate such sweeping generalizations. . . . The demise of the traditional American proprietor has been slightly exaggerated and the much advertised triumph of the organization is far from total.[14]

---

[12] *Forbes*, May 1, 1964, p. 22.

[13] Ferdinand Lundberg, *The Rich and the Super-Rich* (New York: Lyle Stuart, 1968).

[14] Robert Sheehan, "Family Run Corporations: There Are More of Them Than You Think," *Fortune*, June 15, 1967, p. 179.

**TABLE 2-7    Family Dominance in Corporations**

| Corporation | Family |
|---|---|
| E. I. duPont de Nemours | duPont |
| Remington Arms Co., Inc. | Dodge, Rockefeller |
| Ford Motor Co. | Ford |
| Aluminum Co. of America | Mellon |
| Carborundum Co. | Mellon |
| Gulf Oil Co. | Mellon, Scaife |
| Sun Oil Co. | Pew |
| Pittsburgh Plate Glass | Pitcairn |
| Standard Oil (Exxon) | Rockefeller |
| Sears, Roebuck & Co. | Rosenwald |
| Reynolds Metals | Reynolds |
| The Singer Company | Clark |
| Inland Steel Co. | Block |
| Allegheny Corp. | Kirby |
| Scott Paper Co. | McCabe |
| Minnesota Mining & Mfg. Co. | Ordway, McKnight |
| Polaroid Corp. | Land |
| IBM | Watson, Fairchild |
| Dow Chemical Co. | Dow |
| Corning Glass Works | Houghton |
| International Paper Co. | Phipps |
| W. R. Grace & Co. | Grace, Phipps |
| Weyerhaeuser | Weyerhaeuser |
| Winn-Dixie, Inc. | Davis |
| Georgia-Pacific | Cheatharn |
| General Tire & Rubber Co. | O'Neil |
| Campbell Soup Company | Dorrance |
| H. J. Heinz Co. | Heinz |
| Wm. Wrigley Jr. Co. | Wrigley |
| Firestone Tire & Rubber | Firestone |
| National Steel | Hanna |
| Columbia Broadcasting Co. (CBS) | Paley |
| Olin Chemical | Olin |
| Ralston Purina Co. | Danforth |
| Crown-Zellerbach Corp. | Zellerbach |
| Texas Eastern Transmission | Brown |
| Fairchild Camera | Fairchild |
| Smith Kline & French Laboratories | Valentine |
| Allied Chemical Corp. | Burden |
| Merck & Co., Inc. | Rogengarten |
| American Metal Climax | Hochschild, Dodge |
| W. T. Grant Co. | Grant |
| E. J. Korvette | Ferkauf |
| Hilton Hotels | Hilton |
| Howard Johnson Co. | Johnson |
| Great Atlantic & Pacific Tea Co. (A&P) | Hartford |
| S. S. Kresge Co. | Kresge |
| Beech Aircraft Corp. | Beech |
| McDonnell Douglas Aircraft | McDonnell |
| General Dynamics Corp. | Crown |

**TABLE 2–7 (cont.)**

| Corporation | Family |
|---|---|
| Hess Oil & Chemical | Hess |
| Eli Lilly & Co. | Lilly |
| Duke Power Co. | Duke |
| Kaiser Industries | Kaiser |
| Rockwell Mfg. Co. | Rockwell |
| Gerber Products Co. | Gerber |
| Deere & Company | Deere |
| Jos. Schlitz Brewing Co. | Uihlein |
| George A. Hormel & Co. | Hormel |
| Oscar Mayer & Co. | Mayer |

Sources: Ferdinand Lundberg, *The Rich and the Super-Rich* (New York; Lyle Stuart, 1968); *Fortune*, June 15, 1967; updated to *Fortune*, "Directory of the Largest 500 Corporations," May 1975.

Nonetheless, even family controlled corporations recruit professional managers from the ranks. Indeed, a majority of the directors of Ford, Alcoa, Gulf, Standard Oil, Chase Manhattan, E. I. duPont, and other such corporations are professional managers recruited from outside the family.

It really does not matter a great deal whether the "inheritors" or the "managers" really control America's largest corporations; the end policies appear to be the same. Management is motivated by considerations of growth, stability, and profit, and so are prudent family stockholders. Moreover, "managers" themselves usually acquire sizable blocks of stock in their own companies as they move up through the ranks. It is doubtful that the decisions of "managers" differ a great deal from those of "inheritors." *Fortune* magazine agrees:

> It was expected that the demise of the owner-manager would markedly affect the conduct and performance of business. Some have predicted that the new managerial brass, as essentially non-owners, would lack the self-interested maximization of profits that inspired proprietors, would be inclined to curb dividends, and would be tempted to provide themselves with disproportionately large salaries and bonuses. . . .

> Despite these theories, it is extremely doubtful that ownership or the lack of it motivated the conduct of executives in such a direct way. Very few executives agree that the managers of a widely held company run their business any differently from the proprietors of a closely held company. Competition is a great leveler, and both managers and proprietors respond to its pressures with equal spirit and objectivity.[15]

15 *Ibid.,* p. 183.

### Henry Ford II: The Inheritor as Boss

"The first thing you have to understand about the company is that Henry Ford is the boss. . . . He *is* the boss, he always was the boss since the first day I came in and he always will be the boss." These are the words of Arjay Miller, who spent 23 years climbing the rungs of Ford management to become president of the company, only to find that Henry Ford II actually ran things. Miller eventually resigned to become dean of the Graduate School of Business at Stanford University.

Henry Ford II grew up in a very narrow society—he was a member of a rich, insulated family that was dominated by his grandfather, known to be an exceedingly suspicious, prejudiced, and willful man. Young Ford attended Hotchkiss School and later Yale University. But he failed to graduate in 1940 after admitting that he had cheated on a term paper. He enlisted in the Navy and served until his father died in 1943; President Roosevelt directed the Secretary of the Navy to release Ford to return to the family business.

Ford started in the automobile industry at the age of 25 as vice-president of Ford Motors, serving under his aged grandfather. A year later he took over the presidency. His initial decisions were to replace the one-man autocratic rule of the company with a modern management structure, recruiting bright young management types (the famous Ford "Whiz Kids," including Robert S. MacNamara, who later resigned as Ford president to become Secretary of Defense). He also initiated a modern labor relations program and ended the company's traditional hostility toward labor unions. As commonplace as these policies appear today, they were considered advanced, enlightened, and liberal for the Ford Motor Company at the time.

Over the years Ford proved himself a capable director of the company, despite some occasional and even colossal mistakes. (The Edsel fiasco cost the company over $300 million.) Ford works long hours at the company headquarters in Detroit. He personally approves style changes in Ford cars and test-drives them himself. He is active on the board of the Ford Foundation, and conscientiously reviews research and grant proposals with other board members.

In recent years Ford's energies have increasingly turned to public service programs. He helped launch the National Urban Coalition and organized the National Alliance of Businessmen to provide more jobs for minorities. He heads the National Center for Voluntary Action (frequently advertised in spot commercials featuring popular athletes on TV sports programs), which tries to bring volunteer workers into social welfare projects. He has been a prime mover in Detroit's urban renewal and redevelopment program.

Ford explained his leadership in public-benefit programs to a Yale University audience in 1969: "To hire a man because he needs a job rather than because the job needs him is to assure him that he is useless. On the other side of the coin, to help a man because it is in your own interest to help him is to treat him as an equal." Ford supported Lyndon Johnson in 1964 and Hubert Humphrey in 1968; he supported Nixon in 1972 but afterward became "bluntly and profanely" critical of Nixon's performance.

Ford is particularly concerned with energy policy: "I'm more worried about it than any other problem. I'm not worried about gasoline for automobiles, but the whole infra-structure of the U.S. We've got to heat our homes, and run our plants to employ people. People want air conditioning and a lot of other things that they're used to, and I don't see the power system of this country meeting the needs. . . . We need something like the Manhattan Project to solve this energy crisis." [16]

Like many men born to wealth and power, Ford's personal style is far from that of the bland organizational man. He is frequently unpredictable, sometimes abrasive, often profane; he expresses his opinions directly. His public and private actions are often controversial (he divorced his wife of many years and married a beautiful young Italian actress); but his preeminence in America's elite structure is unquestioned.

In 1977, Ford turned 60 years of age and reportedly transferred greater responsibilities to Ford Motor Co. President Lee Iacocca. Ford also resigned from his directorship of the Ford Foundation. In his resignation letter, he pointedly advised the Foundation to direct more attention to strengthening the capitalist system. "The Foundation is a creature of capitalism. . . . I'm just suggesting to the trustees and the staff that the system that makes the Foundation possible very probably is worth preserving." [17] But the Foundation had already cut many of its ties to the Ford Motor Company and the Ford family.

### PERSONAL WEALTH AND ECONOMIC POWER

It is a mistake to equate *personal* wealth with economic power. Men with relatively little personal wealth can exercise great power if they occupy positions that give them control of huge institutional resources. A president of a large company who came through the ranks of management may receive an income of only $200,000 or $300,000 a year, and

---

[16] Dan Cordiz, "Henry Ford, Superstar," *Fortune,* May 1973, p. 191.
[17] *Newsweek,* January 24, 1977, p. 69.

possess a net worth of $1 or 2 million. Yet these amounts are small when you consider that he may control a corporation with annual revenues of $2 *billion* and assets worth $10 or 20 *billion*. (The contrast is even greater in government where $40,000-a-year bureaucrats manage government expenditures of $50 *billion* a year!) The important point is that personal wealth in America is insignificant in comparison to corporate and governmental wealth.

One must occupy top *positions* in large corporate *institutions* to exercise significant economic power. The mere possession of personal wealth, even $100 million, does not guarantee economic power. Indeed, among America's 150 "centimillionaires"—individuals with personal wealth in excess of $100 million—there are many people such as widows, retired persons, and other inheritors who have never played any role in the family business. There are also many "independent operators" who have acquired great wealth in, say, independent oil operations or land speculation, but who do not occupy high positions in the corporate world. Of course, there are many centimillionaires whose personal wealth has come to them through their personal ownership of corporate shares. Familiar names—Ford, Rockefeller, duPont, Mellon—are liberally sprinkled among the nation's top personal wealth-holders. But their personal wealth is a *by-product* of their role, or their ancestor's role, in the corporate structure.

Socialist critics of America usually do not comprehend the insignificance of personal wealth in relation to corporate and governmental resources. They direct their rhetoric against inequality in personal income in the nation, when in fact the greatest inequities occur in the comparisons between corporate and government resources and the resources of individuals.

Let us illustrate our point: If the personal wealth of every one of America's 150 centimillionaires were *completely confiscated* by the government, the resulting revenue (about $30 billion) would amount to less than *10 percent* of the federal budget for a *single year!*

The relationship between personal wealth and institutional power is described well by economist Adolf Berle:

> As of now, in the United States and in Western Europe, the rich man has little power merely because he is rich. . . . [He] amounts to little unless he connects himself with effective institutions. He must master past institutions or must create new ones. . . . However large his bank account, he can do nothing with it but consume. He can build or buy palaces, amuse himself at Mediterranean or Caribbean resorts, become a figure in Monte Carlo, Miami, or Las Vegas. He can amuse himself by collecting books or purchasing bonds. He can give libraries or laboratories to universities and have his name put on them. He can receive the pleasant but powerless rec-

ognition of decorations, honorary degrees, and even titles of nobility. None of these things entitle him to make decisions affecting other men or to give orders (outside his household) with any likelihood they will be fulfilled. Even when he seeks to give his son a career in business, he must ask the assistance of acquaintances and friends who will give the boy a fair chance—and can give him little more. Beyond that, he can leave his son nothing but the ability to live without work and to waste as long as his wealth holds out. All of this does not add up to power.

So, if he wishes a power position, he must find it outside his bank account. He can, it is true, use the bank account to buy into, or possibly create, an institution. He can buy control of a small corporation. (Few rich men are left who are capable of buying individual control of really large ones.) He can undertake the management of that corporation. Then he can derive power from the institution—if, and only if, he is capable of handling it. Whatever power he has comes from the corporation or other institutions, and from such intellectual or organizing skill as he may have—not from his wealth, which is largely irrelevant. He at once discovers that he is subordinate to the institution. It operates under, and in conditions accepted or laid down or directed by, the paramount political power. Then he is tested, not by the dollar value of his wealth, but by his performance as director or manager of the institution.[18]

Of course, income inequality is and has always been a significant component of the American social structure.[19] The top fifth of income recipients in America account for over 40 percent of all income in the nation, while the bottom fifth accounts for only about 5 percent (see Table 2–8). However, the income share of the top fifth has declined since the pre–World War II years. The income share of the top 5 percent of families has declined dramatically from 30 to 14.4 percent. But the bottom fifth of the population still receives a very small share of the national income. The significant rise in income shares has occurred among the middle classes, in the second, third, and fourth income fifths.

Nonetheless, it is interesting to observe who the top personal wealth-holders in America are. The editors of *Fortune* report that in 1957, 45 persons in the United States had fortunes of over $100 million. In the following decade, this "centimillionaire" population tripled, and 66 persons were estimated to have 150 million or more.

Even if personal wealth is not the equivalent of power, the list of top wealth-holders is worthy of study. It includes at least two categories —old and established Eastern families with wealth derived from corporate ownership; and newly rich, self-made Southern and Western

---

[18] From Adolf A. Berle, *Power,* copyright © 1967, 1968, 1969. Reprinted by permission of Harcourt Brace Jovanovich, Inc.

[19] See Gabriel Kolko, *Wealth and Power in America* (New York: Praeger, 1962); see also Clair Wilcox, *Toward Social Welfare* (Homewood, Ill.: Richard D. Irwin, 1969), pp. 7–24.

TABLE 2–8   The Distribution of Family Income in America

*(By quintiles and top 5 percent)*

| Quintiles | 1929 | 1936 | 1944 | 1950 | 1956 | 1962 | 1972 | 1976 |
|---|---|---|---|---|---|---|---|---|
| Lowest | 3.5 | 4.1 | 4.9 | 4.8 | 4.8 | 4.6 | 5.5 | 5.4 |
| Second | 9.0 | 9.2 | 10.9 | 10.9 | 11.3 | 10.9 | 12.0 | 12.0 |
| Third | 13.8 | 14.1 | 16.2 | 16.1 | 16.3 | 16.3 | 17.4 | 17.6 |
| Fourth | 19.3 | 20.9 | 22.2 | 22.1 | 22.3 | 22.7 | 23.5 | 24.1 |
| Highest | 54.4 | 51.7 | 45.8 | 46.1 | 45.3 | 45.5 | 41.6 | 41.0 |
| Total | 100.0 | 100.0 | 100.0 | 100.0 | 100.0 | 100.0 | 100.0 | 100.0 |
| Top 5 Percent | 30.0 | 24.0 | 20.7 | 21.4 | 20.2 | 19.6 | 14.4 | 14.2 |

Source: U.S. Bureau of the Census, *Current Population Reports*, Series P-60 No. 80; data for early years from Edward C. Budd, *Inequality and Poverty* (New York: W. W. Norton and Co., 1967).

centimillionaires whose wealth is derived from "independent" oil operations, real estate speculations, aerospace industries, or technological inventions. (Further contrasts between new wealth and established wealth are found in Chapter 8.) Representative of new-rich, self-made wealth were J. Paul Getty and H. L. Hunt, both now deceased, whose fabulous fortunes were amassed in independent oil operations; Howard Hughes (also now deceased), whose fortune was made in the aerospace industry and is now invested in Las Vegas real estate; and Edwin H. Land, an inventor whose self-developing "Land" camera was the foundation of the giant Polaroid Corporation. Representative of established Eastern wealth derived from stable corporate enterprise are the Mellons, duPonts, Fords, Rockefellers, and others whose wealth extends back through several generations.

## THE LABYRINTH OF CORPORATE OWNERSHIP

If *individuals* no longer own America's corporations, who does? Other corporations. And who owns the owning corporations? Still other corporations. Tracing corporate ownership in America leads one into an endless labyrinth of holding companies, "street names" (camouflage ownership names), banks, insurance companies, and pension funds.

Various federal regulatory agencies require reporting of corporate ownership. But many corporations fall between the jurisdiction of different agencies, and the ownership reports actually submitted generally hide more than they reveal about corporate ownership.

The Securities and Exchange Commission, for example, requires a corporation to report all owners of 5 percent or more of its common stock; but simply by buying several blocks under different names, an owner can escape official reporting. The Federal Communications Commission requires that owners of 1 percent or more of broadcasting companies be publicly accounted for; the Interstate Commerce Commission requires complete ownership reports on the largest railroads; and the Federal Power Commission requires complete ownership reports on the largest utilities.

But consider this report submitted by AT&T, the world's largest corporation, in 1975 of its ten largest owners:

1. Kabo & Co.
2. AT & T
3. Merrill, Lynch
4. Cudd & Co.
5. Kane & Co.
6. Sior & Co.
7. Pitt & Co.
8. Société de Banque Suisse
9. Crédit Suisse
10. Sigler & Co.[20]

Few persons have ever heard of Kabo & Co., Cudd & Co., Sior & Co., or Pitt & Co. (AT&T itself holds its own stock for its shareowner and pension plans; Merrill, Lynch is Wall Street's largest brokerage house). These companies are official owners of record of AT&T, but now we must find out who they are. The addresses given on the official filing forms are worthless—usually only "N.Y., N.Y." and they cannot be found in the New York City telephone directory. These official owners are "street names," or aliases of major banks and insurance companies. For example, it turns out that Kabo & Co. is really Bankers Trust of New York, the nation's seventh largest bank. Sior & Co. is also Bankers Trust. Cudd & Co. is really Chase Manhattan, and so is Kane & Co. Pitt & Co. is Mellon National Bank, and so on.

The *real* owners of AT&T turn out to be: [21]

1. Bankers Trust
2. AT & T
3. Merrill, Lynch
4. Chase Manhattan
5. Morgan Guaranty Trust
6. Citicorp

[20] Committee on Government Operations, "Corporate Ownership and Control," 94th Congress, 2nd Session, November 1976, (Washington: Government Printing Office, 1976), p. 340.

[21] *Ibid.*, p. 402.

7. State Street Bank (Boston)
8. Chemical Bank
9. Manufacturers Hanover
10. Crédit Suisse (Switzerland), which holds stock for anonymous foreign investors

But it is rare that ownership can be traced even to the extent that we have done so here for AT&T.[22]

In short, the nation's largest corporations are "owned" by holding companies, street names, banks, insurance companies, pension funds, and other corporations. These "owners" almost always assign their voting rights as shareholders to the officers and directors of the companies they own. Thus, the officers and directors—"management"—control the decisions of the corporation. The institutional owners rarely try to oust management. If the owning institutions do not like the way a corporation is managed, they simply sell their stockholdings in it on the open market.

Stock *voting* power is even more concentrated than stock ownership. Many, if not most, stockholders turn over their voting power, via "proxies", to management, banks, pension funds, and investment firms. A Congressional investigation in 1978 into the question "Who Votes the Big Blocks?" produced convincing evidence of concentration of voting power in the nation's largest industrial, financial, transportation, insurance, and utility companies.[23] For eample, Morgan Guaranty Trust was

---

[22] For example, Cede & Co. is a front name for Depository Trust Co. of New York, but Depository refuses to reveal the names of anyone it represents. However, it was learned that Cede & Co. held at least the following corporate ownership shares in 1975:

| | |
|---|---|
| Ashland Oil | 8.1% |
| Chrysler | 15.8 |
| LTV Corp | 34.0 |
| Bethlehem Steel | 8.6 |
| Greyhound | 13.8 |
| TransWorld Airlines | 27.4 |
| PanAmerican Airways | 23.8 |
| Eastern Airlines | 31.9 |
| Braniff | 30.0 |
| American Electric Power | 13.4 |
| American Natural Gas | 11.6 |
| Niagara Mohawk Power | 13.5 |
| Western Union | 19.6 |

Nonetheless, despite Cede & Co.'s obvious importance, it has refused to reveal the names of its institutional investors. See Vic Reinemer, "Uniform Reporting Dealing with Corporate Ownership." Paper delivered at the Conference on Government Information Needs, Columbia University Center for Law and Economic Studies, November 1976.

[23] Subcommittee on Reports, Accounting, and Management, U.S. Senate Committee on Government Operations, "Voting in Major Corporations," January 15, 1978; courtesy of Victor Reinemer, staff director. Also reported in *The New York Times* January 19, 1978, p. 59.

identified as the largest *stockvoter* in 56 of the 122 largest corporations studied. Citibank was the largest stockvoter in 25 of these corporations. Moreover, Morgan Guaranty Trust is the largest stockvoter in Citybank (as well as BankAmerica, Manufacturers Hanover, Chemical New York Bank, and Bankers Trust New York). And Citicorp, in turn is the largest stockvoter in Morgan Guaranty Trust! In short, these banks "direct" each other, in that they have the major voting rights in each others' stocks. The study also confirmed that these banks and other large institutional investors generally vote to support management-backed programs and resolutions. They support management not only by voting the stock they own themselves, but also by voting the "proxies" they receive from other investors.

## THE CORPORATE CONSCIENCE

Today those at the top of the corporate world are far more liberal and oriented toward public welfare in their attitudes and decisions than the "robber baron" industrial capitalists of a few decades ago. Radical critics of American business who portray top corporate elites as reactionary, repressive, narrow-minded, or short-sighted vastly underestimate their chosen enemy.

Rugged individualism, laissez-faire, public-be-damned business attitudes are far more characteristic of new-rich, self-made men than of established corporate leaders. The people who head the nation's large corporations—both inheritors and up-from-the-ranks managers—are generally sympathetic to the ideals of social welfare. They are concerned with the public interest and express a devotion to the "corporate conscience." The corporate conscience is, in Adolf Berle's words,

> the existence of a set of ideas, widely held by the community and often by the organization itself and the men who direct it, that certain uses of power are "wrong," that is, contrary to the established interest and value system of the community. Indulgence of these ideas as a limitation on economic power, and regard for them by the managers of great corporations, is sometimes called—and ridiculed as—the "corporate conscience." The ridicule is pragmatically unjustified. The first sanction enforcing limitations imposed by the public consensus is a lively appreciation of that consensus by corporate managements. This is the reality of the "corporate conscience." [24]

These top leaders place great value on social prestige and popular esteem. Thus, although the public has no direct economic control over

[24] Adolph A. Berle, *Power Without Property*, pp. 90–91.

management, and government control is more symbolic than real, society does wield a powerful weapon—the deprivation of prestige—to aid in enforcing its values upon individuals and groups. Moreover, most of the values of the prevailing liberal consensus have already been internalized by corporate managers themselves.

Corporate elites are by no means hostile to big government. Indeed, in his popular book, *The New Industrial State,* John K. Galbraith argues effectively that we are experiencing a gradual blurring of the distinction between corporate versus governmental enterprise with the growth of a giant, bureaucratic "techno-structure." Corporate planning and governmental planning are replacing market competition in America. Corporations avoid vigorous price competition, and the government also endeavors to fix overall prices. Both corporations and the government seek stable relations with large labor unions. Solid, prosperous growth is the keynote of the planned economy, without undue, disruptive, old-style competition. Wars, depressions, or overheated inflations are to be avoided in the interest of stable growth. Big government, big industry, and big labor organizations share in this consensus. Within it, the big quietly grow bigger and more powerful. Government protects this secure, stable world of corporate giants, unless one of them should abuse the accepted standards of behavior or openly try to improve its position.

Thus the interests of the government and the corporate world come together on behalf of a consensus for stable planned growth:

> The state is strongly concerned with the stability of the economy. And with its expansion or growth. And with education. And with technical and scientific advance. And, most notably, with the national defense. These are *the* national goals; they are sufficiently trite so that one has a reassuring sense of the obvious in articulating them. All have their counterpart in the needs and goals of the techno-structure. It requires stability in demand for its planning. Growth brings promotion and prestige. It requires trained manpower. It needs government underwriting of research and development. Military and other technical procurement support its most developed form of planning. At each point the government has goals with which the techno-structure can identify itself.[25]

The new jargon in the board room is "corporate responsibility," "social consciousness," "affirmative action." These notions are more prevalent in larger corporations than in smaller ones, but it is the larger corporations that control the greatest share of America's economic resources. Only a few "classic" economists—most notably, University of Chicago's Milton Friedman—continue to argue that America's corpora-

---

[25] Galbraith, *The New Industrial State,* p. 316.

tions best serve the nation by concentrating on business alone, allocating resources on the basis of profit alone, and striving for optimum efficiency and productivity. In contrast, most top corporate elites are advocates of corporate responsibility—they want a larger social role for industry and generally are willing to sacrifice some profits to perform such a role. They believe that business should undertake positive efforts to expand minority opportunities, abate pollution, assist in the renewal and re-development of the nation's cities, and, in general, *do good*.

Consider, for example, the case of General Motors. The men at the top of GM are aware of the charges against the company; they are concerned with air pollution, congestion in cities, the ugliness of used-car scrap heaps, employment opportunities for blacks, and, of course, the safety record of their cars. In 1970, GM created a Public Policy Committee within its board of directors and elected its first black, Reverend Leon Sullivan, a leader in the creation of on-the-job minority training centers, to its board.[26] The Policy Committee recommended a series of steps to increase safety and pollution-control engineering efforts, speed up minority promotion practices, and improve GM relations with the mass media. When GM engineers wanted to inform the public that pollution-control costs rise exponentially when attempts are made to control the last few grams of pollutants, the Committee vetoed the effort. The engineers argued that spilling half a cup of gasoline at the pump puts more pollutants in the air than burning an entire tankful. They wanted to make public the fact that the added cost of meeting unreasonably high anti-pollution standards ($300 to $600 per car) was not worth the amount of pollutants involved. The GM directors agreed, but they were so sensitive to possible charges of economic self-interest and lack of concern for the environment that they decided *not* to tell the public of the unfavorable cost-benefit tradeoffs involved.

The cost of GM's annual social effort is estimated to be in excess of $600 million, or about one-third of its $2 billion before-tax profits.[27] In other words, earnings could be increased by one-third if GM dropped its "social" efforts. This figure represents a significant commitment to "corporate responsibility," but not a serious threat to the profit motive. Other factors—volume of sales, worker productivity, plant utilization, and so forth—affect profits more significantly than corporate social efforts. But it is wrong to believe that GM directors or other top corporate leaders are unconcerned with social problems.

Of course, the profit motive is still important to corporate elites,

[26] Peter Vanderwicken, "GM: The Price of Being Responsible," *Fortune*, January 1972.
[27] *Ibid.*

because profits are the basis of capital formation within the corporation. Increased capital at the disposal of corporate managers means increased power; losses mean a decrease in the capital available to the managers, a decrease in their power, and perhaps eventual extinction for the organization. But a certain portion of profits can be sacrificed for social concerns. The prudent corporate leader views such expenditures as being in the long-run interest of his corporation and himself.

## SUMMARY

In later chapters, we will examine interlocking, recruitment, conflict, and consensus, as well as corporate involvement in national policy making, in greater detail. Now, however, let us summarize our initial observations of corporate management as one of the key elites in the institutional structure of American society.

Economic power in America is highly concentrated. For example, a small number of corporations control over half the nation's industrial assets; half of all assets in communications, transportation, and utilities; and two-thirds of all insurance assets. This concentration of economic power is increasing gradually over time, as the nation's largest corporations gain ever larger shares of total corporate assets.

Power over corporate assets rests in the hands of about 3500 presidents and directors. These directors, not the stockholders or employees, decide major policy questions, choose the people who will carry out these decisions, and even select their own replacements. However, most of these presidents and directors have climbed the corporate ladder to their posts. These "managers" owe their rise to power to their skill in organizational life, and to their successful coping with the new demands for expertise in management, technology, and planning. Individual capitalists are no longer essential in the formation of capital assets. In fact, four-fifths of industrial capital is raised either within the corporation itself or from institutional borrowing.

It is true that the Rockefellers, Fords, duPonts, Mellons, and other great entrepreneurial families still exercise great power over corporate resources. But a majority of the directors of family-dominated firms have been brought in from outside the family; and only about 150 of the 500 largest corporations are family dominated.

Personal wealth is insignificant in relation to corporate (or governmental) wealth. Individuals may own millions, but institutions control billions. Thus it is necessary for individuals to achieve top corporate positions in order to exercise significant economic power.

Top corporate leaders generally display moderately liberal, socially

responsible attitudes and opinions on public issues. They are not necessarily hostile to government, but generally share with government an interest in stable growth, the avoidance of disruption, and planned scientific and technological development. The notion of "corporate responsibility" involves a willingness to sacrifice some profits to exercise a larger role in social policy making. Profits, however, remain essential to the accumulation of capital and the continued existence of the corporation.

# the governing
# circles

▶▶▶▶▶▶▶▶▶▶▶▶▶▶▶▶▶▶▶▶▶▶▶▶▶▶▶▶▶▶▶▶▶▶▶▶▶▶▶▶▶▶▶▶▶▶▶▶▶▶▶▶▶▶▶▶▶▶▶▶▶▶▶▶

# 3

If there ever was a time when the powers of government were limited—when government did no more than secure law and order, protect individual liberty and property, enforce contracts, and protect against foreign invasion—that time has long passed. Today it is commonplace to observe that governmental institutions intervene in every aspect of our lives—from the "cradle to the grave." Government in America has the primary responsibility for providing insurance against old age, death, dependency, disability, and unemployment; for providing medical care for the aged and indigent; for providing education at the elementary, secondary, collegiate, and postgraduate levels; for providing for public highways and regulating water, rail, and air transportation; for providing police and fire protection; for providing sanitation services and sewage disposal; for financing research in medicine, science, and technology; for delivering the mail; for exploring outer space; for maintaining parks and recreation; for providing housing and adequate food for the poor; for providing for job training and manpower programs; for cleaning the air and water; for rebuilding central cities; for maintaining full employment and a stable money supply; for regulating business practices and labor relations; for eliminating racial and sexual discrimination. Indeed, the list of government responsibilities seems endless, yet each year we manage to find additional tasks for government to do.

## THE CONCENTRATION OF GOVERNMENTAL POWER

Governments do many things that cannot be measured in terms of dollars and cents. Nonetheless, government expenditures are the best available measure of the dimensions of government activity. Such expenditures in the United States amount to about 35 percent of the gross national product. This is an increase from about 8 percent of the GNP at the beginning of the century. (Years ago, the German economist Adolph Wagner set forth the "law of increasing state activity"; in effect, this law states that government activity increases faster than economic output in all developing societies.) Today taxes amount to over $2,300 each year for every man, woman, and child in the nation. The largest governmental cost is "income maintenance"—social security, welfare, and related social services. Defense spending is the second largest governmental cost, followed by education.

Of course, the observation that government expenditures now account for over one-third of the nation's GNP actually understates the great power of government over every aspect of our lives. Government regulatory activity cannot be measured in government expenditures alone. Indeed, large segments of the economy come under direct federal regulation, notably transportation and utilities; yet these are officially classified as private industries and are not counted in the governmental proportion of the GNP.

Concentration of governmental resources is also evidenced in the growing proportion of *federal* expenditures in relation to *state* and *local* government expenditures. There are approximately 80,000 separate governmental units operating in the United States today. (U.S. government—1; state governments—50; counties—3,044; municipalities—18,517; townships—16,991; school districts—15,781; special districts—23,885.) But only one of these, the U.S. government, accounts for *two-thirds* of all governmental expenditures. This means that approximately 21 percent of the GNP is accounted for by federal expenditures alone. This centralization of governmental activity is a twentieth-century phenomenon: At the turn of the century, the federal government accounted for only one-third of all governmental expenditures; local governments carried on the major share of governmental activity.

We have defined our governmental elite as the top executive, congressional, military, and judicial officers of the *federal* government: the President and Vice-President; secretaries, undersecretaries, and assistant secretaries of executive departments; White House presidential advisers; congressional committee chairmen and ranking minority members; congressional majority and minority party leaders in the House and Senate; Supreme Court Justices; and members of the Federal Reserve Board and the Council of Economic Advisers. In the pages that follow we will try to describe some members of the governmental elite, as well as to discuss the power they exercise, and how they came to power.

## THE POLITICIANS: STYLE AND IMAGE

The politician is a professional office-seeker. He knows how to run for office—but not necessarily how to run the government. After victory at the polls, the prudent politician turns to "serious men" to run the government. Pulitzer Prize-winning writer David Halberstam reports a revealing conversation between newly elected President John F. Kennedy and Robert A. Lovett in December 1960, a month before Kennedy was to take office:

> On the threshold of great power and great office, the young man seemed to have everything. He was handsome, rich, charming, candid. The candor was part of the charm: he could beguile a visitor by admitting that everything the visitor proposed was right, rational, proper—but he couldn't do it, not this week, this month, this term. Now he was trying to put together a government, and the candor showed again. He was self-deprecating with the older man. He had spent the last five years, he said ruefully, running for office, and he did not know any real public officials, people to run a government, *serious men*. The only ones he knew, he admitted, were politicians. . . . Politicians *did* need men to serve, to run the government. The implication was obvious. Politicians could run Pennsylvania and Ohio, and if they could not run Chicago they could at least deliver it. But politicians run the world? What did they know about the Germans, the French, the Chinese? [1]

Robert Lovett was "the very embodiment of the Establishment." His father had been chairman of the board of Union Pacific Railroad and a partner of the great railroad tycoon, E. H. Harriman. Lovett attended Hill School and Yale, married the daughter of James Brown, the senior partner of the great banking firm of Brown Brothers, and formed a new and even larger Wall Street investment partnership, Brown Brothers, Harriman, & Co. Lovett urged Kennedy to listen to the advice of his partner and former Governor of New York and ambassador to the Soviet Union, Averell Harriman; to see "Jack McCloy at Chase," and "Doug Dillon too"; to look up a "young fellow over at Rockefeller, Dean Rusk," to head up the State Department; and to get "this young man at Ford, Robert McNamara," to run the Defense Department. Ken-

---

[1] David Halberstam, *The Best and the Brightest* (New York: Random House, 1969) , pp. 3–4. [Italics added.]

nedy gratefully accepted the advice: he turned to these "serious men" to run the government.

Of course, not all politicians are shallow, superficial, office-seekers. Some are "serious men" themselves—that is, they would be influential even if they never won elective office. Following are a few examples of such individuals.

*Nelson A. Rockefeller.* Former Vice-President of the United States, fourterm Governor of New York. Son of John D. Rockefeller. Attended Lincoln School and Dartmouth College. Former president and chairman of the Rockefeller Center of New York City. Former Assistant Secretary of State, special assistant to the President for International Development, Under Secretary of Health, Education and Welfare. Chairman of the board of the Museum of Modern Art, trustee of the Rockefeller Brothers Fund, Government Affairs Foundation, Inc.

*Charles Percy.* U.S. Senator (R. Ill.). Attended University of Chicago. Former president and chairman of the board of Bell & Howell Corporation. Director of Harris Trust and Savings Bank. Outboard Moving Corporation. Former chairman of National Finance Committee of the Republican Party. Trustee of the University of Chicago, Illinois Institute of Technology, California Institute of Technology.

*H. J. Hienz III.* U.S. Senator (R. Pa.) Attended Phillips Exeter Academy, Yale University, and Harvard Law School. Began work with his father's H. J. Hienz Co. as marketing manager. He left the family business to win a congressional seat from Pittsburgh in 1970. In 1976 he won election to the U.S. Senate in the most expensive campaign in the State's history.

*Daniel Patrick Moynihan.* U.S. Senator (D.N.K.) Attended public schools in New York City; received B.A., M.A., and Ph.D. degrees in political science from Fletcher School of Law and Diplomacy. He was professor of education and urban politics at Harvard and director of the Harvard—M.I.T. Joint Center for Urban Studies. Served as Assistant Secretary of Labor under Presidents Kennedy and Johnson, Assistant to the President for Domestic Affairs under President Nixon, ambassador to India, and ambassador to the United Nations under President Ford. He is the author of numerous books and articles and he is listed as one of the nation's elite intellectuals (p. 138).

The backgrounds of these men suggest that they can run a government as well as run for office. But the great majority of politicians—elective officeholders—have had little or no experience in heading major enterprises. Most have devoted their lives to running for public office. They are specialists in vote-getting, public relations, image-making, bargaining and compromise, and coalition-building.

Most politicians in America are lawyers. But they are not usually top professional lawyers. (We will examine these "superlawyers" in Chapter 5.) Instead, the typical politician-lawyer uses his law career as a means of support—one that is compatible with political office-holding. Woodrow Wilson said, "The profession I chose was politics; the profession I entered was the law. I entered one because I thought it would lead to the other." [2] The legal profession provides the free time, the extensive public contacts, and the occupational prestige required for political campaigning. The lawyer's occupation is the representation of clients, so he makes no great change when he moves from representing clients in private practice to representing constituents in public office.

A significant number of top politicians have inherited great wealth. The Roosevelts, Rockefellers, Kennedys, Lodges, Harrimans, and others have used their wealth and family connections to support their political careers. *But it is important to note that a majority of the nation's top politicians have climbed the ladder from relative obscurity to political success.* Many have acquired some wealth in the process, but most started their climb from very middle-class circumstances. In fact, only one of the last six Presidents (John F. Kennedy) was born to great wealth. Thus, as in the corporate world, one finds both "inheritors" and "climbers" in the world of politics.

## GERALD R. FORD: FROM THE ROSE BOWL TO THE WHITE HOUSE

Gerald Ford has always been a team player—from his days as an All-American lineman at the University of Michigan, through his long service and rise to leadership in the Congress, during his years of service and support for the Republican Party, to his presidency. He projects the image of an open, accessible, and consensus-building presidency. Ford was the nation's first President not selected by popular vote (or by vote of presidential electors). He is a man whose career was built in the Congress of the United States. His colleagues there have described him as "solid, dependable, and loyal—a man more comfortable carrying out the programs of others than initiating things on his own." [3] As President, he was thrust into the role of leadership, but there is ample evidence that he acted only after extensive consultation with leaders in Congress, the cabinet, industry, finance, labor, and the mass media.

Gerald Ford was born Leslie King, Jr., but his mother divorced and remarried Gerald R. Ford, a Grand Rapids, Michigan, paint store owner. Ford attended public schools in Grand Rapids, and received his B.A. from the University of Michigan and his law degree from Yale Uni-

[2] Quoted in Heinz Eulau and John Sprague, *Lawyers in Politics* (Indianapolis: Bobbs-Merrill Co., 1964), p. 5.

[3] *Congressional Quarterly,* October 20, 1973, p. 2762.

versity. He was a star lineman on the University of Michigan's national championship and Rose Bowl football teams in 1932 and 1933, and was the team's most valuable player in 1934. He turned down the opportunity to play professional football in order to take a coaching job at Yale that would permit him to attend law school at the same time. Upper-social-class member U.S. Senator William Proxmire, whom Ford coached at Yale says, "Ford is the same kind of man now as he was then— solid and square. He has the kind of wholesome sincerity, the kind of loyal consistency that many voters may be looking for." Ford graduated in the top third of his Yale Law School class in 1941. Following service with the Navy in World War II in the South Pacific, Ford returned home to Grand Rapids and, capitalizing on his football reputation and war service, won election to the House in 1948.

Ford served 25 years in the House as a loyal Republican, winning recognition for his integrity, sincerity, and common sense, rather than his intelligence, initiative, or imagination. He was also careful to cultivate his home constituents with minor services, favors, and visits. In 1965, Wisconsin Congressman Melvin Laird, later to become Secretary of Defense, led a movement among House Republicans to replace the aging Charles Halleck as Minority Leader with the younger, likable Gerald Ford. Ford developed into an excellent House Leader through his engaging personality, honesty, and ability to establish close personal relationships with both allies and opponents. A House colleague explained: "Jerry is an open tactician. He doesn't look for clever ways to sneak in behind you. He does the obvious, which is usually common sense." [4]

Ford's voting record was moderately conservative. He voted *for* the Civil Rights Act of 1964, the Voting Rights Act of 1965, and the Fair Housing Act of 1968. But he opposed many aspects of the "war on poverty" and other social welfare spending measures. He supported defense spending, and supported both Presidents Johnson and Nixon in their conduct in the Vietnam War. Ford denounced ultraliberal Supreme Court Justice William O. Douglas after the Justice wrote an article in the left-wing *Evergreen Review* sanctioning violent revolution in America.

In 1973, as the Watergate Affair expanded and Vice-President Spiro Agnew resigned and pleaded guilty to the charge of tax evasion, President Nixon sought to bring into his administration men of recognized personal integrity who could improve presidential relations with Congress. Nixon's ultimate decision to make Gerald Ford Vice-President under the 26th Amendment was widely applauded in Congress and the news media. But in a sense, Ford was Congress's choice for the vice-

---

[4] *Time*, August 19, 1974, p. 32.

presidency, not Richard Nixon's. Nixon personally preferred former Texas Governor John Connally. Ford was quickly confirmed by the Democratic-controlled Congress.

Ford's style is candid, folksy, unpretentious. His long years in the Congress have developed in him a tolerance of differing views, a desire to accommodate, and a willingness to compromise differences. In his first speech to the nation as President he said, "I have had lots of adversaries, but no enemies that I can remember."

When Ford spoke at the Harvard Club of Boston, he was asked to comment on the exile of the world-renowned Russian novelist Alexander Solzhenitsyn. Ford simply said: "Well, I've never read anything Solzhenitsyn has written, but I understand he's quite superb." [5] Doubtlessly there were many others at the Harvard Club who had never read Solzhenitsyn, but to admit such a fact in these circles is unheard of. Such openness contributed to his rise to the top. Whether this was a sufficient quality to govern a nation remains a crucial question. But after the years of Watergate, and a notable absence of candor in the White House, Ford's most visible quality—open sincerity—appealed to the Congress, the news media, and the general public.

Indeed, despite the Watergate scandal and the split in his own party with the Reagan conservatives, and despite a two-to-one lead in Democratic party registration, Ford nearly won the 1976 Presidential election. The fact that he came so close (49 percent of the two-party vote) under these adverse circumstances is a tribute to his unpretentious style and "good guy" image. Although Ford had spent most of his adult life in politics, he never implied that he personally could run the country. More than most modern politicians, Ford acknowledged the importance of the "serious men" who worked in his administration. Even in the presidency, Ford remained a team player.

## JIMMY CARTER: THE SMILE
## ON THE FACE OF THE ESTABLISHMENT

James Earl Carter, Jr. is usually portrayed as a political "outsider," who was catapulted from a Plains, Georgia, peanut farmer to President of the United States in less than two years. At first glance, Carter's meteoric rise from rustic obscurity to the nation's most powerful office would seem to demolish the elitist notion of selecting leaders from the ranks of seasoned officeholders. But a closer examination of elite concerns in 1976—especially concern over declining public confidence in established elites them-

---

[5] Saul Friedman, "In Praise of Honest Ignorance," *Harpers* (August 1974), p. 16.

selves—together with Carter's establishment connections, provides a better understanding of how and when an "outsider" will be selected for national leadership. Specifically, Carter's rise to the presidency can be attributed to elite concerns with declining public trust in national institutions and national leaders, as well as elite knowledge that Carter's "new" face among the national elite would be cosmetic only and would *not* lead to any fundamental changes in policies, programs, or values.

One year before he was elected President, three-quarters of the American people had never heard of Jimmy Carter. He had served only one lackluster term as Governor of Georgia. He had never served in Congress and, except for seven years in the Navy, he had never worked for the federal government. He was not even a lawyer. His family's four million dollar holdings in Sumter County, Georgia, may have made them *local* influentials, but few *national* leaders had ever heard of Sumter County, Georgia. But Carter judged correctly in early 1974 that these political disadvantages could be turned to his favor in an era of popular discontent with national leadership over Watergate, inflation and unemployment, and defeat and humiliation in Vietnam.

The national news media paid little attention to Carter's December 12, 1974, announcement that he was a presidential candidate. Media executives, and political observers everywhere, expected that established leaders—Hubert H. Humphrey or Edward M. Kennedy—would win the presidency in 1976. However, Carter knew that the first two presidential primaries were in New Hampshire and Florida. The first was a small state where he had two years to engage in face-to-face campaigning, and the second was a neighboring Southern state. These two early primary victories brought Carter the recognition that he needed. In the spring of 1976, discussion within national elite circles turned to the question of whether Humphrey or Kennedy could dispel public doubts about national leadership, or whether these men had been tarnished by past scandals, errors, and humiliations.

Carter defeated weaker candidates in the early primaries—Udall, Jackson, Wallace, Shriver, Harris, Schapp, Bentson—although he lost to Brown and Church in later primaries. The real question, however, throughout early 1976 was whether either of the political heavy-weights, Humphrey or Kennedy, would enter the race and take the prize away from Carter. In the end, consultations with other top leaders convinced both men not to run and to allow Carter to become President.

Jimmy Carter is in the great log cabin tradition of American politics. Like Andrew Jackson, Abraham Lincoln, and many others before him, he emphasized his humble beginnings. But his rural boyhood, his Annapolis training, his years in the Navy, his rebuilding of the family peanut business, his years as a Georgia legislator (1962–67), his

two campaigns for the Georgia governorship (1966 when he lost to conservative Lester Maddox and 1970 when he defeated liberal Carl Sanders),
and his service as Governor (1971–75), all contributed to the development of a tough-minded yet flexible politician. Carter proudly pro-
claimed himself "an ignorant and bigoted redneck" in 1970 in order to
defeat a liberal opponent; [6] but after his election he charmed the black
leaders of Georgia by ceremoniously placing a portrait of Martin Luther
King, Jr. in the state capitol. He correctly calculated that in 1976 both
elites and masses in America would be searching for a new face, an
original style, a high moral tone.

Carter brought a new down-home, god-fearing, peanut farmer image into national politics. But he stuck closely to established liberal
remedies for society's problems: social programs for the poor and the
aged; civil rights commitments for blacks; jobs for the unemployed; a
strong national defense; federal aid for cities; support for large labor
unions; and even governmental reorganization, tax "reform," and a balanced budget.

While Carter was obviously a "climber" in the political world, he
was not really the "outsider" that he presented himself to be in the
election. In fact, Carter had been introduced to the "political and economic elite" several years before he began his race for the presidency.
The Coca Cola Company is the largest industrial corporation headquartered in Atlanta. J. Paul Austin, Chairman of the Board of Coca
Cola and a friend and supporter of Jimmy Carter, nominated the Georgia
Governor to serve as a U.S. representative on the international Trilateral
Commission. The Trilateral Commission was established in 1972 by
David Rockefeller, with the assistance of the Council on Foreign Relations and the Rockefeller Foundation. The Trilateral Commission is a
group of corporate officials of multinational corporations and government officials of several industrialized nations who meet periodically to
coordinate economic policy between the United States, Western Europe,
and Japan. Carter's appointment was made by Rockefeller himself and
came with the support of Coca Cola and Lockheed, both Atlanta-based,
multinational corporations. The executive director of the Commission
was Columbia University Professor Zbigniew Brzezinski (now Carter's
national security adviser). The Commission's membership is a com-
pendium of power and prestige; it included Cal Tech President, Harold
Brown (now Secretary of Defense); Coca Cola's J. Paul Austin; *Time
Magazine* editor Hedley Donovan; Paul Warnke, partner in Clark Clifford's Washington law firm; Alden Clausen, president of BankAmerica,
the nation's largest bank; United Auto Workers president Leonard

[6] *Congressional Quarterly Weekly Report*, July 24, 1976, p. 1983.

Woodcock; Bendix Corporation president, Werner M. Blumenthal (now Secretary of the Treasury); Cyrus Vance, senior Wall Street lawyer (now Secretary of State); and U.S. Senator Walter Mondale (now Vice-President of the United States) .

Thus, after Carter won the Democratic nomination, he could sit down comfortably at New York's exclusive "21" Club as a guest of Henry Ford II to meet with the nation's top corporate elite.[7] He could successfully reassure top business leaders that his brand of "populism" would not hurt big business. As Charles Kirbo, Atlanta corporate attorney and Carter's closest adviser, put it: "My guess is that after a while, businessmen will be very happy with Jimmy as President. . . . Jimmy wants to create a fair tax system. But Jimmy is a businessman himself, and he likes to make money. And once he makes it, he likes to keep it." [8]

Thus, Carter as an "outsider" provided the new face, the smile, the reassuring manner that a worried establishment perceived as essential in winning back mass confidence in national leadership. At the same time, Carter reinforced established programs and policies; he personified traditional American values—humble beginnings, hard work, success in business and politics, deep roots in the soil, the family, and the community, and pronounced Christian morals and principles. He was welcomed into top elite circles as a man who could restore mass confidence in public institutions and national leadership, and do so without changing things much.

Carter's appointments reflect his establishment connections. From the Rockefeller-supported Trilateral Commission he chose Secretary of State Cyrus Vance, Secretary of Defense Harold Brown, Secretary of the Treasury Werner Michael Blumenthal, and National Security Adviser Zbigniew Brzezinski. He chose James R. Schlesinger as the nation's first Secretary of Energy; this is the same Schlesinger who served as Secretary of Defense under President Nixon and director of the C.I.A. Carter chose two women for his cabinet (one more than President Ford); one of these women is black (President Ford also had one black cabinet member) . Patricia Roberts Harris was named Secretary of Housing and Urban Development. Ms. Harris was a successful Washington attorney and law partner of Sargent Shriver, brother-in-law of Edward M. Kennedy. She was U.S. Ambassador to Luxembourg under President Johnson; she is also a director of IBM, Chase Manhattan Bank, Scott Paper Co., and a member of the Council on Foreign Relations. Juanita M. Kreps, vice-president of Duke University, was named Secretary of Commerce. She has an earned Ph. D. in economics from Duke; she is also a director of

---

[7] *Wall Street Journal*, August 12, 1976, p. 1.
[8] *Ibid.*

J. C. Penney Co., Western Electric, Eastman Kodak, Blue Cross–Blue Shield, R. J. Reynolds Tobacco, North Carolina State Bank, and the New York Stock Exchange. So much for Carter's "minority" representation in the Cabinet.

Jimmy Carter's rapid rise to national leadership, and his welcome into top elite circles, represents still another tactic available to an embattled elite—replace old faces associated with past defeats and humiliations with smiling new faces, promising honesty, compassion, and good times. And indeed Carter's subsequent performance as President emphasized style rather than substance. Carter focused the attention of the news media and the general public on presidential visits to small towns, dial-a-President telethons, eliminating limousine service for high officials, selling the presidential yacht, and similar gestures designed to "get close to the people." But on major foreign and defense policy issues—the SALT talks, détente with the USSR, relations with China, a Mideast peace, restoring a strategic nuclear balance—Carter made little substantive progress. Likewise on domestic issues—welfare reform, tax rebates, energy policy, tax reform—Carter made little headway with Congress. This is not necessarily a criticism of the Carter Administration, but a recognition of the fact that style (or "image") has taken precedence over substantive issues. This is true of most politicians; it is particularly true of a President selected for his smile, his self-assurance, his high moral tone.

## TED KENNEDY: CROWN PRINCE

John F. Kennedy once said of his brothers, "Just as I went into politics because Joe [the oldest Kennedy brother, killed in World War II] died, if anything happened to me tomorrow Bobby would run for my seat in the Senate. And if Bobby died, our young brother Ted would take over for him."

Edward M. "Ted" Kennedy's major qualifications for public office are his style, appearance, accent, and name. He is the image of his late brothers, John and Robert. Their deaths by assassins' bullets make the youngest Kennedy brother the sentimental favorite of millions of Americans—the last guardian of the Camelot legend. The Kennedy charisma attaches to Ted despite tragedy, scandal, and defeat at the hands of fellow Democratic senators (Kennedy was unceremoniously ousted as Senate Democratic Whip in 1971). The Kennedy wealth is another major political asset. Ted Kennedy's public tax returns reveal an income of $.5 million per year from interest on his inheritance, suggesting a personal net worth of about $10 million. Total family wealth probably exceeds $100 million.

The Kennedy dynasty began with the flamboyant career of Joseph P. Kennedy, son of a prosperous Irish saloon-keeper and ward boss in Boston. Joseph Kennedy attended Boston Latin School and Harvard, receiving his B.A. in 1912. He started his career in banking, moved into stock market operations, dabbled in shipbuilding, formed a movie-making company (RKO and later Paramount), and married the daughter of the Mayor of Boston. "Old Joe" made the major part of his fortune in stock market manipulations. With his associate, William Randolph Hearst, Kennedy provided key financial backing for the 1932 presidential campaign of Franklin D. Roosevelt. FDR later made Kennedy head of the Securities and Exchange Commission. But making a market speculator head of a commission that was designed to protect investors caused such public outcry that he was forced to resign after one year. FDR then appointed Kennedy head of the Maritime Commission, but rumors of extravagant subsidies to shipbuilding friends forced his resignation after only two months on the job. In 1937, FDR appointed him ambassador to England. His diplomatic career lasted three years and ended over differences with FDR regarding U.S. assistance to the Allies. Old Joe is said to have advised FDR of the likelihood of German victory and the advantages of placating Hitler.

Joseph P. Kennedy, Sr., was a family man, a prominent Catholic, and the father of nine children. (Joseph P., Jr., was killed as a World War II Navy Pilot; President John F. Kennedy was assassinated; Senator Robert F. Kennedy was assassinated: Kathleen died in a plane crash; Rosemary is living in an institution for the mentally retarded; Eunice is married to Sargent Shriver, former director of the Peace Corps and the War on Poverty and replacement for Senator Thomas Eagleton as the Democratic vice-presidential nominee in 1972; Patricia, formerly married to actor Peter Lawford; Jean, wife of Stephen Smith; and the youngest, Edward M. "Ted" Kennedy.)

Although born to great wealth and accustomed to an upper-class style of living (he received his first communion from Pope Pius XII), Ted Kennedy acquired the sense of competition fostered in the large Kennedy household. In 1951, suspended from Harvard for cheating on a Spanish examination, he joined the Army and served two years in Germany. He was readmitted to Harvard, where he played on the Harvard football team and graduated in 1956.

Despite his family background, Harvard Law School rejected Ted Kennedy's application for admission. So he enrolled in the University of Virginia Law School and completed his law degree in 1959. Following graduation and work on his brother's 1960 presidential campaign, he was appointed assistant district attorney for Suffolk County, Massachusetts.

In 1962, when he was just 30 years old, the minimum age for a

U.S. Senator, he announced his candidacy for the Massachusetts Senate seat formerly held by his brother, who was then President. In the Democratic primary he faced Edward J. McCormack, nephew of the then Speaker of the House, John W. McCormack. During a televised debate, McCormack said to Kennedy, "You never worked for a living. You never held elective office. You lack the qualifications and maturity of judgment. . . . If your name were not Kennedy, your candidacy would be a joke." But Kennedy won overwhelmingly and went on to defeat the Republican candidate George Cabot Lodge. (George Cabot Lodge was the son of U.S. Ambassador to South Vietnam and former U.S. Senator Henry Cabot Lodge, Jr. In 1916, Kennedy's grandfather, Boston Mayor John F. Fitzgerald had been defeated in a race for the same Senate seat by Lodge's great-grandfather, Senator Henry Cabot Lodge.) Kennedy's campaign slogan was "I can do more for Massachusetts," which undoubtedly carried the implication to some of political patronage from his brother the President.

Kennedy performed better in the Senate than many had expected. He cultivated Senate friends, appeared at fund-raising dinners, and informed himself about several important policy fields. He worked hard learning about national health problems and eventually became chairman of the Subcommittee on Health of the Senate Labor and Public Welfare Committee. He also devoted considerable attention to problems of the elderly and to the activities of the National Science Foundation. In 1969 he was elected Senate Democratic Whip by his colleagues.

But his personal life was marred by accident, tragedy, and scandal. He nearly died in a 1964 plane crash in which he suffered a broken back. An athletic and handsome 6 foot 2 inches, Kennedy was frequently the object of romantic gossip at Washington cocktail parties. On July 19, 1969, a young woman, Mary Jo Kopechne, died when the car Kennedy was driving plunged off a narrow bridge on Chappaquiddick Island after a late-night party. Missing for ten hours after the accident, Kennedy later made a dramatic national television appearance, saying that the tragedy had been an accident, that he had tried unsuccessfully to save Miss Kopechne, and that he had been too confused to report the tragedy until the next day. The official inquest has been kept secret, and many feel that there are still unresolved discrepancies in Kennedy's story.[9] Kennedy pled guilty to the minor charge of leaving the scene of an accident.

Senate Democrats removed Kennedy from his position as majority Whip. But the national news media never pressed the Chappaquiddick incident and continued favorable reporting of the still charismatic Sen-

[9] See Robert Sherrill, "Chappaquiddick + 5," *New York Times Magazine*, July 14, 1974.

ator. He recovered quickly in public opinion polls and generally leads all other Democrats in presidential preference polling. Kennedy deliberately avoided the Democratic presidential nomination in both 1972 and 1976. But most observers believe he can have the Democratic Party's presidential nomination after Carter leaves office.

Clearly, Ted Kennedy is an "inheritor," rather than a "climber" in the world of politics. Yet, like other successful politicians, his success rests upon his image and style more than his substantive contributions to public policy. He was elected to the Senate solely because he was a Kennedy—an inheritor of a famous political image. The image survived tragedy and scandal, although his fellow Senators seem less impressed with his mystique than the general public. His power today stems not from what he knows about government, but from the realization that he may some day convert his popular image into a successful presidential candidate.

## EXECUTIVE DECISION MAKERS: THE SERIOUS MEN

Politicians deal in style and image. But the responsibility for the initiation of national programs and policies falls primarily upon the top White House staff and the heads of executive departments. Generally, Congress merely responds to policy proposals initiated by the executive branch. The President and his key advisers and administrators have a strong incentive to fulfill their responsibility for decision making: In the eyes of the American public, they are responsible for everything that happens in the nation regardless of whether or not they have the authority or capacity to do anything about it. There is a general expectation that every administration, even one committed to a "caretaker" role, will put forth some sort of policy program.

The President and Vice-President, White House presidential advisers and ambassadors-at-large, cabinet secretaries, under secretaries, and assistant secretaries constitute our executive elite. Let us take a brief look at the careers of some of the people who have served in key cabinet positions in recent presidential administrations.

### Defense

*Charles E. Wilson.* Secretary of Defense, 1953–57; president and member of the board of directors of General Motors.

*Neil H. McElroy.* Secretary of Defense, 1957–59; former president and member of the board of directors of Procter & Gamble; member of the board of directors of General Electric, of Chrysler Corp., and of Equitable Life Assurance Co.; member of the board of trustees of Harvard University, of the National Safety Council, and of the National Industrial Conference.

*Thomas S. Gates.* Secretary of Defense, 1959–60, and Secretary of the Navy, 1957–59; chairman of the board and chief executive officer, Morgan Guaranty Trust Co.; member of the board of directors of General Electric, Bethlehem Steel, Scott Paper Co., Campbell Soup Co., Insurance Co. of North America, Cities Service, Smith Kline and French (pharmaceuticals), and the University of Pennsylvania.

*Robert S. McNamara.* Secretary of Defense, 1961–67; president and member of the board of directors of the Ford Motor Co.; member of the board of directors of Scott Paper Co.; president of the World Bank, 1967 to date.

*Clark Clifford.* Secretary of Defense, 1967–69; senior partner of Clifford & Miller (Washington law firm); member of board of directors of the National Bank of Washington and of the Sheridan Hotel Corp.; special counsel to the President, 1949–50; member of board of trustees of Washington University in St. Louis.

*Melvin Laird.* Secretary of Defense, 1969–73; former Wisconsin Republican Congressman and chairman of Republican Conference in the House of Representatives.

*James R. Schlesinger.* Secretary of Defense, 1973–77; former director, Central Intelligence Agency; former chairman of Atomic Energy Commission; formerly assistant director of Office of Management and Budget, economics professor, and research associate of the RAND Corp.

*Harold Brown.* Secretary of Defense, 1977 to date; former president of the California Institute of Technology. A member of the board of directors of International Business Machines (IBM) and the Times-Mirror Corp. Former Secretary of the Air Force under President Lyndon Johnson, and U.S. representative to the SALT I talks under President Richard Nixon.

## State

*John Foster Dulles.* Secretary of State, 1953–60; partner of Sullivan & Cromwell (one of 20 largest law firms on Wall Street); member of the board of directors of the Bank of New York, Fifth Avenue Bank, American Bank Note Co., International Nickel Co. of Canada, Babcock and Wilson Corp., Shenandoah Corp., United Cigar Stores, American Cotton Oil Co., United Railroad of St. Louis, and European Textile Corp. He was a trustee of New York Public Library, Union Theological Seminary, Rockefeller Foundation, and the Carnegie Endowment for International Peace; also a delegate to the World Council of Churches.

*Dean Rusk.* Secretary of State, 1961–68; former president of Rockefeller Foundation.

*William P. Rodgers.* Secretary of State, 1969–73; U.S. attorney general during Eisenhower Administration; senior partner in Royall, Koegal, Rogers, and Wells (one of the 20 largest Wall Street law firms).

*Henry Kissinger.* Secretary of State, 1973–77; former special assistant to the President for National Security Affairs; former Harvard Professor of International Affairs, and project director for Rockefeller Brothers Fund and for the Council on Foreign Relations.

*Cyrus Vance.* Secretary of State, 1977 to date; senior partner in the New York law firm of Simpson, Thacher and Bartlett. A member of the board of directors of International Business Machines (IBM) and Pan American World Airways; a trustee of Yale University, the Rockefeller Foundation, and the Council on Foreign Relations. Former Secretary of the Army under President Lyndon Johnson.

## Treasury

*George M. Humphrey.* Secretary of the Treasury, 1953–57; former chairman of the board of directors of the M. A. Hanna Co.; member of board of directors of National Steel Corp.; Consolidated Coal Co. of Canada and Dominion Sugar Co.; trustee of M.I.T.

*Robert B. Anderson.* Secretary of the Treasury, 1957–61; Secretary of the Navy, 1953–54; deputy Secretary of Defense, 1954–55; member of board of directors of Goodyear Tire and Rubber Co. and Pan-American Airways; member of the executive board of the Boy Scouts of America.

*Douglas Dillon.* Secretary of the Treasury, 1961–63; chairman of the board of Dillon, Reed, and Co., Inc. (one of Wall Street's largest investment firms) ; member of New York Stock Exchange; director of U.S. and Foreign Securities Corp. and U.S. International Securities Corp.; member of board of governors of New York Hospital and Metropolitan Museum.

*David Kennedy.* Secretary of the Treasury, 1969–71; president and chairman of the board of Continental Illinois Bank and Trust Co.; director of International Harvester Co., Commonwealth Edison, Pullman Co., Abbott Laboratories, Swift and Co., U.S. Gypsum, and Communications Satellite Corp.; trustee of the University of Chicago, the Brookings Institution, the Committee for Economic Development, and George Washington University.

*John B. Connally.* Secretary of the Treasury, 1971–72; former Secretary of Navy, Governor of Texas, administrative assistant to Lyndon B. Johnson; attorney for Murcheson Brothers Investment (Dallas) ; former director of New York Central Railroad.

*George P. Schultz.* Secretary of the Treasury, 1972–74; former Secretary of Labor and director of the Office of Management and Budget; former dean of the University of Chicago Graduate School of Business; former director of Borg-Warner Corp., General American Transportation Co., and Stein, Roe & Farnham (investments) .

*William E. Simon.* Secretary of the Treasury, 1974–77; former director, Federal Energy Office, and former Deputy Secretary of the Treasury; formerly a senior partner of Salomon Brothers (one of Wall Street's largest investment firms specializing in municipal bond trading) .

*Warner Michael Blumenthal.* Secretary of the Treasury, 1977 to date. Former president of the Bendix Corporation; former vice-president of Crown Cork Co. A trustee of Princeton University and the Council on Foreign Relations.

It makes relatively little difference whether a President is a Democrat or a Republican: he must call on the same type of "serious men" to run the government.

## INTELLECTUALS IN POWER: KISSINGER AND BRZEZINSKI

Only one person meets *daily* with the President to discuss questions of war and peace—the Assistant to the President for National Security Affairs. This presidential adviser coordinates all of the information coming from the C.I.A., the State Department, and the Defense Department; briefs the President daily on national security affairs; heads the staff of the National Security Council; and presents alternative policies for the President's selection. Interestingly, over the last 20 years, this most important post in the White House has been filled by "intellectuals" —men drawn from the nation's leading universities who have demonstrated their competence in elite circles. McGeorge Bundy, dean of arts and sciences at Harvard University, held the job under President Kennedy; Henry Kissinger, professor of government at Harvard, held the post under President Nixon; and Zbigniew Brzezinski, professor of government at Columbia University, holds the position in the Carter Administration. It is interesting to observe how intellectuals have risen to such positions of power and to examine the way in which they use this power.

### Henry Kissinger

Heinz Alfred Kissinger (he changed his name to Henry after coming to the United States) was born in Furth in Bavaria, Germany. His father was a teacher in the local *Gymnasium,* or prep school. The Kissingers were an educated, middle-class German Jewish family. When the Nazis came to power in the early 1930s, the Kissingers were subjected to increasing persecution. Young Henry was denied entrance to the *Gymnasium* and forced to attend an all-Jewish school. He and his fellow Jewish students were frequently beaten up on their way to and from school. His father was humiliated and then dismissed from his teaching post. At his mother's urging, the family emigrated to New York City in 1938. His father found work as a clerk and bookkeeper and his mother worked as a cook. Henry attended George Washington High School in New York; he was a straight-A student, but his heavy accent and unhappy experiences in Germany caused him to be withdrawn.

After graduation, Kissinger took a job in a shaving brush factory and took evening courses at the City University of New York in hopes of becoming an accountant. He was drafted in 1943, and as a private in the 84th Infantry Division saw action in France and Germany. But his comrades still described him as "totally withdrawn."

Kissinger once observed about his own early career: "Living as a Jew under the Nazis, then as a refugee in America, and then as a private in the Army isn't exactly an experience that builds confidence." But it was in the Army that Kissinger first made his mark. When his division moved into Germany, he was made interpreter for the division's commanding general. Later he was placed in charge of the military government of the small German town of Drefeld and promoted to staff sergeant. One of his officers urged him to return home after his service and complete his college education. He also advised him that "gentlemen do not go to the College of the City of New York." Kissinger took the advice, returned home, won a New York State scholarship, and was admitted to Harvard University.

Kissinger graduated as a Phi Beta Kappa, summa cum laude government major in 1950, and continued his studies at the Harvard Graduate School. He received his M.S. in 1952 and his Ph.D. in 1954, writing his dissertation on the efforts of conservative statesmen to create a new world balance of power at the Conference of Vienna in 1815. (This was later published as *A World Restored: Castlereagh, Metternich, and the Problems of Peace* [1957].)

Kissinger reportedly turned down a professorship at the University of Chicago to stay at Harvard as a temporary instructor. But shortly thereafter he was appointed to head an important study by the Council on Foreign Relations to develop methods short of all-out war for coping with the perceived Soviet challenge to Western Europe. Key members of this influential Council had become disenchanted with the "massive retaliation" doctrine of then Secretary of State John Foster Dulles. In 1957 Kissinger produced his major work, *Nuclear Weapons and Foreign Policy*,[10] which argued persuasively that strategy must determine weapons rather than vice versa, and that the U.S. should strive for greater flexibility in weapons development, including tactical nuclear weapons.

The book established Kissinger as a leading "defense intellectual." He was named associate professor (1959), and professor (1962), in Har-

---

[10] Henry Kissinger, *Nuclear Weapons and Foreign Policy* (New York: Council on Foreign Relations, 1957). Published also as an Anchor Book by Doubleday, 1958.

vard's Government Department and director of Harvard's Defense Studies Program. He became a consultant to the Joint Chiefs of Staff, the National Security Council, Arms Control and Disarmament Agency, and the State Department, as well as the RAND Corporation. His close association with the Rockefellers began when Nelson A. Rockefeller asked him to direct a Rockefeller Brothers Foundation special study of foreign policy. The resulting book, *The Necessity of Choice: Prospects of American Foreign Policy* (1961), warned against undue optimism about U.S.-Soviet relations but also recommended ways of avoiding the ultimate confrontation between these superpowers. Later Kissinger became foreign policy adviser to Nelson Rockefeller and drafted his key statements on world affairs during the New York Governor's unsuccessful bid for the presidency in 1968.

Although Nixon viewed himself as an expert on world affairs, one of his earliest moves after assuming the presidency in 1968 was to ask the Rockefellers, the Council of Foreign Affairs, and the Harvard University intellectuals for their choice of a foreign affairs specialist. They recommended Kissinger and, even though Nixon had only met him once, Kissinger was appointed Special Assistant to the President for National Security Affairs.

Kissinger's performance as the President's national security adviser and special emissary can only be described as spectacular. He met secretly with North Vietnamese representatives over a prolonged period of negotiations which eventually ended the Vietnam War. He undertook his now-celebrated clandestine trip to Peking to arrange the President's historic visit to that nation. In trips to Moscow he paved the way for the President's visit and the establishment of a new Soviet-American détente. He played the major role in the Strategic Arms Limitation Talks (SALT), which resulted in the world's first agreement to limit strategic nuclear weapons. His performance overshadowed that of Secretary of State William P. Rodgers. In 1974, upon the resignation of Rodgers, Kissinger was appointed Secretary of State.

Kissinger's power and reputation generally survived the demise of the Nixon presidency. The new President, Gerald Ford, with little experience in foreign policy, seemed to rely on Kissinger as much or more than had Nixon. As Secretary of State, Kissinger continued to engage in personal travel and face-to-face diplomacy. He did not retreat within the State Department bureaucracy. But with the presidency weakened by Watergate, with a Democratic Congress suspicious of presidential power, and with the mass media increasingly critical of foreign commitments, it became evident that America's power in world affairs was declining. Kissinger's efforts to maintain American influence were frustrated not only by Communist victories in Southeast Asia but also by internal politics, which placed domestic concerns ahead of national defense and international affairs.

One final note: Kissinger's rise to power depended more upon his affiliation with Nelson Rockefeller, the Rockefeller Foundation, and the Council on Foreign Affairs than his intellectual achievements.

### Zbigniew Brzezinski

Brzezinski is the son of an upper-class Polish diplomat who was consul in Montreal, Canada, when the Nazis overran his country in 1939. Brzezinski was educated in private schools in Canada and received his B.A. from McGill University. He went to Harvard for his Ph.D. in Eastern European studies. He married the niece of the last democratic President of Czechoslovakia, Edward Benes. Brzezinski was well-known among upper-class emigrant families from Eastern Europe. He was an assistant professor at Harvard and later professor of government at Columbia.

Although Brzezinski produced eight books and scores of articles on world politics, his work was never accorded the scholarly praise of Kissinger's books. The result was a distinct feeling of academic competitiveness between the two men. Brzezinski was noted for his quick summaries of complicated questions, his development of balanced approaches to world problems, and his ability to come up with useful slogans to describe national policies. This latter ability is greatly appreciated by political leaders. Brzezinski served for two years on the State Department's policy planning staff in the Johnson Administration where he gained a reputation as a "hawk." As late as February 1968, he was quoted as saying, "We must make it clear to the enemy [North Vietnam] that we have the staying power—we're willing to continue for 30 years and we happen to be richer and more powerful." [11] But when Nixon became President, Brzezinski returned to Columbia and became a "dove."

At Columbia, Brzezinski became a close confidant of David Rockefeller. (Brzezinski's Northeast Harbor, Maine, summer home is near Rockefeller's Seal Harbor, Maine, estate.) When Rockefeller became chairman of the Council on Foreign Relations, he turned principally to Brzezinski for assistance. When top bankers and businessmen in the United States, Western Europe, and Japan decided in 1972 to form a group to study their mutual problems, it was Brzezinski who coined the term "trilateralism." The resulting Trilateral Commission was formed with elite representatives from the advanced industrial world, funded by David Rockefeller, and directed by Zbigniew Brzezinski. At the request

[11] *U.S. News and World Report,* February 1968.

of J. Paul Austin, the head of the Atlanta-based Coca Cola Company, Rockefeller named the then little-known Governor of Georgia, Jimmy Carter, to the new, prestigious Commission.

Carter never missed a meeting of the Trilateral Commission.[12] He relied heavily on Brzezinski's counsel on world affairs; Carter himself had no experience in international diplomacy. As the Carter presidential campaign rolled into high gear, the word went out to the campaign staff: "Clear it with Zbig." All of Carter's foreign and defense policy statements were either written by, or approved by Brzezinski. Carter's competent performance on the television debate with President Ford on foreign policy is generally attributed to Brzezinski's coaching.

Brzezinski became Special Assistant to the President for National Security Affairs immediately upon Carter's taking office in 1977. In contrast to Kissinger's spectacular style of personal diplomacy and international celebrity, Brzezinski maintains a low profile—he rarely makes public appearances, avoids dramatic announcements, maintains strict personal privacy, shuns social gatherings, and does not engage in personal diplomacy. (Indeed, he declines to provide biographical material for *Who's Who, Current Biography,* and other standard reference works.) While Kissinger overshadowed all those around him, one insider reports, "I was shocked to see how much Zbig defers to Jimmy. He seems to be telling Jimmy what he wants to hear. He comes on as sort of a brilliant yes man. But no doubt Jimmy trusts and relies on him in foreign policy more than anyone else." [13] Yet despite their differences in social background and personal style, Brzezinski and Kissinger share the view that U.S. power has waned in the world and that America must seek a new world order. This includes détente with the Soviet Union, normalization of relations with China, and greater interdependence with the industrialized nations of Western Europe and Japan. It is difficult to identify any basic policy differences between the two men.

Both Kissinger and Brzezinski owe their rise to power to their relationships with the Rockefellers: Kissinger with Nelson Rockefeller; Brzezinski with David Rockefeller. But the upper-class Brzezinski resents comparisons between his and Kissinger's relationship to the Rockefellers: "Henry Kissinger worked closely but also for Nelson Rockefeller. I worked closely but *with* David Rockefeller. I didn't work *for* David Rockefeller. He is not my employer." [14] Nonetheless, despite these personal differences, both intellectuals rose to power through their establishment connections.

[12] *Los Angeles Times,* January 24, 1977, p. 13.
[13] *Los Angeles Times,* January 23, 1977, p. 3.
[14] *Los Angeles Times,* January 24, 1977, p. 13.

## THE PROFESSIONAL BUREAUCRATS

The federal bureaucracy, comprised of nearly three million people, and the professional federal executives who supervise it occupy a uniquely influential position in American society. They advise the President on decisions he must make; they present and defend legislative recommendations before the Congress; and they supervise the day-to-day decisions of the hundreds of departments, agencies, commissions, and boards that influence the lives of every American. A powerful bureaucratic elite is comprised of these federal executives—particularly the secretaries, assistant secretaries, and under secretaries of the thirteen federal departments (State, Treasury, Defense, Justice, Post Office, Interior, Agriculture, Commerce, Labor, HEW, Housing and Urban Development, Energy, and Transportation); the same officials for the Army, Navy, and Air Force departments; administrators of important independent agencies in the executive office of the President (including the Office of Management and Budget, the National Security Council, and the Council of Economic Advisers); and members of key regulatory commissions and boards (Federal Reserve Board, Civil Aeronautics Board, Federal Communications Commission, Federal Power Commission, Federal Trade Commission, Interstate Commerce Commission, National Labor Relations Board, and Securities and Exchange Commission). Nearly all of these top federal executive positions are filled by presidential appointment with Senate confirmation.

What kind of men head the federal bureaucracy? In an interesting study [15] of over 1000 men who occupied the positions listed above during the presidential administrations of Roosevelt, Truman, Eisenhower, Kennedy and Johnson, the Brookings Institution reports that 36 percent of these top federal executives came up through the ranks of the government itself, 26 percent were recruited from law, 24 percent from business, 7 percent from education, and 7 percent from a variety of other fields. A plurality of top federal executives are *career bureaucrats.* Moreover, most of these people have served in only one government agency,[16] slowly acquiring seniority and promotion in the agency in which they eventually became chief executives. A total of 63 percent of the top federal executives were federal bureaucrats at the time of their appointment to a top post; only 37 percent had no prior experience as federal bureaucrats.[17] (If experience in *state* bureaucracies is counted, a total of 69 percent of the

---

[15] David T. Stanley, Dean E. Mann, and Jameson W. Doig, *Men Who Govern* (Washington: Brookings Institution, 1967).

[16] *Ibid.,* p. 8.

[17] *Ibid.,* p. 45.

top federal executives can be said to have been government bureaucrats at the time of their appointment.)

Thus, a majority of top federal executives are themselves career bureaucrats. The federal bureaucracy itself is producing its own leadership, with some limited recruitment from business and law. (Later in this volume, see Table 7–4, we will compare our own data for the 1970s on governmental and military elites with the earlier Brookings Institution's data: but we can say now that our figures are roughly comparable.) The federal bureaucracy, then, is an independent channel of recruitment to positions of governmental power in America. Consider, for example, the careers of the following individuals.

> *Joseph A. Califano, Jr.* Secretary of Health, Education, and Welfare. The grandson of an Italian immigrant who owned a fruit store in Brooklyn, New York, and the son of a middle echelon administrator of IBM. Califano attended Catholic schools in New York and graduated from Holy Cross College in 1952. He went on to Harvard Law School and graduated in 1955 with honors, and with the prestige of having edited the *Harvard Law Review*. After serving as a legal officer in the Navy, Califano was recruited by the prestigious Wall Street law firm of Dewey, Ballantine, Bushby, Palmer, and Wood. After two years on Wall Street and the election of John F. Kennedy as President, Califano wrote to the new administration seeking a job. He said he was "bored with splitting stocks."[18] His letter was answered by another former Wall Street lawyer and establishment figure, Cyrus Vance, who was then general counsel for the Department of Defense. Califano became Vance's assistant. Like many bureaucrats who aspire to climb the rungs of the Washington ladder, Califano's success was based in part upon the success of his mentor, Cyrus Vance.
>
> When Vance became Secretary of the Army, Califano became general counsel for the Department of the Army and later special assistant to the Secretary of Defense. His work for the Defense Department included liaison with the White House, and he was brought into close contact with top White House staff and President Lyndon Johnson. (Another lesson for aspiring bureaucrats, besides finding a highly placed mentor, is to establish contact with the White House as soon as possible.) In 1965, President Johnson chose Califano as special assistant to the president for domestic affairs. In this capacity, Califano shepherded much of the Great Society legislation through Congress. Thus, Califano helped to create the giant bureaucracy at HEW that he administers today. As President Johnson became preoccupied with the war in Vietnam, Califano came to exercise a great deal of independent power over domestic affairs in the White House. When Republicans captured the White House in 1968, Califano joined the prestigious Washington law firm of Arnold and Fortas (which included Abe Fortas, Lyndon Johnson's close personal friend and unsuccessful nominee to the Supreme Court). Later Califano worked with the well-known criminal lawyer Edward Bennett Williams. His years in the Washington bureaucracy brought him wealthy clients including Washington

[18] *Current Biography* (June 1977), p. 14.

Post–Newsweek, Inc. His 1976 income was reported at $560,000. He toured the world on Ford Foundation money and wrote two lackluster books. He kept a hand in politics by serving as general counsel for the Democratic National Committee, and he joined the Carter campaign as an adviser in early 1976. He was named Secretary of Health, Education, and Welfare in January 1977. Thus, while Califano was associated with two of the nation's top law firms (see Chapter 5), his rise to the top was achieved primarily through his mastery of the Washington bureaucracy.

*Elliot Richardson.* Former Secretary of Health, Education, and Welfare, Secretary of Defense, and Attorney General. He attended Harvard College, Harvard Law School. Millionaire descendant of six generations of Boston doctors (father was chief of surgery at Massachusetts General Hospital) and to the Boston Brahmin family of Shattuck, which had played a key role in the history of Harvard University. Richardson graduated cum laude from Harvard Law School and edited the *Harvard Law Review*. He did his law clerkship under Supreme Court Justice Felix Frankfurter, then joined a prestigious Boston law firm. He served briefly as an assistant to Republican U.S. Senator Leverett Saltonstall of Massachusetts, and was Assistant Secretary of Health, Education, and Welfare in the Eisenhower Administration. Richardson ran successfully for Lieutenant Governor of Massachusetts in 1964 and for State Attorney General in 1966. Nixon appointed Richardson as Secretary of Health, Education, and Welfare in 1971. The appointment was based more on Richardson's proven administrative abilities than on his political association with Nixon. Richardson managed well, despite pressure upward from a liberal and Democratic HEW bureaucracy and pressure downward from a conservative and Republican White House staff. Richardson's upper-class, Eastern, liberal convictions set him apart from the Nixon team, but improved his relations with Congress. In 1973 Nixon asked Richardson to take over the Defense Department to rebuild it after the Vietnam debacle. But Watergate events soon overtook the White House and Nixon found himself in need of an Attorney General whose integrity was unchallenged and who had the confidence of Eastern liberals in the news media and Congress. In an apparent agreement with congressional leaders, Nixon appointed Richardson as Attorney General, who in turn appointed his old Harvard Law Professor Archibald Cox as special Watergate prosecutor. But Cox recruited a staff of young liberals as prosecutors, expanded his investigations of the White House far beyond the original Watergate break-in, and finally went to court to subpoena the President to produce the famous White House tapes. Nixon fired Cox, and Richardson resigned his office in protest. The ejection of Richardson and Cox from his administration initiated the impeachment movement which eventually led to Nixon's resignation. President Ford thereafter appointed Richardson Ambassador to Great Britain where he served until the end of the Ford Administration. Despite the election of Carter and the installation of a Democratic administration, Richardson remains a powerful figure in Washington. Richardson is a trustee of Massachusetts General Hospital, Radcliffe College, and Harvard University.

Note that these men rose to prominence primarily in government service. They were not recruited from the corporate or financial world.

Of course, top federal bureaucrats are recruited primarily from the middle- and upper-middle-class segments of the population, as are leaders in other sectors of society. The Brookings Institution reports that the percentage of college-educated top executive bureaucrats rose from 88 percent in the Roosevelt Administration to 99 percent in the Johnson Administration. Moreover, 68 percent had advanced degrees—44 percent in law, 17 percent with earned master's degrees, and 11 percent with earned doctorates. But the class composition of the top bureaucrats is better reflected in information on *which* schools and colleges were attended. The Brookings Institution reports that the Ivy League schools plus Stanford, Chicago, Michigan, and Berkeley educated over 40 percent of the top federal executives, with Yale, Harvard, and Princeton leading the list.[19] Moreover, this tendency has increased over time; there were larger proportions of Ivy Leaguers in top posts in 1965 than in 1945. Perhaps more importantly, the Brookings study reports that 39 percent of the top federal executives attended *private* schools (compared to only 6 percent of the U.S. population) ; and 17 percent went to one of only 18 "name" prep schools.[20] The Brookings Institution study also reports that most top federal executives come from large Eastern cities.

There is little difference between Republican and Democratic administrations in the kind of men who are appointed to top executive posts. It is true, of course, that Republican Presidents tend to appoint Republicans to top posts, and Democratic Presidents tend to appoint Democrats; only about 8 percent of the top appointments cross party lines. However, the Brookings study reports few discernible differences in the class backgrounds, educational levels, occupational experiences, or previous public service of Democratic or Republican appointees.

One troublesome problem at the top of the federal bureaucracy is the shortness of tenure of federal executives. *The median tenure in office of top federal executives is only two years.*[21] Only on the regulatory commissions do we encounter significantly longer tenure. Of course, top federal executives have had significant federal bureaucratic experience before coming to their posts. But such a short tenure at the top has obvious disadvantages; it is generally estimated that a top federal executive needs a year or more to become fully productive, to learn the issues, programs, procedures, technical problems, and personalities involved in his work. If he resigns after his second year, the federal bureaucracy is not getting continuous, knowledgeable direction from its top officials.

[19] Stanley, Mann, and Doig, *Men Who Govern*, p. 21.

[20] Avon Old Farms, Choate, Deerfield, Groton, Hill, Hotchkiss, Kent, Lawrenceville, Loomis, Middlesex, Milton, Phillips Andover, Phillips Exeter, St. George's, St. Mary's, St. Paul's, Taft, Thatcher.

[21] Stanley, Mann, and Doig, *Men Who Govern*, p. 57.

According to the Brookings study, of the top bureaucrats who leave office, 60 percent go into private law practice or private business, 25 percent stay in the federal service in some other capacity, and 15 percent retire or die.[22] The data on short tenure suggest that we have created too many conflicting pressures on top federal executives—from the White House, Congress, interest groups, other government agencies, and particularly the mass media. Top federal executive positions are becoming less attractive over time.

## THE MILITARY ESTABLISHMENT

In his farewell address to the nation in 1961, President Dwight D. Eisenhower warned of "an immense military establishment and a large arms industry." He observed:

> In the councils of government, we must guard against the acquisition of unwarranted influence, whether sought or unsought, by the military-industrial complex. The potential for the disastrous rise of misplaced power exists and will persist. We must never let the weight of this combination endanger our liberties or democratic processes. We should take nothing for granted. Only an alert and knowledgeable citizenry can compel the proper meshing of the huge industrial and military machinery of defense with our peaceful methods and goals, so that security and liberty may prosper together.

These words were prepared by political scientist Malcolm Moos, an Eisenhower adviser who was later to become president of the University of Minnesota. But they accurately reflect Eisenhower's personal feelings about the pressures that had been mounting during his administration from the military and from private defense contractors for increased military spending. The "military-industrial complex" refers to the Armed Forces, the Defense Department, military contractors, and congressmen who represent defense-oriented constituencies.

While radicals view the military-industrial complex as a conspiracy to promote war and imperialism, it is not really anything like that. Economist John K. Galbraith portrays the military-industrial complex as a far more subtle interplay of forces in American society:

> It is an organization or a complex of organizations and not a conspiracy. . . . In the conspiratorial view, the military power is a coalition of generals and conniving industrialists. The goal is mutual enrichment: they arrange elaborately to feather each other's nests. The industrialists are the

[22] *Ibid.*

*deus ex machina;* their agents make their way around Washington arranging the payoff. . . .

There is some enrichment and some graft. Insiders do well. . . . Nonetheless, the notion of a conspiracy to enrich the corrupt is gravely damaging to an understanding of military power. . . .

The reality is far less dramatic and far more difficult of solution. The reality is a complex of organizations pursuing their sometimes diverse but generally common goals. The participants in these organizations are mostly honest men. . . . They live on their military pay or their salaries as engineers, scientists, or managers, or their pay and profits as executives, and would not dream of offering or accepting a bribe. . . .

The problem is not conspiracy or corruption, but unchecked rule. And being unchecked, this rule reflects not the national need but the bureaucratic need. . . .[23]

What are real facts about the military-industrial complex? Total defense spending runs about $110 billion per year—less than 25 percent of the federal government's budget and only about 5 *percent of the gross national product*. The 100 largest industrial corporations in the United States depend on military contracts for *less than 10 percent of their sales*. In other words, American industry does *not* depend upon war or the threat of war for any large proportion of its income or sales.

Nonetheless, there are a few powerful companies that depend heavily on defense contracts—Lockheed Aircraft, General Dynamics, McDonnell-Douglas, Boeing Co., Martin-Marietta Co., Grumman Aircraft, Thiokol, and Newport News Shipbuilding. But these firms are not really the nation's largest corporations. (McDonnell-Douglas is listed as 73 and Boeing as 84 in the top 100 industries on Table 2–1. The others do not appear in the top 100 at all.) While Exxon, General Motors, General Electric, and American Telephone and Telegraph, among the real corporate giants, appear near the top of defense contract lists, their military sales are only *a small proportion of total sales*. Yet there is enough military business to make it a real concern of certain companies, the people who work for them, the communities in which they are located, and the congressmen and other public officials who represent these communities.

But American business in general is not interested in promoting war or international instability. The defense industry is considered an unstable enterprise—a feast or famine business for industrial companies. The price-earnings ratios for military-oriented companies are substan-

[23] John Kenneth Galbraith, *How to Control the Military* (New York: Signet Books, 1969), pp. 23–31.

**TABLE 3-1**   **Companies Awarded Military Contracts Totaling in Excess of $1 Billion**

| Ranking by Total Dollar Amounts of Military Contracts | Percent of Total Sales |
|---|---|
| 1.  Lockheed Aircraft | 88% |
| 2.  General Dynamics | 67 |
| 3.  McDonnell-Douglas | 75 |
| 4.  Boeing Co. | 54 |
| 5.  General Electric | 19 |
| 6.  Rockwell International | 57 |
| 7.  United Aircraft | 57 |
| 8.  AT & T | 9 |
| 9.  Martin-Marietta | 62 |
| 10.  Sperry-Rand | 35 |
| 11.  General Motors | 2 |
| 12.  Grumman Aircraft | 67 |
| 13.  General Tire | 37 |
| 14.  Raytheon | 55 |
| 15.  AVCO | 75 |
| 16.  Hughes Tool Co. (Howard Hughes) | u |
| 17.  Westinghouse Electric | 13 |
| 18.  Ford (Philco) | 3 |
| 19.  RCA | 16 |
| 20.  Bendix | 42 |
| 21.  Textron | 36 |
| 22.  Ling-Temco-Vought | 70 |
| 23.  IT&T | 19 |
| 24.  IBM | 7 |
| 25.  Raymond International * | u |
| 26.  Newport News Shipbuilding | 90+ |
| 27.  Northrop | 61 |
| 28.  Thiokol | 96 |
| 29.  Exxon | 2 |
| 30.  Kaiser Industries | 45 |
| 31.  Honeywell | 24 |
| 32.  General Tel. | 25 |
| 33.  Collins Radio | 65 |
| 34.  Chrysler | 4 |
| 35.  Litton | 25 |
| 36.  Pan-Am. World Air. | 44 |
| 37.  FMC | 21 |
| 38.  Hercules | 31 |

u-Unavailable

* Includes Morrison-Knudsen, Brown & Root, and J. A. Jones Construction Co.

Source: Dr. Ralph E. Lapp, *The Weapons Culture* (New York: W. W. Norton and Co., 1968), pp. 187–188.

tially lower than for civilian-oriented companies. More importantly, corporate America seeks planned stable growth, secure investments, and guaranteed returns. These conditions are disrupted by war. The stock market, reflecting the aspirations of businessmen, goes *up* when peace is announced, not *down*.

A frequent criticism of the military-industrial complex is that defense-oriented industries have become dependent on military hardware orders. Any reduction in military spending would result in a severe economic setback for these industries, so they apply great pressure to keep defense spending high. This is particularly true of the industries that are almost totally dependent upon defense contracts. The military, always pleased to receive new weapons, joins with defense industries in recommending to the government that it purchase new weapons. Finally, congressmen from constituencies with large defense industries and giant military bases can usually be counted on to join with the armed forces and defense industries in support of increased defense spending for new weapons.

But the military-industrial complex has been notably *unsuccessful* in recent years in influencing the federal budget. Federal spending for defense has *declined* from 49.8 percent of the budget in 1960, to 40.8 percent in 1970, and down to 25 percent of the budget in 1978. Federal spending for social security and welfare surpassed defense spending long ago. The B-1 bomber, at a total cost of 22 billion dollars for 220 aircraft was supposed to be the largest single defense contract. Rockwell International was the prime contractor, but many subcontractors stood to gain also. But the B-1 was shot down by a critical report by the Brookings Institution (see Chapter 9), and the President cancelled the project despite military support for it. This suggests that the American military-industrial complex is *not* a very powerful conspiracy.

How many top federal executives come to Washington from employment by large defense contractors? The Brookings Institution reports that of 1,000 top federal executives studied from 1954 through 1965, *only 4 percent* had been employed by major defense contractors before their employment by the federal government.[24] Of course, there were slightly more people with defense industry backgrounds in the Defense Department itself, but even here, the Brookings study reports that only 12 percent of all top executives in the Defense Department and the Departments of the Army, Navy, and Air Force had had previous employment with defense contractors.

It seems clear in retrospect that C. Wright Mills placed too much

[24] *Ibid.*, p. 38.

importance on the military in his work, *The Power Elite.*[25] Mills was writing in the early 1950s when military prestige was high following victory in World War II. After the war a few high-level military men were recruited to top corporate positions: General Douglas MacArthur became chairman of the board of Remington-Rand (now Sperry-Rand Corporation). General Lucius D. Clay, who commanded American troops in Germany after the war, became board chairman of Continental Can Company; General James H. Doolittle, head of the Air Force in World War II, became vice-president of Shell Oil, General Omar M. Bradley, Commander of the 12th Army Group in Europe in World War II, became board chairman of Bulova Research Laboratories. General Leslie R. Groves, head of the Manhattan Project, which developed the atomic bomb, became vice-president of Remington-Rand. General Walter Bedell Smith, Eisenhower's Chief of Staff, became vice-president of the board of directors of American Machine and Foundry Company. General Matthew B. Ridgeway, Army Chief of Staff during the Korean War, became chairman of the board of the Mellon Institute of Industrial Research.

But as sociologist Morris Janowitz points out, "The practice of appointing military personnel to politically responsible posts, although it continues, has declined sharply since 1950. Much of the political debate about military personnel in government policy positions centers on a few conspicuous cases where civilian leadership sought to make use of prestigious military officers to deal with difficult political problems." [26] Indeed, the contrast between the political prestige of the military in the 1950s and the 1970s is striking: the Supreme Allied Commander in Europe in World War II, Dwight D. Eisenhower, was elected President of the United States; the U.S. Commander in Vietnam, William Westmoreland, was defeated in his bid to become Governor of South Carolina!

Moreover, in contrast with corporate and governmental elites, military officers do *not* come from the "upper classes" of society. Janowitz reports that a general infusion of persons from lower- and lower-middle-class backgrounds has occurred in all branches of the Armed Services (particularly the Air Force). He also reports that military leaders are more likely to have rural and Southern backgrounds than corporate or governmental elites: "In contrast with almost 70 percent of contemporary military leaders with social backgrounds with rural settings, only 26 percent of business leaders have rural backgrounds." [27]

[25] C. Wright Mills, *The Power Elite* (New York: Oxford, 1956).

[26] Morris Janowitz, *The Professional Soldier* (New York: Free Press, 1960), p. 378.

[27] *Ibid.*, p. 87.

While national policies are developed outside Congress, Congress is no mere "rubber stamp." Key congressmen do play an independent role in national decision making: thus key congressional leaders must be included in any operational definition of a national elite.

But the congressional role is essentially a deliberative one. Congress accepts, modifies, or rejects the policies and programs developed by the President and White House staff, executive departments, influential interest groups, and the mass media.

Many important government decisions, particularly in foreign and military affairs, are made without any direct participation by Congress. The President, with the support of top men in his administration, the mass media, the foundations, and civic associations, can commit the nation to foreign policies and military actions that Congress can neither foresee, prevent, or reverse. Congress had little or no role in the Korean War and the Vietnam War, other than to appropriate the necessary funds. Détente with the Soviet Union, new relationships with Communist China, the U.S. role in the Middle East, and similarly important policy directions are decided with little congressional participation. Often congressional leaders are told of major foreign policy decisions or military actions only a few minutes before they are announced on national television.

Congress is more influential in domestic affairs than in foreign or military policy. It is much freer to reject presidential initiatives in education, welfare, health, urban affairs, civil rights, agriculture, labor, business, or taxing and spending. Executive agencies—for example, the Office of Education, the Social Security Administration, the Housing Assistance Administration, the Department of Agriculture, the Office of Economic Opportunity—must go to Congress for needed legislation and appropriations. Congressional committees can exercise power in domestic affairs by giving or withholding the appropriations and the legislation wanted by these executive agencies.

Finally, congressional committees are an important communication link between governmental and nongovernmental elites; they serve as a bridge between the executive and military bureaucracies and the major nongovernmental elites in American society. Congressional committees bring department and agency heads together with leading industrial representatives—bankers, cotton producers, labor leaders, citrus growers, government contractors.

Political scientists have commented extensively on the structure of power *within* the Congress. They generally describe a hierarchical struc-

ture in both houses of the Congress—a "congressional establishment" which largely determines what the Congress will do. This "establishment" is composed of the Speaker of the House and President Pro Tempore of the Senate; House and Senate Majority and Minority Leaders and Whips; and committee chairmen and ranking minority members of House and Senate standing committees. Party leadership roles in the House and Senate are major sources of power in Washington. The Speaker of the House and the Majority and Minority Leaders of the House and Senate direct the business of Congress. Although they share this task with the standing committee chairmen, these leaders are generally "first among equals" in their relationships with committee chairmen. But the committee system also creates powerful congressional figures, the chairmen of the most powerful standing committees—particularly the Senate Foreign Relations, Appropriations, and Finance Committees, and the House Rules, Appropriations, and Ways and Means Committees.

"Policy clusters"—alliances of leaders from executive agencies, congressional committees, and private business and industry—tend to emerge in Washington. Committee chairmen, owing to their control over legislation in Congress, are key members of these policy clusters. One policy cluster might include the chairmen of the House and Senate committees on agriculture, the Secretary of Agriculture, and the leaders of the American Farm Bureau Federation. Another vital policy cluster would include the chairmen of the House and Senate Armed Services Committees; the Secretary and Under Secretaries of Defense; key military leaders, including the Joint Chiefs of Staff; and the leadership of defense industries such as Lockheed and General Dynamics. These alliances of congressional, executive, and private elites determine most public policy within their area of concern.

Senators and prominent reporters have described a Senate "establishment" and an "inner club" where power in the Senate and in Washington is concentrated (see Table 3–2). Ralph K. Huitt describes the Senate "establishment" type as

> a prudent man, who serves a long apprenticeship before trying to assert himself, and talks infrequently even then. He is courteous to a fault in his relations with his colleagues, not allowing political disagreements to affect his personal feelings. He is always ready to help another Senator when he can, and he expects to be repaid in kind. More than anything else he is a Senate man, proud of the institution and ready to defend its traditions and prerequisites against all outsiders. He is a legislative workhorse who specializes in one or two policy areas. . . . He is a man of accommodation who knows that "you have to go along to get along"; he is

**TABLE 3–2    The Congressional Establishment 1977–78**

### Senate Leadership

| | |
|---|---|
| President Pro Tempore | James O. Eastland (D. Miss.) |
| Majority Leader | Robert C. Byrd (D. W. Va.) |
| Majority Whip | Alan Crauston (D. Calif.) |
| Minority Leader | Howard H. Baker (R. Tenn.) |
| Minority Whip | Ted Stevens (R. Alaska) |

### House Leadership

| | |
|---|---|
| Speaker | Thomas P. O'Neill, Jr. (D. Mass.) |
| Majority Leader | Jim Wright (D. Tex.) |
| Majority Whip | John Brademas (D. Ind.) |
| Minority Leader | John J. Rhodes (R. Ariz.) |
| Minority Whip | Robert H. Michel (R. Ill.) |

### Senate Committees

| | |
|---|---|
| Appropriations | John L. McClellan (D. Ark.) |
| Armed Services | John C. Stennis (D. Miss.) |
| Labor and Public Welfare | Harrison A. Williams (D. N.J.) |
| Banking, Housing, and Urban Affairs | William Proxmire (D. Wis.) |
| Foreign Relations | John Sparkman (D. Ala.) |
| Government Operations | Abraham Ribicoff (D. Conn.) |
| Judiciary | James O. Eastland (D. Miss.) |
| Finance | Russell B. Long (D. La.) |
| Agriculture | Herman E. Talmadge (D. Ga.) |
| Budget | Edmund Muskie (D. Maine) |

### House Committees

| | |
|---|---|
| Rules | James J. Delaney (D. N.Y.) |
| Ways and Means | Al Ullman (D. Ore.) |
| Interstate Commerce | Harley O. Staggers (D. W. Va.) |
| Judiciary | Peter W. Rodino (D. N.J.) |
| Government Operations | Jack Brooks (D. Texas) |
| International Relations | Clement J. Zablocki (D. Wis.) |
| Banking and Currency | Henry S. Reuss (D. Wis.) |
| Armed Services | Melvin Price (D. Ill.) |
| Appropriations | George Mahon (D. Texas) |
| Agriculture | Thomas S. Foley (D. Wash.) |
| Budget | Robert N. Giaimo (D. Conn.) |

a conservative, institutional man, slow to change what he has mastered at the expense of so much time and patience.[28]

But viewed within the broader context of a *national elite,* congressional leaders appear "folksy," parochial, and localistic. Because of the local constituency of a congressman, he is predisposed to concern

---

[28] Ralph K. Huitt, "The Outsider in the U.S. Senate: An Alternative Role," *American Political Science Review,* 65 (June 1961), 568.

himself with local interests. Congressmen are part of local elite structures "back home"; they retain their local businesses and law practices, club memberships, and religious affiliations. Congressmen represent many small segments of the nation rather than the nation as a whole. Even top congressional leaders from safe districts, with many years of seniority, cannot completely shed their local interests. Their claim to *national* leadership must be safely hedged by attention to their local constituents. Consider, for example, the parochial backgrounds of these top congressional leaders.

*Robert C. Byrd,* Senate Majority Leader. Former Senate Majority Whip and chairman of the Judiciary Committee. Born in 1918, and then adopted and raised by relatives in West Virginia. Attended small Beckeley College and later Marshall College in West Virginia for three years. Elected to the West Virginia legislature in 1946, and to the U.S. House of Representatives in 1952. Earned a law degree from American University in 1963 after ten years of night school while serving in Congress. He won his U.S. Senate seat in 1958. For many years he served quietly on the Rules, Administration, and Judiciary committees, mastering parliamentary knowledge and performing small favors for his colleagues. His voting record was conservative: he voted against the Civil Rights Act of 1964, the Voting Rights Act of 1965, and the confirmation of Thurgood Marshall as Supreme Court Justice. In 1967, with the support of then Majority Leader Mike Mansfield, Byrd was made secretary to the Senate Democratic Caucus. Edward M. Kennedy was Majority Whip, but Kennedy was too busy with his national aspirations to tend to his job of lining up votes for the leadership. Byrd, by contrast, put in long hours and devoted much hard work to his Senate assignments. After Kennedy's involvement in the Chappaquiddick scandal, Byrd decided to challenge the Massachusetts senator for the Whip's job. To the surprise of many, Byrd won. Apparently Kennedy's disregard of the unwritten rules of senatorial behavior, combined with Byrd's intense devotion to the work of the Senate, gave the little-known West Virginian an impressive victory over the nation's leading Democratic political figure. As Whip, Byrd continued to work quietly behind the scenes to consolidate his position with his Senate colleagues. In 1977, when Mansfield retired from the Senate, Byrd confronted the challenge of another leading national Democrat, Hubert H. Humphrey. Again, Byrd's "insider" accomplishments in the Senate brought him victory over Humphrey in the race for Majority Leader. Thus, the little-known West Virginian defeated the two most popular Democratic politicians in the nation in his climb to top of the Senate.

*Thomas P. "Tip" O'Neill.* Speaker of the House, former House Majority Leader. O'Neill has been a politician and Democratic party loyalist all of his life. Immediately after graduation from Boston College in 1936, he ran for the Massachusetts state legislature and won. He served there as a party organization loyalist, becoming Democratic leader of the state general assembly in 1947. When Democrats captured control of the legislature in 1948, O'Neill became Speaker of the Massachusetts House. When John F. Kennedy vacated his Boston seat in U.S. House of Representatives in 1952 to run for U.S. Senate, O'Neill cashed in on his own party alliances and state house prestige to win that seat for himself. Upon arriving in Washington, O'Neill quickly aligned himself with John McCormack, another Boston Irish politician who had risen to Majority Leader and later served as Speaker of the House. McCormack gave O'Neill key committee memberships, and the tall, burly Irishman began his slow rise through the ranks of the House. O'Neill was never known for initiating important new laws, but rather for party loyalty, service to constituents, and political "flexibility" (changing sides when it seemed expedient to do so). O'Neill served many years on the important Rules Committee and in 1971 was the choice of Speaker Hale Boggs as new Majority Leader. When Boggs died in a plane crash in 1972, O'Neill was the unanimous choice for Speaker of the House.

*Howard H. Baker, Jr.* (R. Tenn.) Senate Minority Leader. Born in 1925 into a political family. Baker's father was a Congressman from Tennessee from 1950 until his death in 1964; Baker's mother completed his father's term in the Congress. Baker attended a private academy, Tulane University, and the University of Tennessee, where he earned his law degree. He served in the Navy in World War II. He married the daughter of U.S. Senator Everett M. Dirkson (R. Ill.), former Republican leader of the Senate. He is a former chairman of the First National Bank of Oneida, Tennessee, and former president of Colonial Gas Co. of Wytheville, Virginia. Baker passed up the opportunity to win his father's congressional seat in order to run for the U.S. Senate in 1964. He lost this first bid in a close vote, but he succeeded in winning his Senate seat (and first public office) in 1966. As son-in-law of the Senate Minority Leader, he received a great deal of public attention and good committee assignments—Foreign Relations, Public Works, and later the Select Committee on Intelligence. But he was defeated by Hugh Scott (R. Pa.) in an attempt to become Minority Leader, after the death of his father-in-law. His Senate colleagues resented his efforts to move up too quickly in the Senate hierarchy. His career in the Senate was resuscitated, however, by his brilliant performance as co-chairman of the Senate Select Committee on Campaign Practices (the Watergate investigation committee). Baker received national television prominence by pressing the question: "What did the President know, and when did he know it?" When Hugh Scott, who had defended President Nixon until almost the end of the investigation, retired, Senator Robert P. Griffin (R. Mich.), as Minority Whip, was next in line to succeed Scott, But when President Ford lost to Jimmy Carter in 1976, Griffin lost an important ally in the White House, and many Republicans believed the party should turn to a younger, "new face" for leadership. Baker was elected Minority Leader in a close vote over Griffin in January 1977.

*Russell B. Long* (D. La.) U.S. Senator, chairman, Senate Finance Committee. The son of Huey Long, Louisiana's most famous politician and a national figure in the 1930s. Russell Long received his bachelor's and law degrees from Louisiana State University, which his father had been instrumental in building. He served in the Navy in World War II and returned to practice law in the capital at Baton Rouge. At age 33, he was elected to the U.S. Senate without having held previous office, clearly on the popularity of his family name. But Long applied himself to the work of the Senate under the tutelage of Harry F. Byrd (D. Va.), the long-time chairman of the Senate Finance Committee. Long became a Senate "insider" with close connections to Lyndon Johnson. When Byrd retired in 1965, Long succeeded him in the chairmanship of the Senate Finance Committee. (Long then had 14 years of seniority.) Senator Herman Talmadge, another Senate insider and the son of one of Georgia's most flamboyant politicians of the 1930s, "Old Gene" Talmadge, is second in line in seniority and influence on the Finance Committee. Long's chairmanship assures him of control over all bills affecting taxation—including jurisdiction over tax reform, energy, welfare, social security, national health insurance, revenue sharing, and anything else that costs money. (At one time, Long's preeminence was shared with Wilbur Mills of the House Ways and Means Committee; but Mills' downfall after acknowledged alcoholic problems left Long the leading figure on Capitol Hill in tax matters.) In conference committees with Al Ullman's (D. Ore.) House Ways and Means Committee, Long usually wins his battles.

*Henry M. Jackson,* (D. Wash.) U.S. Senator, chairman, Senate Internal Affairs Committee, member of Senate Government Operations and Armed Services committees. Son of Norwegian immigrants in Everett, Washington. Attended the University of Washington and received law degree in 1935. Was popularly elected Snohomish County Prosecuting Attorney, and four years later (1940) was elected to the House of Representatives. Served in the House until election to the Senate in 1952. Has never lost an election, and has been reelected to the Senate by record margins of over 80 percent. Is the leading spokesman in the Senate on national defense. Boeing Aircraft, a major defense contractor, is a major employer in his district; however, a fellow congressman once remarked: "If the State of Washington did not have a single defense contract or a single military base, Jackson would still be strong for defense." Is co-author of the Environmental Protection Act and leading advocate of environmental protection. Belongs to the Everett, Washington, American Legion, Elks, Eagles, Masons, and Sons of Norway.

*John J. Rhodes.* (R. Ariz.) House Minority Leader. Attended Kansas State University and Harvard Law School. Opened law practice in Mesa, Arizona, after service in the Air Force. First elected to House of Representatives in 1952. Served three terms before appointment to the Appropriations Committee in 1959, where he developed an important specialty— defense appropriations—and rose in power within Republican ranks in Congress. In 1965, he became chairman of the House Republican Policy Committee and also helped swing crucial support behind Gerald Ford in his successful bid to unseat aging Charles Halleck as House Republican Leader. In 1973, when Ford became Vice-President under the 26th Amendment to the Constitution, Rhodes won easy election as House Republican Leader. "Johnny won because of his close ties with Ford and the ranking members. He's had his little group in the policy committee. He's been easy to get along with. He's been very patient, almost overdue. So he was ready to roll."[29] Rise to congressional leadership fits the traditional mold of the loyal, hard-working, friendly, patient party man who eventually rises in

[29] *Congressional Quarterly,* December 15, 1973, p. 3293.

seniority and influence. His political views are generally labeled as "independently conservative." Member of Mesa, Arizona Masons, Elks, Rotary, Mesa Junior Chamber of Commerce, American Legion, and Sons of the American Revolution.

## THE JUDGES

Nine men—none of whom is elected and all of whom serve for life—possess ultimate authority over all the other institutions of government. The Supreme Court of the United States has the authority to void the acts of popularly elected Presidents and Congresses. There is no appeal from their decision about what is the "supreme law of the land," except perhaps to undertake the difficult task of amending the Constitution itself. Only the good judgment of the Justices themselves—their sense of "judicial self-restraint"—limits their power over government elites. It was the Supreme Court, rather than the President or the Congress, that took the lead in such important issues as eliminating segregation from public life, insuring voter equality in representation, limiting the powers of police, and declaring abortion to be a fundamental right of women.

Social scientists have commented on the class bias of Supreme Court Justices. John R. Schmidhauser reports that over 90 percent of the Supreme Court Justices serving on the Court between 1789 and 1962 were from socially prominent, politically influential, upper-class families.[30] Over two-thirds of the Supreme Court Justices ever serving on the Court attended well-known or Ivy League law schools (most notably, Harvard, Yale, Columbia, Pennsylvania, N.Y.U., Michigan, Virginia). No blacks served on the Supreme Court until the appointment of Associate Justice Thurgood Marshall in 1967. Henry Abraham depicts the typical Supreme Court Justice: "White; generally Protestant. . . ; fifty to fifty-five years of age at the time of his appointment; Anglo-Saxon ethnic stock. . . ; high social status; reared in an urban environment; member of a civic-minded, politically active, economically comfortable family; legal training; some type of public office; generally well educated."[31] Of course, social background does not necessarily determine judicial philosophy. But as Schmidhauser observes: "If . . . the Supreme Court is the keeper of the American conscience, it is essentially the conscience of the American upper-middle class sharpened by the imperative of individual social

---

[30] John R. Schmidhauser, *The Supreme Court* (New York: Holt, Rinehart and Winston, 1960), p. 59.

[31] Henry Abraham, *The Judicial Process* (New York: Oxford University Press, 1962), p. 58.

responsibility and political activism, and conditioned by the conservative impact of legal training and professional legal attitudes and associations." [32]

But not all Justices conform to this upper-class portrait. Indeed, several current Justices of the Supreme Court are middle-class rather than upper-class in social origin. Their appointments to the Supreme Court have been more closely related to their political activities than either their social backgrounds or their accomplishments in the law.

*Warren E. Burger.* Chief Justice, U.S. Supreme Court. Son of a successful Swiss-German farmer near St. Paul, Minnesota. Worked his way through the University of Minnesota and St. Paul College of Law, receiving law degree in 1931. Developed a successful 22-year private practice in Minneapolis–St. Paul with a wide range of civil and criminal cases. An early political associate of Minnesota Republican Governor Harold E. Stassen, he brought himself to the attention of Eastern Republicans in national GOP conventions in 1940 and 1952. President Eisenhower appointed him Assistant Attorney General in 1953, then to U.S. Court of Appeals in 1956. Served on the Court of Appeals until appointed Chief Justice by President Nixon in 1969 on the resignation of Earl Warren.

*Byron R. White.* U.S. Supreme Court Justice. Son of the mayor of Wellington, Colorado. Attended public schools and University of Colorado. At Colorado, was Phi Beta Kappa, a Rhodes Scholar, and an All-American halfback. Attended Yale Law School while playing halfback for the Pittsburgh Steelers and Detroit Lions; was the NFL leading ground gainer in 1938. In World War II served in Navy in the Pacific, where he met John F. Kennedy. After the war, completed law degree at Yale, served legal clerkship under U.S. Supreme Court Chief Justice Fred M. Vinson, and opened a law practice in Denver, Colorado. His law practice was undistinguished, but in 1960 the Kennedys called on him to organize Colorado for JFK's presidential campaign. White was credited with delivering Colorado's convention votes to Kennedy. Was JFK's only appointment to the Supreme Court.

*Thurgood Marshall.* U.S. Supreme Court Justice. Son of a Pullman car steward. Educated at Lincoln University and Howard University Law School. Shortly after graduation in 1933, became counsel for Baltimore chapter of NAACP. From 1940 to 1961, served as director and chief counsel of NAACP's semi-autonomous Legal Defense and Educational Fund. During that period, he argued 32 cases before the Supreme Court, winning 29. His notable victory (indeed, perhaps the black man's most notable judicial victory) came in *Brown* v. *Board of Education of Topeka* in 1954.

President Kennedy chose Marshall as a judge for the U.S. Circuit Court of Appeals in 1961; President Johnson appointed him U.S. Solicitor General in 1965. As the latter, Marshall argued 19 more cases before the U.S. Supreme Court. When President Johnson announced Marshall's appointment to the Supreme Court in 1967, he accurately noted that "prob-

---

[32] Schmidhauser, *The Supreme Court*, p. 59.

ably only one or two other living men have argued as many cases before the court—and perhaps less than half a dozen in all the history of the nation."

## THE POLITICAL CONTRIBUTORS

Political campaigns cost money—usually a great deal more than candidates themselves are willing or able to spend. In 1976, Ford and Carter each spent $22 million on the general election; Ford spent an additional $14 million defeating Reagan in the Republican primaries, while Reagan spent nearly $18 million in his losing effort. Carter spent an additional $13 million defeating his Democratic opponents in primary elections. Nonetheless 1976 campaign spending is *down* from 1972: Richard Nixon spent $60 million in his reelection campaign, and his "power" opponent Senator George McGovern spent $30 million. Few candidates can even begin a political career for state or local office without first securing financial support from wealthy "angels." Far-sighted men of wealth may choose to back a promising young politician early in his career and continue this support for many years.[33] There are few congressmen or senators who do *not* have wealthy financial sponsors.

Prior to 1976, the spiraling costs of political campaigns (particularly the high costs of television advertising), placed extreme pressure on candidates and potential candidates to secure the backing of wealthy financial contributors. For example, in 1972 Richard Nixon's top financial backers included W. Clement Stone, centimillionaire chairman of Combined Insurance Company of America, who contributed $2 million; Richard Mellon Scaife, director of Mellon National Bank and Trust and Gulf Oil Corporation, and centimillionaire heir to the Mellon fortune ($1 million contribution); Arthur K. Watson, former chairman of the board of IBM ($300,000 contribution). Other large Nixon contributors included John DuPont (DuPont Corp.), Harvey Firestone (Firestone Tire and Rubber), Henry Ford II (Ford Motors); Howard Hughes, J. Willard Marriot (motels), Henry J. Heinz II (ketchup), Bob Hope, and Frank Sinatra.

Democrats do not usually receive as much money from the corporate world as Republicans, commonly deriving about half of their funds from this source. The Xerox Corporation, for example, has been

---

[33] Richard Nixon was long supported by Chicago insurance tycoon W. Clement Stone. George McGovern was backed for many years by Stewart Mott, heir to the General Motors fortune. Jimmy Carter was backed in his early races in Georgia by J. Paul Austin, chairman of the board of Coca Cola, Charles Kirbo, Atlanta attorney, and Thomas B. (Bert) Lance, former president of the National Bank of Georgia and director of the Office of Management and Budget.

a major source of support for Democratic candidates. Traditionally, Democrats have turned to big labor for support, notably the Committee on Political Education (COPE) of the AFL–CIO and the larger international unions, among them the United Automobile Workers and the United Steel Workers. Liberal Democrats have also been supported by upper-class liberal philanthropists. These "limousine liberals" provided much of the financial support for the civil rights movement, the peace movement, and other liberal causes. For example, in 1972, Senator George McGovern's campaign was supported by such wealth-holders as Stewart Mott (heir to the General Motors fortune), Max Palevsky (former chairman of the board of the Xerox Corporation), Nicholas and Daniel Noyes (wealthy students who are heirs to the Eli Lilly Pharmaceutical fortune), and Richard Saloman (president of Charles of the Ritz, Inc.).

Yet over the years the Democratic deficit in campaign finances has provided a stimulus to "reform" of campaign funding, especially when Democrats controlled both houses of Congress by overwhelming margins and a close presidential election was on the horizon. In 1974, Congress passed a comprehensive campaign spending law, with the following provisions:

1. A Presidential Election Campaign Fund was created from the voluntary one dollar per person check-offs from individual income taxes.
2. A Federal Election Commission was created to oversee federal election spending.
3. The Commission would distribute campaign monies from the fund (a) to candidates in the primaries; (b) to the Democratic and Republican parties for their national conventions; (c) and to the Republican and Democratic candidates in the general election.
4. Individuals are limited to a $1,000 contribution in any single election, and organizations are limited to $5,000. All contributions must be reported to the Federal Elections Commission.

The Supreme Court modified these provisions by declaring that an individual, as an exercise of his 1st Amendment rights, can spend as much of his *own* money on his *own* election as he wishes. Moreover, as an exercise of 1st Amendment rights, any individual may *independently* spend any amount of money to advertise his own political views. As long as these independent expenditures are not tied directly to a political campaign, they are not to be counted against the maximum limits set by the law. While the campaign spending law, as modified by the Supreme Court, reduces the role of the large financial "angels," it permits men of wealth to spend large amounts on their own campaigns.

We have made a composite listing of the heavy political contributors in the 1968 and 1972 presidential elections.³⁴ About one-third of these contributors were presidents or directors of the nation's largest corporations and banks. (These were the same top economic elites identified in Chapter 2.) Another third were inheritors of large fortunes. The remainder appeared to be wealthy, upper-middle-class, successful people whose names were not directly linked to large corporations or recognized great family fortunes.

What do contributors get for their money? Perhaps the most important payoff is simply *access* to the political officeholder—in the presidency, Senate, Congress, or state government. The big contributor can expect to see and talk with the officeholder to discuss general issues confronting the nation as well as the contributor's specific problems with the government. This access assures that the views of top contributors will at least be heard. Another payoff is *assistance* with government-related problems. Large contributions generally insure speedy consideration of requests, applications, contracts, bids, and so forth, by government bureaucracies. Assistance does not necessarily mean favoritism, but it does mean a reduction of standard red tape, bureaucratic delays, and cumbersome and time-consuming administrative reviews. Of course, *favoritism* itself is a frequent motive for large contributions by individuals and corporations who are dependent upon government contracts, licenses, or regulatory decisions. But despite occasional sensational cases, blatant favoritism is a politically dangerous game avoided by most officeholders.³⁵ Generally it is only when the contributor's contract, bid, or license ap-

---

³⁴ Political scientist Herbert Alexander provides a list of 424 contributors of $20,000 or more to the 1968 presidential campaigns of candidate Nixon and Humphrey. The *Congressional Quarterly* published a list of 50 contributors of $50,000 or more (obtained from the U.S. General Accounting Office) to the 1972 presidential campaigns of candidates Nixon and McGovern. And an out-of-court settlement of a suit by the lobbying group Common Cause against the Committee to Re-Elect the President produced a list of 105 additional Nixon contributors. But discrepancies in these listings are numerous; contributions are often listed under the names of wives and relatives; large contributions are frequently split into smaller unidentified gifts to numerous separate campaign committees and organizations; and finally, some contributions have remained secret by design. In sum, then, there were 424 contributors of $20,000 or more in 1968, and 150 contributors of $50,000 or more in 1972.

³⁵ For example, the jury found in the trial of former Attorney General John Mitchell and former Republican Campaign Chairman Maurice Stans that the contribution of financier Robert Vesco merely bought the assistance of John Mitchell in presenting Vesco's argument to the Security and Exchange Commission. The SEC actually decided *against* Vesco, despite his secret $100,000 contribution to President Nixon's reelection. It was Vesco himself who expected White House intervention on his behalf and when he did not get it, threatened to "blow the lid" on his secret contribution. Vesco's top lieutenant attempted to implicate Mitchell and Stans by charging their complicity in bribery. But the jury decided their actions did not constitute illegal acts.

plication is substantially equal to that of the noncontributor that favoritism plays a decisive role. Another motive of contributors is the *status* a large contribution provides—the opportunity to rub shoulders with the great and near-great in American politics, to be invited to the President's inaugural ball, to visit the White House for dinner and tell one's friends about it, and even to boast of the size of one's contribution at cocktail parties.

Perhaps the most important motive in campaign contributions, however, is *political ideology*. Most of the top contributors, including conservatives W. Clement Stone, Richard Mellon Scaife, Arthur K. Watson, Cornelius Vanderbilt Whitney, John DuPont, and Bob Hope, and liberals Stewart Mott, Max Palevsky, Averell Harriman, and Jacqueline Onassis, expect no direct personal gain from their contributions. They believe their contributions are helping to guide the nation's government in the proper direction.

## SUMMARY

Governmental power may be even more concentrated than corporate power in America. One indicator of its growing concentration is the increasing proportion of the Gross National Product produced by government. All governmental expenditures now account for one-third of the GNP and *federal* expenditures account for two-thirds of these. Fewer than 250 people occupy *all* of the influential posts in the combined executive, legislative, and judicial branches of the federal government.

Presidents must depend upon "serious men" to run the government, for skill in campaigning does not necessarily prepare individuals for the responsibility of governing. Key government executives must be recruited from industry, finance, the law, the universities, and the bureaucracy itself. These "serious men" do not appear to differ much in background or experience from one administration to another.

The federal bureaucracy, an independent channel of recruitment to positions of power, is now producing its own leadership. The declining percentage of federal expenditures devoted to the military and the small percentage of corporate sales devoted to arms suggest that the military-industrial complex has been notably *un*successful in recent years. There has been a sharp decline since the 1950s in the exchange of military and corporate personnel, and a sharp decline in the power and prestige of the military generally.

Congress seldom initiates programs, but rather responds to the initiatives of the President, the executive departments, influential interest groups, and the mass media. Power *within* Congress is concentrated in the House and Senate leadership and the chairmen and ranking minority members of the standing committees. Compared to other national elites, congressional leaders appear localistic. Their claim to national leadership must be safely hedged by attention to their local constituencies. Congressmen are frequently recruited from very modest, middle-class backgrounds.

Nine men on the Supreme Court have the authority to void the acts of popularly elected Presidents and Congresses. It was the Supreme Court, rather than the President or Congress, which took the lead in eliminating segregation from public life, insuring voter equality in representation, limiting the powers of police, and declaring abortion to be a fundamental right of women. Although most Justices have been upper-class in social origin, their appointment has generally been related to their political activities rather than to their experience in the law.

Political contributions are important linkages between corporate wealth and the political system. About one-third of the heavy political contributors in presidential elections are presidents or directors of large corporations and banks; one-third are inheritors of large fortunes; and one-third are wealthy upper-middle-class individuals who are not directly linked to large corporations or great family fortunes. Their contributions are usually given in support of their political views rather than for direct personal gain.

# the newsmakers

▶▶▶▶▶▶▶▶▶▶▶▶▶▶▶▶▶▶▶▶▶▶▶▶▶▶▶▶▶▶▶▶▶▶▶▶▶▶▶▶▶▶▶▶▶▶▶▶▶▶▶▶▶▶

# 4

Television is the major source of information for the vast majority of Americans, and the people who control this flow of information are among the most powerful in the nation. Indeed, today the leadership of the mass media has successfully established itself as equal in power to the nation's corporate and governmental leadership.

The rise of the mass media leadership to a position of preeminence among men of power is a relatively recent phenomenon. It is a direct product of technological change: the development of a national television communication network extending to nearly every home in America. (In 1952 only 19.8 percent of all American homes had TV sets, compared to 99.8 percent in 1972.) [1] Newspapers had always reported wars, riots, scandals, and disasters, just as they do today. But the masses of Americans did not read them—and fewer still read the editorials on these topics. But today television reaches the masses: it is really the first form of *mass* communication devised by man. And it presents a *visual* image, not merely a printed word. Nearly everyone watches TV, and over two-thirds of the American public testify that television provides "most of [their] views about what's going on in the world today." [2] Over two-thirds of the American people say that television is the best way to follow candidates for national office. [3]

Network television news not only reaches a larger audience than

[1] *Statistical Abstract of the United States, 1973*, p. 693.

[2] The Roper Organization, *What People Think of Television and Other Mass Media: 1959–1972* (New York: Television Information Office, 1973), p. 2.

[3] *Ibid.*

newspapers, but perhaps more importantly, it reaches children, functional illiterates, the poor, and the uneducated. The television viewer *must* see the news, or else turn off his set; the newspaper reader can turn quickly to the sports and comics without confronting the political news. But the greatest asset of television is its *visual* quality—the emotional impact that is conveyed in pictures. Scenes of burning and looting in cities, sacks of dead American GIs being loaded on helicopters, terrorists holding frightened hostages, all convey *emotions* as well as *information*.

## CONCENTRATION OF POWER IN THE MASS MEDIA

The power to determine what the American people will see and hear about their world is vested in three private corporations—the American Broadcasting Company (ABC), the National Broadcasting Corporation (NBC), and the Columbia Broadcasting System, Inc. (CBS). These networks determine what will be seen by the mass viewing audience; there is *no* public regulation whatsoever of network broadcasting. Individual television stations are privately owned and licensed to use public broadcast channels by the Federal Communications Commission. But these stations are forced to receive news and programming from the networks because of the high costs involved in *producing* news or entertainment at the local station level. The top officials of these corporate networks, particularly the people in charge of the news, are indeed "a tiny, enclosed fraternity of privileged men." [4] Nicholas Johnson, a member of the Federal Communications Commission and a self-professed liberal, has said:

> The networks, in particular . . . are probably now beyond the check of any institution in our society. The President, the Congress of the United States, the FCC, the foundations, and universities are reluctant even to get involved. I think they may now be so powerful that they're beyond the check of anyone. [5]

The men at the top of the news media do not doubt their own power. They generally credit themselves with the success of the civil rights movement: the dramatic televised images of the nonviolent civil

[4] The phraseology is courtesy of former Vice-President Spiro Agnew, who also used the more colorful description of the network top brass—"super-sensitive, self-anointed, supercilious electronic barons of opinion." See *Newsweek*, November 9, 1970, p. 22.

[5] Quoted by Edward Jay Epstein, *News from Nowhere* (New York: Random House, 1973), p. 6.

rights demonstrators of the early 1960s being attacked by police with night-sticks, cattle prods, and vicious dogs helped to awaken the nation and its political leadership to the injustices of segregation. These leaders also credit TV with "decisively changing America's opinion of the Vietnam War," and forcing Lyndon Johnson out of the presidency. The director of CBS News in Washington proudly claims:

> When television covered its "first war" in Vietnam, it showed a terrible truth of war in a manner new to mass audiences. A case can be made, and certainly should be examined, that this was cardinal to the disillusionment of Americans with this war, the cynicism of many young people towards America, and the destruction of Lyndon Johnson's tenure of office.[6]

Television news, together with the Washington press corps, also lays claim, of course, to the expulsion of Richard Nixon from the presidency. The *Washington Post* conducted the "investigative reporting" that produced a continuous flow of embarrassing and incriminating information about the President and his chief advisers. But it was the television networks that maintained the continuous nightly attack on the White House for nearly two years and kept Watergate in the public eye. Richard Nixon's approval rating in public opinion polls dropped from an all-time high of 68 percent in January 1973 following the Vietnam Peace Agreement to a low of 24 percent less than one year later.

Yet the leadership of the mass media frequently claim that they do no more than "mirror" reality. Although the "mirror" argument contradicts many of their more candid claims to having righted many of America's wrongs (segregation, Vietnam, Watergate), the leadership of the three television networks claim that television "is a mirror of society." Frank Stanton, president of CBS, told a House committee: "What the media does is hold a mirror up to society and try to report it as factually as possible." When confronted with charges that television helped to spread urban rioting in the late 1960s, Julian Goodman, president of NBC, told the National Commission on the Cause and Prevention of Violence that "the medium is being blamed for the message."[7]

Of course, the mirror analogy is nonsense. Newsmen decide what the news will be, how it will be presented, and how it will be interpreted. As David Brinkley explained, "News is what I say it is. It's something worth knowing by my standards."[8] Newsmen have the power to create some national issues and ignore others; elevate obscure men to national prominence; reward politicians they favor and punish those they dis-

[6] *Ibid.*, p. 9.
[7] *Ibid.*
[8] *TV Guide*, April 11, 1964.

favor. The best description of the newsmaking power of television is found in a book significantly entitled *News from Nowhere* by Edward Jay Epstein, who explains:

> The mirror analogy further tends to neglect the component of "will," or decisions made in advance to cover or not to cover certain types of events. A mirror makes no decisions, it simply reflects what occurs in front of it; television coverage can, however, be controlled by predecisions or "policy." . . .
>
> Policy can determine not only whether or not a subject is seen on television but also how it is depicted. . . .
>
> Intervention by the producer or assistant producers in decisions on how to play the news is the rule rather than the exception.[9]

The principal source of distortion in the news is caused by the need for drama, action, and confrontation to hold audience attention. NBC news executive producer Reven Frank advised his producers in a memorandum: "The highest power of television journalism is not in the transmission of information but in the transmission of experience—joy, sorrow, shock, fear—these are the stuff of news." [10]

Ninety percent of the national news that reaches the American television public arrives from ABC, NBC, and CBS.[11] Local television stations do not have the resources to produce their own national news, and consequently largely restrict themselves to local news coverage. The three networks "feed" approximately 600 local affiliated stations, with "The Evening News." These stations generally videotape network programs for rebroadcast later in the evening, usually in truncated form, on the local news program. Moreover, the networks also *own* key television stations in the nation's largest cities. While the Federal Communications Commission limits station ownership by the networks to no more than seven stations, these network-owned stations are concentrated in the largest "market" cities. The twelve largest "market" cities contain 38 percent of all "TV households" in the nation, and these cities have network-owned stations.[12]

The nation's 1,748 daily newspapers get most of their national news from the Associated Press (AP) and United Press International (UPI)

[9] Epstein, *News from Nowhere*, pp. 16–17.

[10] *Ibid.*, p. 39.

[11] See Lewis H. Lapham, "The Temptation of a Sacred Cow," *Harpers* (August 1973), pp. 43–54.

[12] Ben H. Bagdikian, *The Information Machines* (New York: Harper & Row, 1971), pp. 171–172.

wire services, although the larger newspapers and newspaper chains also disseminate their own national news. Radio stations also rely heavily on AP and UPI. One large radio station admitted to filling its newscasts "90 percent with verbatim items from UPI teletype." [13] Of course, local newspapers can "rewrite" national news stories to fit their own editorial slant, and they usually write their own headlines on the national news. But the news itself is generated from an extremely small cadre of people at the top of the media industry.

Concentration of newspaper ownership is increasing, as more and more local papers are being taken over by the major newspaper chains. Nine newspaper chains account for one-third of the total newspaper circulation in the United States. These chains, in order of their total daily circulation, are: Tribune Company, Newhouse, Scripps-Howard, Knight-Ridder Newspapers, Hearst Corporation, Gannett Newspapers, Times Mirror Company, Dow Jones, and Cox Enterprises.[14]

Our operational definition of leaders in positions of power in the mass media include the presidents and directors of

Columbia Broadcasting System, Inc. (CBS owns five TV stations, 14 radio stations, 22 magazines, Columbia records, and more)

American Broadcasting Company (ABC television)

National Broadcasting Company (NBC television is a subsidiary of RCA with five TV stations and four publishing companies)

New York Times Company (*New York Times* plus nine daily newspapers in the South)

Washington Post Company (*Washington Post–Newsweek* plus five TV stations)

Time, Inc. (*Time, Sports Illustrated, Fortune,* and *People* magazines plus five TV stations)

Associated Press

United Press International

Newhouse (*Denver Post, Cleveland Plain Dealer, etc.*)

Hearst Corporation (Los Angeles, San Francisco, Baltimore, Boston, Albany, Seattle, San Antonio, etc.)

Scripps-Howard

Tribune Company (*Chicago Tribune, New York Daily News, Orlando Sentinal, etc.*)

Field Enterprises (*Chicago Sun-Times, Chicago Daily News, etc.*)

Dow Jones (*Wall Street Journal*)

Times Mirror (*Los Angeles Times, etc.*)

---

[13] Edwin Emery, *The Press in America* (Englewood Cliffs, N.J.: Prentice-Hall, Inc., 1972), p. 481.

[14] Raymond B. Nixon, "Nation's Dailies in Group Ownership," *Editor & Publisher,* July 17, 1971, pp. 7, 32.

Knight-Ridder Newspapers, Inc. (*Detroit Free Press, Miami Herald, Philadelphia Inquirer,* etc.)
Cox

There are 213 presidents and directors of these institutions.

## THE NEWSMAKERS

Who are the men who govern the flow of information to the nation? Let us examine a few brief sketches of those in the top leadership positions in the major media institutions.

*William S. Paley.* Chairman of the board, Columbia Broadcasting System Inc. Attended Western Military Academy, University of Pennsylvania. Began work in father's cigar company, but in 1928 at age 27 purchased CBS for $400,000. Recruited Edward R. Murrow to develop news policy for CBS, and supported Murrow's successful efforts to make television news an independent political force in America. Paley actively opposed creation of Federal Communications Commission and over the years helped to prevent its intrusion into network broadcasting. Established the first regular schedule of television broadcasting in the U.S. in 1941. A trustee of the Museum of Modern Art, Columbia University, Resources for the Future, Inc., Bedford-Stuyvesant Development Corp. Past chairman of the United Jewish Appeal.

*Roy E. Larson.* Chairman of the board of Time, Inc., publishers of *Time, People, Fortune, Sports Illustrated.* Attended Boston Latin School, Harvard College. Was hired by classmate Henry Luce, owner of Time, Inc., in 1922 to handle financial matters; rose to president in 1939. Is a trustee of Committee for Economic Development, Ford Foundation, New York Public Library, and a former trustee of Harvard University.

*Arthur Ochs Sulzberger.* Publisher and president, *New York Times.* Son of the *Times* board chairman and grandson of the newspaper's founder. Attended Loomis school and Columbia University. A corporal in World War II, but assigned as headquarters aid to General Douglas MacArthur. Began as a reporter with the *Times* in 1953 and became president in 1963. A director of the New York Times Co., the Chattanooga Publishing Co., the Spruce Falls Power and Paper Co. of Toronto, and the Gaspesia Pulp and Paper Co. of Canada. A trustee of the Boy Scouts of America, American Association of Indian Affairs, Columbia University, and the Metropolitan Museum of Art.

*Julian Goodman.* President, NBC. Attended public schools in Glasgow, Kentucky, and Western Kentucky University. Began as a newswriter for NBC in 1945; moved up to become Washington news manager in 1950. Recruited Chet Huntley and David Brinkley and pioneered in television coverage of national party conventions. Produced the Nixon-Kennedy TV debates in 1960, and became president of NBC in 1966. Helped to inaugurate the "news special" and the "documentary"; is a leading exponent of the notion that television should pay "more attention to analysis and interpretation."

*Robert W. Sarnoff.* President of RCA (Radio Corporation of America). Former president and director of NBC. Son of David Sarnoff, chairman of Board of RCA (which owns NBC). Attended Phillips Andover Academy and Harvard. Served in the Navy in World War II as communications officer for the Chief of Naval Operations, joined NBC in 1948, and became president in 1955. Regards his own documentary *Victory at Sea* as most personally satisfying undertaking. Is also director of Manufacturer's Hanover Trust, and Random House, Inc., and a trustee of John F. Kennedy Library, Boston University, Franklin and Marshall College, Roper Public Opinion Research Center, and Williams College.

*Leonard H. Goldenson.* President, ABC. Attended Harvard College and Harvard Law School. Began as an attorney for Paramount Pictures in Hollywood and became president of Paramount Pictures and United Paramount Theatres. In 1953, merged Paramount and ABC and became president of ABC. Also invested in Walt Disney Productions, started the popular *Mickey Mouse Club* TV shows. Hired top ABC news commentators himself. Is a director of United Cerebral Palsy Association, John F. Kennedy Library, Lincoln Center for Performing Arts, Will Rogers Memorial Hospital, and United Jewish Appeal.

*Frank Stanton.* President CBS. Attended public schools in Dayton, Ohio, then Ohio Wesleyan University; Ph.D. in psychology, Ohio State University, 1935. Sent his dissertation on radio listening behavior to CBS and won a job in its research department. Later worked with Paul F. Lazarfeld of Columbia to develop better methods of rating program audiences. In 1946, William S. Paley asked Stanton, then 38, to become CBS president. Paley and Stanton together established CBS as the largest advertising and communications corporation in the world. Stanton introduced diversification in CBS; invested in a Broadway show, *My Fair Lady,* and earned $100 million. Later purchased the New York Yankees. Is a leading opponent of the "equal-time" rule of the FCC requiring stations to give equal time to political candidates. A chairman of the RAND Corp., and trustee of Rockefeller Foundation, Center for Advanced Study of the Behavioral Sciences, Lincoln Center for the Performing Arts, and Stanford Research Institute.

*Hedley Donovan.* Editor-in-chief, Time, Inc. University of Minnesota, Rhodes scholar, Oxford. Began as reporter for *Washington Post,* and later *Fortune* magazine. Became Time, Inc. editor-in-chief, 1964. Trustee of New York University, Carnegie Foundation. Member of Council of Foreign Relations.

Other top corporate directors of the media include Robert Lovett, CBS (former Secretary of Defense, senior partner of Wall Street investment firm of Brown Brothers, Harriman & Co., a director of North American Rockwell, Union Pacific Railroad, Carnegie Foundation and M.I.T.); Frank Pace, *Time* (former Secretary of the Army, a director of Fidelity Life Insurance, Colgate-Palmolive, Continental Oil). Pace has also been named chairman of board of the Corporation for Public Broadcasting designed to use federal funds to produce shows for public TV stations. Also John W. Gardner, who serves on the Time, Inc. board; he was former Secretary of Health, Education, and Welfare and now heads Washington's heaviest spending lobby group, the liberal-oriented Common Cause.

## KATHERINE GRAHAM:
## THE MOST POWERFUL WOMAN IN AMERICA

Katherine Graham, the owner and publisher of the *Washington Post* and *Newsweek* magazine, was probably the most powerful woman in America even *before* Watergate. But certainly her leadership of the *Post,* which did more than any other publication to force the resignation of the President of the United States, established Ms. Graham as one of the most powerful figures in Washington. The *Washington Post* is the capital's most influential newspaper, and it vies with the *New York Times* as the world's most influential newspaper. These are the papers read by all segments of the nation's elite; and both papers feed stories to the television networks and wire services.

Ms. Graham inherited her position from her father and husband, but since 1963, when she became president of the Washington Post Company, she has demonstrated her own capacity to manage great institutional power. She is the daughter of a wealthy New York banker, Eugene Meyer. Like many elites, her education was in the fashionable private preparatory schools; she also attended Vassar College and the University of Chicago. In 1933 her father bought the *Washington Post* for less than one million dollars. Katherine Meyer worked summers on her father's paper, and then took a job as a reporter with the *San Francisco News*. After one year as a reporter, she joined the editorial staff of the *Washington Post*. "Father was very strong. There was a great deal of emphasis on not behaving rich and a lot of emphasis on having to *do* something. It never occurred to me that I didn't have to work." [15]

In 1940, she married Philip L. Graham, a Harvard Law School graduate with a clerkship under Supreme Court Justice Felix Frankfurter. After service in World War II, Philip Graham was made publisher of the *Washington Post* by his father-in-law. Meyer later sold the paper to the Grahams for one dollar. The Washington Post Company proceeded to purchase other competitive papers in the nation's capital; it also bought *Newsweek* magazine from the Vincent Astor Foundation, as well as some television stations (including Washington's WTOP-TV) and several pulp and paper companies.

In 1963, Philip Graham committed suicide, and Katherine Graham took control of the *Washington Post–Newsweek* enterprises. By the early 1970s the *Washington Post* was challenging the *New York Times* as the nation's most powerful newspaper.

Both the *Washington Post* and the *New York Times* published the *Pentagon Papers,* stolen from the files of the Defense and State Departments by Daniel Ellsberg, and led the fight against the Vietnam War. But it was the *Washington Post* that developed the Watergate story and brought about Richard Nixon's humiliation and resignation.

Indeed the Washington Post Company's domination of the Washington scene gives it great power over federal officials and agencies. As conservative columnist Kevin Phillips observes: "We might note the quasi-governmental role played by the Washington Post Company. The Post Company has a five-level presence in Washington—a newspaper (the *Washington Post*), a radio station (WTOP), a television station (WTOP-TV), a news magazine (*Newsweek*), and a major news service (L.A. Times–Washington Post). Not only does the Washington Post Company play an unmatched role as a federal government information system—from the White House to Congress to the bureaucracy and back —it serves as a cue card for the network news, and it plays a huge role in determining how the American government communicates to the American people." [16]

Ms. Graham is a director of Bowaters Mersey Paper Company, the John F. Kennedy School of Government of Harvard University, and a member of the Committee for Economic Development. She is a trustee of George Washington University, the American Assembly, the University of Chicago, and St. Alban's School.

## LIBERAL BIAS IN THE NEWS

When TV newscasters insist that they are impartial, objective, and unbiased, they may sincerely believe that they are, because in the world in which they live—the New York–Washington world of newsmen, writers, intellectuals, artists—the established liberal point of view has been so uniformly voiced. TV news executives can be genuinely shocked and affronted when they are charged with slanting the news toward the prevailing established liberal values.

Network entertainment programming, newscasts, and news specials

[16] Kevin Phillips, "Busting the Media Trusts," *Harpers* (July 1977), p. 30.

are designed to communicate established liberal values to the masses. These are the values of the elite; they include a concern for liberal reform and social welfare, an interest in problems confronting the poor and blacks, a desire to educate the ignorant and cure the sick, and a willingness to employ governmental power to accomplish these ends.

Admittedly, there are some restraints on television communication of elite values—the most important of which is the need to capture and retain the attention of the audience. Television must entertain. To capture the attention of jaded audiences, news must be selected which includes emotional rhetoric, shocking incidents, dramatic conflict, overdrawn stereotypes. Race, sex, violence, and corruption in government are favorite topics because of popular interest. More complex problems—inflation, government spending, foreign policy—must be simplified and dramatized or ignored. To dramatize an issue, the newsmakers must find or create a dramatic incident; film it; transport, process, and edit the film; and write a script for the introduction, the "voice-over," and the "recapitulation." All this means that "news" must be created well in advance of scheduled broadcasting.

But television has made some serious tactical mistakes in its (conscious or unconscious) advancement of liberal values. For example, for several years the national networks decided that incidents of violence, disruption, and civil disorder in American cities were to be treated as "news." Generally the media chiefs believed that the civil rights movement had to be carried to Northern black ghettos, that urban conditions had to be improved, that ghetto blacks deserved greater public attention to their plight. Televised riots and disorders dramatized black discontent, and "voice-overs" generally gave legitimacy to such discontent by citing various social evils as causes of the riots—poverty, racism, poor housing, police brutality. The purpose was to pave the way for mass acceptance of urban renewal programs, especially with a view to improving the plight of minority groups.

But the strategy backfired. Whites saw the visual image of black violence, and ignored the social message attached to it by the commentators. Images of black violence remained in their minds, while words of explanation were ignored. White mass hostilities and prejudices were actually *reinforced* by the urban violence shown on the media. The liberal network executives had created exactly what they did *not* want: a strong "law and order" movement and a surge of support for George C. Wallace as a presidential candidate.[17]

[17] A study of newsmakers' bias toward presidential candidates was made by journalist Edith Efron in a book bluntly entitled *The News Twisters* (Los Angeles: Nash Publishing Co., 1971). Efron carefully counted words spoken for and against the 1968 presidential candidates—Nixon, Humphrey, and Wallace—

For a long time there were two basic issues in national politics: foreign policy, a traditional advantage to the Republicans, and economics, a plus for the Democrats. Now there is a third: Law and Order—shorthand for street crime, race, protest tactics, and "revolution." It has been forty years since American politics generated an issue so intense that it could change partisan loyalties for vast numbers of citizens. Law and Order may be such an issue. Where did it come from?

We suggest that the essential midwives in the birth of this issue are Mssrs. Cronkite, Brinkley, and their brethren—television newsmen who, we hasten to add, are probably as strongly revolted by the appearance of Law and Order as any group in America.[18]

There is far *less* diversity of news presented on television than one finds in the press. There are only three national television network corporations. But there are thousands of newspapers and hundreds of magazines throughout the land for Americans to choose from. Newspapers and magazines present a fairly wide spectrum of views because they represent a wider variety of such things as geographical area, communication policies, and above all, more diversified groups deciding their news presentation. Conventionally, "liberal" and "conservative" viewpoints are found in such publications as the *New York Times* versus the *Chicago Tribune; Time* magazine versus *U.S. News and World Report;* the *Washington Post* versus the *Wall Street Journal;* the *New Republic* versus the *National Review;* the *Village Voice* versus *Barron's Weekly.* But television is so important in mass socialization that diversity of views is avoided, and a single Eastern, liberal "establishment" interpretation prevails in all three network presentations.

In an especially candid interview with *Playboy* magazine, Walter Cronkite commented on both the power and the bias of the television networks: [19]

> *Playboy:* A great deal of economic and social power is concentrated in the networks. CBS, for example, does research and development in military and space technology, owns two publishing houses, and has phonograph-record, record club, and film communications divisions.
>
> *Cronkite:* That's right. We're big. And we're powerful enough to thumb our nose at threats and intimidation from Government. I hope it stays that way.

---

in the nightly news broadcasts of ABC, CBS, and NBC. She also counted words revealing a friendly or unfriendly disposition of the networks toward particular groups.

[18] Byron Shafer and Richard Larson, "Did TV Create the Social Issue?" *Columbia Journalism Review* (September/October 1972), p. 10. Also see Richard Scammon and Ben Wattenberg, *The Real Majority* (New York: Coward, McCann, Geohegan, 1970), p. 162.

[19] "Playboy Interview: Walter Cronkite," *Playboy* (June 1973), pp. 68–90.

*Playboy:* Implicit in the Administration's attempts to force the networks to "balance" the news is a conviction that most newscasters are biased against conservatism. Is there some truth in the view that television newsmen tend to be left of center?

*Cronkite:* Well, certainly liberal, and possibly left of center as well. I would have to accept that. . . . But I don't think there are many who are *far* left. I think a little left of center probably is correct.

The federal government has made only a very feeble attempt to insure pluralism in television coverage of public affairs. The Federal Communications Commission has developed a Fairness Doctrine that requires all licensed broadcasters of public affairs messages to provide equal air time to present "all sides of controversial issues." The Fairness Doctrine does not restrict reporting or editorializing on television in any way, but it tries to guarantee access to airings of views not shared by the stations. But the Doctrine has proven impossible to enforce in newscasts, and no station has ever lost its license for violation of the Fairness Doctrine. Yet it is bitterly opposed by the broadcasting corporations. Their argument is that the First Amendment gives them the right to be biased, just as it protects the right of individuals or newspapers to be biased.

## HOW NEWSMAKERS CREATE NEWS

In general, newsmakers are more liberal in their views than other segments of the American establishment. (We will compare the liberalism of various segments of the nation's elite in Chapter 9.) But how are these views expressed on the tube itself? The primary source of bias is in the selection of topics to be presented as "news." Topics selected weeks in advance for coverage reflect, or often create, as we have seen, current liberal issues: concern for poor and blacks, women's liberation, opposition to defense spending and the CIA, ecology, migrant farm labor, tax loopholes, Indian rights,[20] and for nearly two years, Watergate. The Chappaquiddick incident involving Senator Edward M. Kennedy was given one or two weeks' coverage, but barely mentioned thereafter, despite a closed judicial inquiry and many available witnesses to the pre-accident party.

[20] The 1972 Wounded Knee incident was planned in advance by television producers and Indian leaders and then presented on cue as television "news." See Terri Schultz, "Bamboozle Me Not at Wounded Knee," *Harpers* (June 1973), pp. 46–56.

But there are other techniques of creating bias in the news:

Invoking anonymous "high Washington sources" who express the newscasters' own opinions, or using phrases such as "observers point out . . ." and "experts believe . . ." to express their opinions.

Suppressing information that might clash with a liberal interpretation of the news. Thus Eldridge Cleaver's criminal conviction as a rapist was never mentioned, and he was presented as "a noted black nationalist."

Presenting glamorous, articulate spokesmen for the liberal side of an argument and "balancing" it with ugly, harsh, offensive spokesmen for the other side.

Winding up coverage of a controversy by a "summary" or "recapitulation" which directs humor, sarcasm, or satire at the other side.

"Mind-reading," in which newscasters glibly describe the motives and aspirations of large numbers of people—students, blacks, suburbanites, or whatever—and express the causes of society's discontents and other social and political ideologies.

Deliberate deception is less frequent, but it does occur. One of the most impressive "news specials" ever produced by CBS was "Hunger in America"—a 1968 production presumably designed to increase support for the food stamp program and the fading war on poverty. The film began by showing a dying baby, pitifully thin and malformed, being given resuscitation in a hospital. The narrator, Charles Kuralt, said: "Hunger is easy to recognize when it looks like this. The baby is dying of starvation. He was an American. Now he is dead." [21] This image couldn't help having a tremendous impact on the viewer, who naturally assumed the baby died of starvation or malnutrition. But a subsequent investigation by newsmen and others disclosed that the dying baby was a three-month premature infant weighing less than three pounds at birth, whose parents were neither poor nor starving. Edward J. Epstein writes: "The mother, a schoolteacher, had the premature birth after an automobile accident. There was no medical reason to suspect that malnutrition or starvation was in any way connected with the death of the child." Later, CBS News President Richard Salant admitted that "new evidence came to light" regarding the death of the baby. However, he added his *belief* that "in that area, at that time, in that hospital, babies were dying of malnutrition." [22] In short, it appears as if CBS was so convinced that babies were dying of starvation that even though CBS could not find one to televise, there was no harm done in picturing a baby who *looked* like it was starving. Moreover, throughout the broadcast, mothers were asked

[21] Edward Jay Epstein, *News from Nowhere* (New York Random House), p. 21.
[22] Letter to Prentice Hall, Inc. December 15, 1977. Mr. Salant also stated that *at the time* CBS news officials had been told by a "hospital authority" that the baby was dying of malnutrition. Only later, after the broadcast, did CBS learn that such was not the case.

what food was available for their children, and the mothers all answered to the effect that little or no food was available. But CBS never asked *why:* Were these mothers turned away from the federal Aid to Families with Dependent Children (AFDC) program (in existence since 1935)? Or were they simply ignorant of available services? Or had they spent their public assistance checks for something other than food for their children? The broadcast never mentioned the variety of federal and state programs available to the poor. Viewers were left with the strong impression that the poor in America have no alternative except starvation.

## SELECTIVE PERCEPTION: "ALL IN THE FAMILY"

Many have argued, however, that the viewer's psychological mechanism of "selective perception" defends him against some portion of television bias. Indeed, one of the reasons why political scientists pay little heed to the political impact of television newscasting is their belief in the theory of selective perception. This is the notion that viewers mentally screen out information, statements, or images with which they disagree, and see only what they want to see on the tube. The proponents of this theory argue that television rarely produces attitudinal or behavioral changes in viewers.[23] If this theory is true, newsmakers exercise little real power. But many of these studies have directed their inquiries to political *campaigns,* not to *issues* and *policies.* Many have ignored the *visual* impact of television. Only recently has a small number of political scientists come to grips with the real power of the mass media. Political scientists Gary Wamsley and Richard Pride cite Spiro Agnew's attack on TV—"No medium has a more powerful influence over public opinion. Nowhere in our system are there fewer checks on vast power." [24]

But there is just enough evidence of selective perception, and enough evidence of network executive blunders, to keep alive the notion that television cannot completely control public opinion. Consider the example of the enormously popular CBS television show, "All In The Family." Producer Norman Lear and the leadership of CBS believed that the crude, bumbling, working-class, conservative, superpatriotic, racist Archie Bunker would be an effective weapon against prejudice. Bigotry

[23] See Herbert Simon and Frederick Stern, "The Effect of Television upon Voting Turnout in Iowa in the 1952 Election," *American Political Science Review,* 49 (1955), 470–477; J. Blumer and T. McQuail, *Television in Politics* (Chicago: University of Chicago Press, 1969) ; Harold Mendelsohn and Irving Crespi. *Polls, Television and the New Politics* (Scranton: Chandler, 1970).

[24] Gary L. Wamsley and Richard A. Pride, "Television Network News: Rethinking the Iceberg Problem," *Western Political Quarterly,* 25 (September 1972), 434–450.

would be made to appear ridiculous; Archie would always end up suffering some defeat because of his bigotry; and the masses would be instructed in liberal reformist values. But evidence soon developed that many viewers applauded Archie's bigotry, believing he was "telling it like it is." [25] They missed the satire altogether. Sixty percent of the viewers liked or admired the bigoted Archie more than his liberal son-in-law, Mike. Vidmar and Rokeach's study indicated that highly prejudiced people enjoy and watch the show *more* than less-prejudiced people; and few people believed that Archie was being "made fun of." When these trends in public opinion became apparent, the show was sharply attacked by the *New York Times*.[26] But by that time "All In The Family" had become the number one rated show on television. CBS optimistically predicted that eventually the humor of the program would help break down bigotry.[27] But it seems clear that the network vastly underestimated "selective perception."

## "TELEVISION MALAISE"

The networks' concentration on scandal, abuse, and corruption in government has not always produced the desired liberal, reformist notions in the minds of the masses of viewers. Contrary to the expectations of network executives, their focus on governmental scandals—Watergate, illicit C.I.A. activities, F.B.I. abuses, congressional sex scandals, and power struggles between Congress and the executive branch—has produced feelings of general political distrust and cynicism toward government and "the system." These feelings have been labeled "television malaise"—a combination of social distrust, political cynicism, feelings of powerlessness, and disaffection from parties and politics which seems to stem from television's emphasis on the negative aspects of American life.[28]

Network executives do not *intend* to create "television malaise" among the masses. But scandal, sex, abuse of power, and corruption attract large audiences and increase "ratings." "Bad" news is placed up

---

[25] See Neil Vidmar and Milton Rokeach, "Archie Bunker's Bigotry: A Study in Selective Perception and Exposure," *Journal of Communication* (Winter 1974), pp. 36–47.

[26] I. Z. Hobson, "As I Listened to Archie say 'Hebe,'" *New York Times*, September 12, 1972.

[27] Norman Lear, "As I Read How Laura Saw Archie," *New York Times*, October 10, 1971.

[28] Michael J. Robinson, "Public Affairs Television and the Growth of Political Malaise," *American Political Science Review*, 70 (June 1976), 409–432; and "Television and American Politics," *The Public Interest* (Summer 1977), pp. 3–39.

front in the telecast, usually with some dramatic visual aids. Negative television journalism ". . . is concerned with what is *wrong* with our governmental system, our leaders, our prisons, schools, roads, automobiles, race relations, traffic systems, pollution laws, every aspect of our society. In Europe, there is much less emphasis on exposing what is wrong, much more satisfaction with the status quo." [29] The effect of negative television coverage of the American political system is to "turn off" the masses from participation in government. The long-run effects of this elite behavior may be self-defeating, in terms of elite interest in maintaining a stable political system.

## SUMMARY

The people who control the flow of information in America are among the most powerful in the nation. Television network broadcasting is the first form of truly *mass* communication; it carries a visual image with emotional content as well as information. Television news reaches virtually everyone, and for most Americans it is the major source of information about the world.

Control of the television media is highly concentrated. Three private corporations (CBS, NBC, and ABC) determine what the people will see and hear about the world; they feed 600 local TV stations that account for 90 percent of the news and entertainment broadcasts. Most of the nation's 1,748 daily newspapers receive their news from the AP and/or UPI wire services. The ten largest newspaper chains account for one-third of the total newspaper circulation in the country.

Those at the top of the mass media include both inheritors and individuals who worked their way up the management ladder. Among the media elite are the heads of CBS, NBC, and ABC; AP and UPI; the *New York Times*; *Washington Post–Newsweek*; Time, Inc.; and the ten largest newspaper chains.

Television programming is uniformly liberal—within an establishment framework—which means that elite values of those in positions of power predominate. Bias is introduced primarily in the selection of topics to be treated as "news," but there are other ways in which liberal values are incorporated into newsmaking. While claiming to present merely a "mirror of society," newsmakers credit themselves with the success of the civil rights movement, ending the Vietnam War, exposing Watergate, and ousting two Presidents from office.

The major counterbalance to the power of the media is the "selec-

---

[29] Merritt Panitt, "America Out of Focus," *TV Guide,* January 15, 1972, p. 6.

tive perception" of the mass viewing audience. Viewers often mentally screen out information or images they do not want to see. Network executives have blundered in creating certain undesired issues and attitudes by underestimating selective perception, as in the case of the law and order movement stemming from media coverage of urban riots.

# the civic
# establishment

▶▶▶▶▶▶▶▶▶▶▶▶▶▶▶▶▶▶▶▶▶▶▶▶▶▶▶▶▶▶▶▶▶▶▶▶▶▶▶▶▶▶▶▶▶▶▶▶▶▶▶▶▶▶▶▶▶▶▶▶

# 5

In a complex, industrial society, there are many specialized institutions and organizations that exercise power. In addition to economic organizations (corporations, banks, insurance companies, and utilities), governmental and military bureaucracies, television networks and news services, there are other less visible institutions which also provide bases of power in American society. An operational definition of a national elite must include individuals who occupy positions of power in influential law firms, major philanthropic foundations, recognized national civic and cultural organizations, and prestigious private universities. We shall refer to these institutions collectively as the civic establishment.

The identification of a "civic establishment" involves many subjective judgments. We shall try to defend these judgments, but we recognize that equally valid defenses of alternative judgments might be made in many cases.

## THE "SUPERLAWYERS"

As modern societies grow in scale and complexity, the need for rules and regulations increases geometrically, and so does the power of people whose profession it is to understand those rules and regulations. As early as 1832, de Tocqueville felt that the legal profession in this country would become the "new aristocracy" of the Republic. C. Wright Mills asserts that lawyers are indeed a key segment of the nation's aristocracy of power:

The inner core of the power elite also includes men of the higher legal and financial type from the great law factories and investment firms who are professional go-betweens of economic, political, and military affairs, and who thus act to unify the power elite.[1]

The predominance of lawyers among political elites has already been noted. Within the corporate elite—presidents and directors of the nation's largest industries, banks, utilities, and insurance companies—over 15 percent are lawyers. But neither the politician-lawyer nor the businessman-lawyer really stands at the top of the legal profession. The "superlawyers" are the senior partners of the nation's largest and most highly esteemed New York and Washington law firms. These are the firms that represent clients such as General Motors, AT&T, DuPont, CBS, and American Airlines,[2] not only in the courts, but perhaps more importantly, before federal regulatory agencies. Of course, the nation's largest corporate and financial institutions have their own legal departments; but attorneys in these departments, known as "house counsels," usually handle routine matters. When the stakes are high, the great corporations turn to the "superlawyers."

Sociologist Erwin O. Smigel argues persuasively that the largest New York and Washington law firms are emerging as the dominant force in the legal profession:

> As our society has grown increasingly complex, the legal tools for social control have indeed increased beyond the possible total comprehension of a single individual. And the lawyers, like the scientists, have increasingly, although on a much smaller scale, met the problem of specialization within large law firms.[3]

Identification of the "top" New York and Washington law firms is necessarily a subjective task. Professional ethics prevent firms from listing their clients; so we cannot be certain what firms actually represent the nation's largest corporations. The listing in Table 5–1 was compiled from a variety of sources and represents our best estimate of the nation's legal elite.

We have identified 176 senior partners of these firms—our "superlawyers." The names of the firms themselves, of course, do not always identify the senior partners. Firms often retain the names of deceased founders, and most large firms have so many senior partners (20 or 30 is not uncommon) that it would be impossible to put all their names in

---

[1] C. Wright Mills, *The Power Elite* (New York: Oxford, 1956), p. 289.

[2] Quoted as clients of Covington and Burling by Joseph C. Goulden, *The Superlawyers* (New York: Dell Publishing Co., 1971), p. 27.

[3] Erwin O. Smigel, *The Wall Street Lawyer* (New York: Free Press, 1964), p. 9.

**TABLE 5–1    The Top Law Firms**

| Wall Street | Washington |
|---|---|
| Shearman & Sterling | Arnold & Porter |
| Cravath, Swaine & Moore | Covington & Burling |
| White & Case | Arent, Fox, Kintner, Plotkin & Kahn |
| Dewey, Ballantine, Bushby, Palmer & Wood | Wilmer, Cutler & Pickering |
| Simpson, Thacher & Bartlett | Clifford, Warnke, Glass, McIlwain & |
| Davis, Polk, & Wardwell |     Finney |
| Milbank, Tweed, Hadley & McCloy | |
| Cahill, Gordon & Reindel | |
| Sullivan & Cromwell | |
| Chadbourne, Parke, Whiteside & Wolff | |
| Breed, Abbott & Morgan | |
| Winthrop, Stimson, Putnam & Roberts | |
| Cadwalader, Wickersham & Taft | |
| Wilkie, Farr & Gallagher | |
| Donovan, Leisure, Newton & Irvine | |
| Lord, Day & Lord | |
| Dwight, Royall, Harris, Koegel & Caskey | |
| Mudge, Rose, Guthrie & Alexander | |
| Kelley, Drye & Warren | |
| Cleary, Gottlieb, Steen & Hamilton | |

the title of the firm. Then, too, some firms change names upon the resignation of partners, so it is sometimes difficult to maintain the identity of a firm over time.[4]

The great law firms are, of course, the "spokesmen" for big business. But it would be naive to believe that they oppose government regulation, consumer laws, antitrust laws, labor laws, or corporate tax legislation. On the contrary, the top law firms gain in power and influence as the interaction between business and government heightens. New laws mean new business for lawyers.

The superlawyers are philosophically liberal and tend to favor welfare socialism. Even the founder of one of Washington's most conservative

[4] For example, Mudge Stern Baldwin & Todd placed the name of Richard M. Nixon at the head of the firm during his Wall Street years, and later added John Mitchell's name to the firm. The result was "Nixon Mudge Rose Guthrie Alexander & Mitchell." When Nixon became President and Mitchell became Attorney General, the firm went back to Mudge Rose Guthrie & Alexander. Despite the legal difficulties of its former partners, the firm remains one of the most powerful on Wall Street. Likewise, when one of Arnold, Fortas & Porter's clients, Lyndon Johnson, became President of the United States, and named his personal attorney Abraham Fortas to the Supreme Court (and then later tried unsuccessfully to make him chief justice), the Fortas name was removed from the firm. The firm is now Arnold & Porter—but it is still one of the most powerful in Washington.

and dignified firms, Judge J. Harry Covington of Covington and Burling, confided before his death: "I disagreed with the New Deal strongly. But it was a great benefit to lawyers because so many businessmen all over the country began squealing about what was happening and had to have lawyers. So when you ask me about bureaucracy, I say 'Oh, I'm for it. How would I eat otherwise?' " [5]

The senior partners of the nation's top law firms generally feel an obligation to public service. According to superlawyer Arthur Dean, the experience of serving in such a firm provides "an exceptional opportunity to acquire a liberal education in modern government and society. Such partnerships are likely in the future, as they have in the past, to prepare and offer for public service men exceptionally qualified to serve." The arrogance of such an assertion has too much basis in fact to be dismissed as mere self-congratulation.

Earlier we identified several superlawyers among the "serious men" who have been called upon for governmental leadership:

John Foster Dulles, Secretary of State (Sullivan & Cromwell)
Dean Acheson, Secretary of State (Covington & Burling)
Clark Clifford, Secretary of Defense (Clifford, Warnke, Glass, McIlwain & Finney)
Cyrus Vance, Secretary of State (Simpson, Thacher & Bartlett)

In an even earlier era, the New York Wall Street law firms supplied presidential candidates:

John W. Davis, Democratic Party nominee for President of the United States, 1928 (Davis, Polk, Wardwell, Sunderland & Kiendl) [6]
Wendell Willkie, Republican Party nominee for President of the United States, 1940 (Willkie, Farr, Gallagher, Walton & Fitzgibbon)
Thomas E. Dewey, Republican Party nominee for President of the United States, 1944 and 1948 (Dewey, Ballantine, Bushby, Palmer & Wood)

Equally important are the top lawyers who are called upon to represent the United States itself in periods of crisis where matters are too serious to be left to State Department bureaucrats.

*Paul Warnke.* Arms control and disarmament adviser under President Carter. U.S. negotiator in the Strategic Arms Limitation Talks (SALT). Partner in Clifford, Warnke, Glass, McIlwain & Finney. Former Assistant

[5] Quoted in Goulden, *The Superlawyers*, p. 36.
[6] Davis unsuccessfully argued the case for racial segregation on behalf of the Board of Education of Topeka, Kansas, in the famous case of *Brown* v. *Board of Education* (1954); opposing counsel for Brown, of course, was Supreme Court Justice Thurgood Marshall.

Secretary of Defense, 1967–69. A member of the Trilateral Commission and a director of the Council on Foreign Relations.

*John J. McCloy.* Special Adviser to the President on disarmament, 1961–63. Chairman of the Coordinating Committee on the Cuban Crisis, 1962. Member of the President's commission on the assassination of President Kennedy. U.S. High Commissioner for Germany, 1949–52. President of the World Bank, 1947–49. Partner in Milbank, Tweed, Hadley & McCloy. Member of the board of directors of Allied Chemical Corp., AT&T, Chase Manhattan Bank, Metropolitan Life Insurance Co., Westinghouse Electric, E. R. Squibb and Sons. Member of the board of trustees of the Ford Foundation, Council on Foreign Relations, and Amherst College.

*Arthur H. Dean.* Chairman of the U.S. Delegation on Nuclear Test Ban Treaty. Chief U.S. negotiator of the Korean Armistice Agreement. Partner, Sullivan and Cromwell. Member of the board of directors of American Metal Climax, American Bank Note Co., National Union Electric Corp., El Paso Natural Gas Co., Crown Zellerbach Corp., Lazard Fund, Inc., and Bank of New York. Member of the board of trustees of New York Hospital, Cornell Medical Center, Cornell Medical College, Cornell University, Carnegie Foundation, and Council on Foreign Relations.

The typical path to the top of the legal profession starts with a Harvard or Yale Law School degree, clerkship with a Supreme Court Justice, and then several years as an attorney with the Justice Department or a federal regulatory commission. Young government lawyers who are *successful* at defeating a top firm in a case are *more* likely to be offered lucrative junior partnerships than those who lose to big firms. Poorly paid but talented younger government lawyers are systematically recruited by the top firms.

### CLARK CLIFFORD: WASHINGTON SUPERLAWYER

Flavor the style of the nation's top Washington lawyer, Clark Clifford:

> There is one point I wish to make clear. This firm has no influence of any kind in Washington. If you want to employ someone who has influence, you will have to go somewhere else. . . . What we do have is a record of working with the various departments and agencies of the government, and we have their respect and confidence, and that we consider to be a valuable asset.[7]

Clifford's "valuable assets" bring him such clients as Standard Oil of California, American Broadcasting Company, Hughes Tool Co. (Howard Hughes), Time, Inc., General Electric, Penn Central Railroad,

---

[7] Quoted in Goulden, *The Superlawyers,* p. 78.

DuPont Corporation, Phillips Petroleum, W. R. Grace Shipping, El Paso Natural Gas, TWA, and so forth. A former personal client was John F. Kennedy. The Clifford firm is Clifford, Warnke, Glass, McIlwain & Finney.

Clifford was the son of an auditor for the Missouri-Pacific Railroad. He attended Washington University and St. Louis Law School, graduating in 1928. He promptly established a successful law practice in St. Louis, and included in his contacts Missouri Senators Harry S. Truman and Stuart Symington. Clifford enlisted in the Navy in World War II, but when Truman became President, he was called to the White House as counsel to the President. Clifford's title never changed, but he soon became a dominant figure on Truman's staff. He supervised foreign and domestic policy in the White House, as well as Truman's successful 1948 presidential campaign. In 1950, he left the White House, after five years of service, to open his own Washington firm. The decision to leave was fortunate, since the White House staff was shortly thereafter shaken by scandal.

Bureaucrats had become accustomed to answering Clifford's phone calls when they came from the White House, so they answered them when he called from his firm. His first big clients were Phillips Petroleum, Pennsylvania Railroad, Standard Oil of California, and Howard Hughes. Even during the Republican years under President Dwight Eisenhower, Clifford prospered: his close friend Senator Stuart Symington was chairman of the Senate Armed Forces Committee. McDonnell-Douglas Aircraft became a Clifford client. After duPont had lost its complex ten-year antitrust case and was ordered to sell its ownership of General Motors, it called upon Clifford in desperation. (Covington & Burling had unsuccessfully represented duPont.) If duPont were forced to sell its stock in GM immediately, the price of GM stock would plummet, and income from the sale would be heavily taxed. Clifford obtained passage of a special congressional act allowing distribution of the GM stock to duPont stockholders as a capital gain—and a tax savings to duPont of one-half billion dollars (which of course was a tax loss to the U.S. Treasury of an equal amount). Clifford's modest legal fee—$1 million.

When President Kennedy prepared to take over the reins of government from his predecessor Dwight Eisenhower, he sent his personal attorney Clark Clifford to arrange the transition. He also sent Clifford to investigate the Bay of Pigs disaster and reorganize the CIA and Defense intelligence operations. Later he sent Clifford to the headquarters of U.S. Steel to force a rollback of steel prices by threatening tax audits, contract cancellations, and FBI investigations. But Clifford did not accept any formal government appointment under Kennedy; by then his annual earnings regularly exceeded $1 million per year.

When the Vietnam War controversy had shattered the Johnson Administration and Robert McNamara was forced to resign as Secretary of Defense, Johnson persuaded his friend Clark Clifford to assume leadership of the Defense Department. Clifford reluctantly accepted the position of Secretary of Defense, reversed the policy of escalation in Vietnam, and began America's slow and painful withdrawal. Thus, the policy of military disengagement from Southeast Asia had already been started under Clifford when the Nixon Administration came to Washington.

In 1969 Clifford returned to his Washington law firm; he subsequently accepted the directorships of Phillips Petroleum and the Knight-Ridder newspapers. His partner, Paul Warnke, is arms control and disarmament adviser to President Carter, with special responsibilities for the SALT negotiations with the Soviet Union. When President Carter's personal friend and banker, Bert Lance, who Carter had named as Director of the Office of Management and Budget, was charged with banking irregularities, Lance turned to Clifford to get him out of trouble. Lance was forced to resign his office, but so far he has avoided prosecution under banking laws. Clifford himself remains at the top of the hierarchy of Washington "superlawyers."

## THE FOUNDATIONS

The power of the nation's largest foundations derives from their support of significant *new* research projects in the social sciences, arts, and humanities. Actually the foundations spend far less for research and development than does the federal bureaucracy. But the principal research components of the federal bureaucracy—the National Science Foundation, Energy Research and Development Administration, U.S. Public Health Service, the National Institute of Education—are generally conservative in their support of social research. These government agencies frequently avoid sensitive, controversial issues or overlook findings that would lead to major social innovations. Thus, it has been the role of the nation's largest foundations to support and direct innovations in the scientific, intellectual, and cultural life of the nation.

Most foundations consider themselves to be in the forefront of national policy making. "The foundations' best role," said Dr. Douglas D. Bond of the W. T. Grant Foundation, "is to identify, support, and bring to fruition certain ideas that government may later implement. . . . Government is beset by crises of a social and political nature that divert it and its money from the nurturing of new ideas and new discoveries. It is the foundation's task to remain steady in its aim and to sacrifice immediate goals for the more distant." [8]

The foundations channel corporate and personal wealth into the policy-making process, providing both financial support and direction for university research and the activities of various policy-planning groups. Foundations are tax-exempt: Contributions to foundations may be deducted from federal corporate and individual income taxes, *and* the foundations themselves are not subject to federal income taxation.

Foundations can be created by corporations or by individuals. These corporations or individuals can name themselves and their friends as directors or trustees of the foundations they create. Large blocks of corporate stock or large amounts of personal wealth can be donated as tax-exempt contributions to the foundations. The foundations can receive interest, dividends, profit shares, and capital gains from these assets without paying any taxes on them. The directors or trustees, of course, are not allowed to use foundation income or assets for their personal expenses, as they would their own taxable income. But otherwise they have great latitude in directing the use of foundation monies—to underwrite research, investigate social problems, create or assist universities, establish "think tanks," endow museums, theaters, operas, symphonies, and so on.

According to *The Foundation Directory*, there are 2,533 foundations large enough to deserve recognition and listing; these are the foundations with at least one million dollars in assets or $500,000 in yearly distributions. (There are tens of thousands of other smaller foundations and trusts, some established as tax dodges by affluent citizens and therefore not having any appreciable effect on public policy except to reduce tax collections.) In 1975 these foundations controlled $31.5 billion in assets.

But as in other sectors of society, these foundation assets are concentrated in a small number of large foundations. *The Foundation Directory* reports: "One of the outstanding facts concerning assets is the degree of their concentration in a small number of large organizations." [9] The 38 foundations each with more than $100 million in assets control 44.4 percent of all foundation assets in the nation (see Table 5–2).

Historically, the largest and most powerful foundations have been those established by the nation's leading families—Ford, Rockefeller, Carnegie, Mellon, Kresge, Pew, Duke, Lilly, Danforth. Over the years, some foundations—for example, the Carnegie Corporation—have become

[8] "Medicine's Philanthropic Support," *Medical World News,* December 8, 1972, p. 65.

[9] *The Foundation Directory,* 3rd ed. (New York: Russell Sage Foundation, 1967), p. 16.

independent of their original family ties; independence occurs when the foundation's own investments prosper and new infusions of family money are not required. However, Rockefellers, Fords, Mellons, Lillys, Danforths, Kresges, and other wealthy individuals still sit on the boards of directors of their family foundations. A number of foundations limit

TABLE 5–2    The 38 Foundations with Assets Greater than $100 Million

| Assets (millions of dollars) | | Foundation |
|---|---|---|
| 1 | $3146 | Ford Foundation, The |
| 2 | 1302 | Johnson (The Robert Wood) Foundation |
| 3 | 1142 | Lilly Endowment, Inc. |
| 4 | 840 | Rockefeller Foundation, The |
| 5 | 658 | Kresge Foundation, The |
| 6 | 636 | Mellon (The Andrew W.) Foundation |
| 7 | 582 | Pew Memorial Trust, The |
| 8 | 577 | Kellogg (W. K.) Foundation |
| 9 | 366 | Duke Endowment, The |
| 10 | 336 | Carnegie Corporation of New York |
| 11 | 322 | Mott (Charles Stewart) Foundation |
| 12 | 286 | Mellon (Richard King) Foundation |
| 13 | 284 | Sloan (Alfred P.) Foundation |
| 14 | 230 | Rockefeller Brothers Fund |
| 15 | 217 | Houston Endowment, Inc. |
| 16 | 206 | Woodruff (Emily and Ernest) Foundation |
| 17 | 198 | Danforth Foundation, The |
| 18 | 193 | New York Community Trust, The |
| 19 | 169 | Cleveland Foundation, The |
| 20 | 163 | Penn (The William) Foundation |
| 21 | 156 | Longwood Foundation, Inc. |
| 22 | 150 | Gannett (Frank E.) Newspaper Foundation, Inc. |
| 23 | 147 | Bush Foundation, The |
| 24 | 142 | Brown Foundation, Inc., The |
| 25 | 120 | Hartford (The John A.) Foundation, Inc. |
| 26 | 119 | Hill (Louis W. and Maud) Family Foundation |
| 27 | 118 | Atlantic Foundation, The |
| 28 | 117 | Moody Foundation, The |
| 29 | 116 | Surdna Foundation, Inc., The |
| 30 | 111 | Dow (The Herbert H. and Grace A.) Foundation |
| 31 | 111 | Commonwealth Fund, The |
| 32 | 108 | DeRance, Inc. |
| 33 | 108 | Alcoa Foundation |
| 34 | 107 | Kenan (William R., Jr.) Charitable Trust |
| 35 | 106 | Board of Directors of City Trusts, City of Philadelphia |
| 36 | 104 | Guggenheim (John Simon) Memorial Foundation |
| 37 | 104 | Fleischmann (Max C.) Foundation |
| 38 | 102 | Welch (The Robert A.) Foundation |

Source; *The Foundation Directory*, 5th ed. (New York: Russell Sage Foundation, 1976).

their contributions to specific fields; The Johnson Foundation, for example, sponsors research in medicine, and the Lilly Foundation supports advances in education and religion. This, however, tends to reduce a foundation's power to shape national goals and policy directions. In contrast, the Ford, Rockefeller, and Carnegie foundations deliberately attempt to focus on key national policy areas. This latter group of foundations plays a more influential role in national policy making because they concentrate their attention on broad social issues as poverty, health care, welfare reform, and foreign affairs.

*The Rockefeller Foundation.* A glance at the members of the Rockefeller Foundation board of directors confirms its ties to other top institutions.

*John D. Rockefeller, III.* Oldest son of John D. Rockefeller, II. Chairman of the Rockefeller Foundation, United Negro College Fund, Lincoln Center for the Performing Arts, and the Population Council.

*C. Douglas Dillon.* Former Secretary of the Treasury and Under Secretary of State; a director of Chase Manhattan.

*Cyrus Vance.* Secretary of State and former director of Chase Manhattan.

*W. Michael Blumenthal.* Secretary of the Treasury and former president of Bendix.

*Theodore Hesburgh.* President of Notre Dame and chairman of the U.S. Civil Rights Commission.

*Robert S. Goheen.* President of Princeton.

*Robert H. Ebert.* Dean of Harvard Medical School.

*Clifford M. Hardin.* Former Secretary of Agriculture and chairman of Ralston Purina.

*Vernon Jordan.* Executive director of the National Urban League.

*Lane Kirkland.* Secretary-treasurer of the AFL–CIO.

*Clifton W. Wharton, Jr.* President of Michigan State University and a director of Ford Motors, Burroughs Corp., and Equitable Life Assurance.

*Clark Kerr.* Former president of University of California and chairman of the Carnegie Commission on Higher Education.

*William Moyers.* Former presidential press secretary under Lyndon B. Johnson.

*Robert V. Roosa.* Partner, Brown Brothers, Harriman & Co., investment firm.

*Robert Seitz.* President of Rockefeller University. Former president of the National Academy of Sciences.

*The Ford Foundation.*  The president of the Ford Foundation is McGeorge Bundy, former dean of Harvard's College of Arts and Sciences, and Special Assistant to the President for national security affairs under both Presidents Kennedy and Johnson. Until his resignation in 1977, the driving force behind the foundation was Henry Ford II himself. His brother Benson Ford also serves on the board, as do:

> *Walter A. Hass.* President of Levi Strauss & Co. and a director of Bank-America.

> *Edward H. Land.* Former president and chairman of the board of Polaroid Corp.

> *John H. Loudon.* Former chairman of the board of Shell Oil Co.

> *Robert S. McNamara.* Former president of Ford Motor Co., Secretary of Defense, and president of the World Bank.

> *Alexander Heard.* President of Vanderbilt University.

> *Joseph Irwin Miller.* Chairman of Irwin-Union Bank & Trust and a director of AT&T, Purity Stores, Equitable Life Insurance, Chemical Bank of New York.

> *Andrew F. Brimmer.* Former Federal Reserve Board member; a director of duPont and Equitable Life Assurance.

> *Vivian W. Henderson.* President of Clark College, Atlanta.

> *Patricia M. Wald.* Partner, Arnold & Porter.

*The Carnegie Foundation.*  For many years the president of the Carnegie Foundation was John W. Gardiner, who went on to become Secretary of Health, Education, and Welfare under President Lyndon B. Johnson. Gardiner now uses his top connections to solicit support for the nation's heaviest spending congressional lobby, Common Cause.

The Carnegie Corporation board includes such men at the top as:

> *Charles M. Spofford.* Senior partner, Davis, Polk, Wardwell, Sunderland, and Kiendl.

> *Caryl P. Haskins.* Former president of Carnegie Foundation; a director of DuPont, RAND Corp., Yale University, Smithsonian Institution, and the Council on Foreign Relations.

> *Amyas Ames.* Former governor of the New York Stock Exchange.

> *Robert F. Bacher.* Former provost, California Institute of Technology and member of the Atomic Energy Commission; a director of Detroit Edison, Bell and Howell Co., and TRW, Inc.

> *Malcolm A. MacIntyre.* Former president, Eastern Airlines.

> *Franklin A. Thomas.* A director of Citicorp, CBS, New York Telephone, Cummins Engine, New York Life Insurance Co.

*Harding F. Bancroft.* Executive vice-president of the New York Times Company.

*Louis W. Cabot* (of the original Boston Cabots who explored America). Chairman of the board of the Cabot Corp.

*David A. Shepard.* Executive vice-president of Exxon and chairman of the board of trustees of the RAND Corp.

*Marta Valle.* Puerto Rican activist in New York City civic affairs.

## THE CULTURAL ORGANIZATIONS

The identification of the nation's leading civic and cultural institutions requires qualitative judgments about the prestige and influence of a variety of organizations. Six cultural organizations were selected:

Metropolitan Museum of Art
Museum of Modern Art
Lincoln Center for the Performing Arts
Smithsonian Institution
National Gallery of Art
John F. Kennedy Center for the Performing Arts

It is difficult to measure the power of particular institutions in the world of art, music, and theater. Certainly there are a number of viable alternatives that might be added to or substituted for our choices.

*The Metropolitan Museum of Art.* This organization in New York City is the largest art museum in the United States, with a collection of nearly one-half million *objets d'art.* Decisions of the Metropolitan Museum regarding exhibitions, collections, showings, and art objects have tremendous impact on what is or is not to be considered valued art in America. These decisions are the formal responsibility of the governing board. This board includes names such as:

*Arthur A. Houghton.* President and chairman of the board of Corning Glass.

*C. Douglas Dillon.* Former Secretary of Treasury, Under Secretary of State, and a director of Chase Manhattan.

*Mrs. McGeorge Bundy.* Wife of the former presidential assistant for national security affairs under Kennedy and Johnson. Former president of the Ford Foundation.

*Arthur Ochs Sulzberger.* Publisher and president of the *New York Times.*

*Nelson A. Rockefeller.* Former Governor of New York and Vice-President of the United States.

*Henry S. Morgan.* Son of J. P. Morgan, who founded U.S. Steel Corp. and International Harvester and became one of the world's wealthiest men in the 1920s through his control of Morgan Guaranty Bank.

*The Museum of Modern Art.*  This museum in New York City is the leading institution in the nation devoted to collecting and exhibiting contemporary art. It houses not only paintings and sculpture, but also films, prints, and photography. Its loan exhibitions circulate art works throughout the world. The determination of what is to be considered "art" in the world of modern art is extremely subjective. The directors of the Museum of Modern Art, then, have great authority in determining what is or is not to be viewed as art. Its directors include such illustrious names as:

*David Rockefeller.* Chairman of the board of Chase Manhattan.

*John Hay Whitney.* Centimillionaire, former publisher of the *New York Herald Tribune* and ambassador to Great Britain.

*William S. Paley.* Chairman of the board of CBS.

*Mrs. C. Douglas Dillon.* Wife of Douglas Dillon.

*Mrs. Edsel B. Ford.* Widow of Edsel B. Ford (son of Henry Ford) and mother of Henry Ford II.

*Mrs. John D. Rockefeller III.* Wife of oldest of four sons of John D. Rockefeller, Jr.

*The Lincoln Center for the Performing Arts.*  The Lincoln Center in New York City is a major influence in the nation's serious theater, ballet, and music. The Lincoln Center houses the Metropolitan Opera, the New York Philharmonic, and the Juilliard School of Music. It also supports the Lincoln Repertory Company (theater), the New York State Theater (ballet), and the Library-Museum for Performing Arts. These component parts exercise some independence, but the Lincoln Center's board of directors has considerable formal responsibility over all of these activities. The chairman of the board of Lincoln Center is John D. Rockefeller III, the oldest of the Rockefeller brothers.

The Metropolitan Opera, which opened in 1883, is the nation's most influential institution in the field of serious operatic music. Decisions about what operas to produce influence greatly what is, or is not, to be considered serious opera in America and indeed the world. Such decisions are the formal responsibility of a board that includes such luminaries as the following:

*Mrs. August Belmont.* A daughter of the Saltonstalls of Massachusetts.

*William Rockefeller.* A cousin of the Rockefeller brothers. A senior partner of Shearman and Sterling, a top Wall Street law firm.

*The Smithsonian Institution.* The Smithsonian Institution in Washington supports a wide variety of scientific publications, collections, and exhibitions. It also exercises nominal control over the National Gallery of Art, the John F. Kennedy Center for Performing Arts, and the Museum of Natural History, although these component organizations have their own boards of directors. The Smithsonian itself is directed by a board consisting of the Vice-President of the United States, the Chief Justice of the Supreme Court, three U.S. Senators, three U.S. Representatives, and six "private citizens."

Its "private citizens" turn out to be people such as:

*Crawford Greenewalt.* Former chairman of the board of E. I. DuPont De Nemours, and a trustee of the DuPont's Christiana Securities Corp. and Morgan Guaranty Trust Co.

*Thomas J. Watson, Jr.* Chairman of the board of IBM.

*William A. M. Burden.* A descendant of the Vanderbilts of New York City. Investor in and director of Allied Chemicals, CBS, Lockheed Aircraft, Manufacturers Hanover Trust, and American Metal Climax. Also served as ambassador to Belgium.

*Carl P. Haskins.* President of the Carnegie Foundation and a trustee of the Council on Foreign Relations, RAND Corp.

*James Edwin Webb.* Former director of the U.S. Bureau of the Budget and Under Secretary of State. Former director of the National Aeronautics and Space Administration. A director of Kerr McGee Oil Corp. and Sperry Rand, and trustee of the Committee for Economic Development.

*The National Gallery of Art.* The capital's leading art institution was begun in 1937 when Andrew W. Mellon made the original donation of his art collection together with $15 million to build the gallery itself. Since then it has accepted other collections from wealthy philanthropists and exercises considerable influence in the art world. Its directors include:

*Paul Mellon.* A son of Andrew Mellon and a director of Mellon National Bank and Trust and the Mellon Foundation.

*John Hay Whitney.* Centimillionaire, former publisher of the *New York Herald Tribune* and ambassador to Great Britain.

*Stoddard M. Stevens.* Senior partner, Sullivan and Cromwell, top Wall Street law firm.

*The John F. Kennedy Center for the Performing Arts.*   The Kennedy Center in Washington, which was begun in 1964, also has a considerable influence on the arts in America. Its board is largely "political" in origin, including:

*Edward M. Kennedy.* U.S. senator from Massachusetts.

*Mrs. J. W. Marriott.* Wife of president of Marriott Motor Hotels, himself a heavy financial contributor to political candidates.

*Jacqueline Kennedy Onassis.* The former Mrs. John F. Kennedy.

*Charles H. Percy.* U.S. senator from Illinois.

*Elliott M. Richardson.* Former Secretary of Health, Education, and Welfare, Secretary of Defense, and Attorney General.

*Arthur Schlesinger, Jr.* Former Special Assistant to President John F. Kennedy.

## THE CIVIC ASSOCIATIONS

Our judgments about power and influence in the civic arena are necessarily qualitative, as they were for cultural organizations. We shall focus particular attention on the political power of the nation's leading policy-planning organizations—the Council on Foreign Relations, the Committee on Economic Development, and the Brookings Institution—both in this chapter and later in Chapter 9. These organizations are central coordinating mechanisms in national policy making. They bring together people in top positions from the corporate world, the universities, the law firms, and the government, to develop explicit policies and programs for submission to Congress, the president, and the nation.

*The Council on Foreign Relations.*   The most influential policy-planning group in foreign affairs is the Council on Foreign Relations. It was founded in 1921 and supported by grants from the Rockefeller and Carnegie Foundations and later the Ford Foundation. Its early directors were internationally minded Wall Street corporation leaders such as Elihu Root (who was Secretary of State); John W. Davis (1924 Democratic presidential nominee); and Paul Cravath (founder of the famous law firm of Cravath, Swaine & Moore).

The CFR is designed to build consensus among elites on foreign policy questions. Its commissions make investigations concerning foreign policy and set major directions of official U.S. policy. On it rests in large measure the decision of when to reassess U.S. foreign or military policy. Its studies are usually made with the financial support of foundations.

The history of the CFR accomplishments are dazzling: It developed the Kellogg Peace Pact in the 1920s, stiffened U.S. opposition to Japanese Pacific expansion in the 1930s, designed major portions of the United Nations' charter, and devised the "containment" policy to halt Soviet expansion in Europe after World War II. It also laid the groundwork for the NATO agreement and devised the Marshall Plan for European recovery.

CFR publishes the journal *Foreign Affairs,* considered throughout the world the unofficial mouthpiece of U.S. foreign policy. Few important initiatives in U.S. policy have not been first outlined in articles in this publication. It was in *Foreign Affairs* in 1947 that George F. Kennan, chief of the policy-planning staff of the State Department, writing under the pseudonym of "X", first announced U.S. intentions of "containing" Communist expansion in the world. When top elites began to suspect that the U.S. was over-reliant on nuclear weapons in the late 1950s, and unable to fight theater-type wars, the CFR commissioned a young Harvard professor to look into the matter. The result was Henry Kissinger's *Nuclear Weapons and Foreign Policy,* urging greater flexibility of response to aggression.

The CFR limits itself to 700 individual resident members (New York and Washington) and 700 nonresident members. There are few individuals in top positions in American institutions with an interest in foreign affairs who are *not* CFR members. The CFR's list of former members include every person of influence in foreign affairs from Elihu Root, Henry Stimson, John Foster Dulles, Dean Acheson, Robert Lovett, George F. Keenan, Averell Harriman, and Dean Rusk to Henry Kissinger and Cyrus Vance.

Evidence of CFR interaction with the corporate and financial world, as well as with universities, foundations, the mass media, and government, is found in extensive interlocking between the leadership of CFR and the leadership of these other elements of the policy-making process. In 1976, the CFR board of directors included:

*David Rockefeller.* Chairman of the board of directors of the Council on Foreign Relations. Chairman of board and chief executive officer, Chase Manhattan Bank. He is a director or trustee of the Rockefeller Foundation, Museum of Modern Art, Harvard University, and the University of Chicago. He is also a director of Chase International Investment Corporation Morningside Heights, Inc., Rockefeller Center, Inc., Downtown Lower Manhattan Association.

*John J. McCloy.* Former chairman of the board of Chase Manhattan Bank and senior partner of the New York law firm of Milbank, Tweed, Hadley, & McCloy. Special adviser to the President on disarmament, 1961–63; chairman of the Coordinating Committee on the Cuban Crisis, 1962; member of the President's Commission on the Assassination of President Kennedy; U.S. High Commissioner for Germany, 1949–52; president of the World Bank, 1947–49. He is a director of Allied Chemical Corporation, American Telephone and Telegraph Company, Chase Manhattan Bank, Metropolitan Life Insurance Company, Westinghouse Electric Corporation, E. R. Squibb and Sons, and a trustee of the Ford Foundation and Amherst College.

*Gabriel Hauge.* President, Manufacturers Hanover Trust Co., former editor of *Business Week.* A director of New York Life Insurance, America Metal Climax, American Home Products. A trustee of the Committee for Economic Development, Juilliard School of Music, and the Carnegie Endowment for International Peace.

*James P. Perkins.* President of Cornell University. A trustee of Carnegie Corporation and the RAND Corporation, and a director of Chase Manhattan.

*Hedley Donovan.* Editor-in-chief, *Time* magazine. A trustee of New York University and the Carnegie Foundation.

*William P. Bundy.* Editor of the Council on Foreign Relations' official journal *Foreign Affairs.* Senior partner, Covington & Burling (Washington law firm). Former deputy director C.I.A., Assistant Secretary of Defense, 1961–64; assistant secretary of state for Far East, 1964–68. A trustee of the Committee on Economic Development, the American Assembly, and Yale University. (His brother McGeorge Bundy was dean of Harvard College, Special Assistant to President Johnson for national security affairs, and president of the Ford Foundation.)

*Robert O. Anderson.* Chairman of the board, Atlantic Richfield Co. A director of the American Petroleum Institute. He is trustee of the California Institute of Technology, University of Chicago, and the University of Denver.

*Nicholas DeB. Kaizenbach.* Former Attorney General of the United States, 1964–66. Former University of Chicago law school professor. He is director and general counsel of the IBM Corporation.

*Douglas Dillon.* Chairman of the board of the New York investment firm of Dillon, Reed, and Co.; a director of U.S. Foreign Securities Corp., U.S. International Securities Corp., Rockefeller Foundation, Brookings Institution, New York Hospital, and Metropolitan Museum of Art. He was Secretary of the Treasury, 1961–63.

*Theodore M. Hesburgh.* President of University of Notre Dame. Former chairman, U.S. Civil Rights Commission. A director of American Council on Education, Rockefeller Foundation, Carnegie Foundation, Woodrow Wilson National Fellowship Foundation, United Negro College Fund, and the Freedom Foundation.

*Robert V. Roosa.* Senior partner of New York investment firm of Brown Brothers, Harriman & Co. (which was founded by Averell Harriman). A director of American Express Co., Anaconda Copper, Owens–Corning Fiberglass, and Texaco. He was former Under Secretary of the Treasury.

*Peter G. Peterson.* Chairman of the New York investment firm of Lehuan Bros. Former chairman of the board of Bell and Howell, Co. and former assistant to the President for international economic affairs 1971–72. A director of Minnesota Mining & Mfg., General Foods, and Federated Department Stores. He is a trustee of the Museum of Modern Art and the University of Chicago.

*Paul C. Warnke.* Now U.S. arms control and disarmament adviser and SALT negotiator. Senior partner, Washington law firm of Clifford, Warnke, Glass, McIlwain & Finney and former Assistant Secretary of Defense, 1967–69. He is a member of the Trilateral Commission.

*Cyrus Vance.* Now Secretary of State. Vice-chairman of the board of directors of the Council on Foreign Relations. Senior partner of New York law firm of Simpson Thacher & Bartlett. A director of Pan-American World Airways, American Life Insurance Co., IBM, American Red Cross, University of Chicago, and the Rockefeller Foundation. He was formerly Secretary of the Army and Under Secretary of Defense; also a U.S. negotiator at the Paris Peace Conference on Vietnam during the Johnson Administration.

*W. Michael Blumenthal.* Now Secretary of the Treasury. President of the Bendix Corporation. A naturalized U.S. citizen whose parents fled Nazi Germany in 1938. An earned Ph.D. in economics from Princeton. Former director of Crown Cork Co. and special representative on trade negotiation under President Kennedy. A trustee of Princeton University.

*Robert O. Anderson.* Chairman of the board, Atlantic Richfield.

*William S. Anderson.* Chairman of the board, National Cash Register.

*Roy L. Ash.* Former director, Office of Management and Budget, 1973–75. Former chief financial officer, Hughes Aircraft Co., and later co-founder and president of Litton Industries. A director of BankAmerica, Global Marine, Inc., and a trustee of the California Institute of Technology.

*James F. Bere.* Chairman of the board, Borg-Warner Corporation. A director of Abbott Laboratories and Continental Illinois National Bank and Trust Co.

*Edward W. Carter.* President of Broadway Hale Stores. A director of AT & T, Southern California Edison, Del Monte Corporation, Western Bankcorporation, and Pacific Mutual Life Insurance Co.

*Frank T. Cary.* Chairman of the board, IBM.

*Clifton C. Garvin, Jr.* Chairman of the board, Exxon Corporation, and a director of Citicorp and the American Petroleum Institute.

*H. J. Heinz II.* Chairman of the board, H. J. Heinz Co. He is a director of Mellon National Bank and Trust and a trustee of Carnegie-Mellon University. His son, H. J. Heinz III, is U.S. Senator from Pennsylvania.

*Edward R. Kaye.* President E. I. DuPont De Nemours & Co. and a director of Morgan Guaranty Trust Co. An earned Ph.D. in chemistry from M.I.T.

*C. Peter McColough.* Chairman of the board, Xerox Corporation and a director of Citicorp.

*Richard D. Wood.* Chairman of the board, Eli Lilly & Co. A director of Chemical Bank of New York, Elizabeth Arden, Inc., Standard Oil of Indiana, and the Lilly Endowment.

*Ralph Lazarus.* President, Federated Department Stores, Inc. A director of Chase Manhattan Bank, Scott Paper Co., General Electric. He also is a trustee of Dartmouth College.

*Zbigniew Brzezinski.* Now Special Assistant to the President for national security affairs. Professor of Government at Columbia University. Son of a Polish diplomat with an earned Ph.D. in government from Harvard. Executive director of the Trilateral Commission.

Of the twenty-five current (1976) directors and sixteen "directors emeriti," the Council now, according to fashion, boasts of one woman and one black. The woman is Elizabeth Drew, *Washington Post–Newsweek* journalist and commentator on Washington's WTOP-TV (which is also owned by *Washington Post–Newsweek*). The black is Franklin Hall Williams, former NAACP attorney and U.S. ambassador to Ghana (1965–68) under President Johnson. He is also a director of the Chemical Bank of New York and Consolidated Edison.

*Committee on Economic Development.*   There are several private policy-planning groups that are influential in domestic affairs. None, however, is really as influential in *domestic* affairs as the CFR is in *foreign* affairs. But the Committee on Economic Development (CED) is a central organization for developing consensus among business and financial leaders on public policy, and communicating their views to government officials. The CED does not restrict itself to fiscal and monetary policy, or to business regulation, but instead works on a wide range of domestic and foreign policy issues. There are many interlocks between CFR and CED members. A brief listing of CED trustees indicates their extensive interlocking with business, financial, foundation, and governmental institutions. The trustees include such men as:

*William H. Franklin.* Chairman of the board of trustees of the Committee on Economic Development. He is chairman of the board of Caterpillar Tractor Co. and a director of Exxon Corp.

*George C. McGhee.* Sole owner, McGhee Oil Company. Former U.S. ambassador to Turkey, former chairman of the Policy Planning Council of the Department of State, and former Under Secretary of State and U.S. ambassador to West Germany. Former chairman of Urban Coalition and a director of Brookings Institution and Vassar College.

*Chauncey J. Medberry III.* Chairman of the board, BankAmerica and a director of Getty Oil Co.

*John B. M. Place.* Chairman of the board, Anaconda Copper Co. and a director of Celanese Corp., Chemical Bank of New York, Communications Satellite Corp., Lever Brothers, and the Union Pacific Railroad.

*Peter G. Peterson.* Chairman of the New York investment firm of Lehman Bros. Former chairman of the board of Bell and Howell Co. and former assistant to the President for international economic affairs, 1971–72. A director of Minnesota Mining & Mfg., General Foods, and Federated Department Stores. He is a trustee of the Museum of Modern Art and the University of Chicago.

*J. L. Scott.* Chairman of the board, Great Atlantic and Pacific Tea Co. (A & P).

*George P. Schultz.* Former Secretary of Labor, 1969–70. Director of the Office of Management and Budget, 1970–72; and Secretary of Treasury, 1972–74. Currently president of Bechtel Corporation and a director of J. P. Morgan & Co. and the Morgan Guaranty Trust Co. Former dean of the Graduate School of Business, University of Chicago; an earned Ph.D. in economics from M.I.T.

*Joseph L. Black.* Chairman and chief executive officer, Inland Steel Company. A director of the Chicago Board of Trade, Commonwealth Edison Co., Chicago First National Bank. A trustee of the National Merit Scholarship Fund, Illinois Institute of Technology, American Iron and Steel Institute.

*Jevis J. Babb.* Former president and chairman of the board of Lever Brothers. A director of Sucrest Corporation, Universal Foods, Gruen Industries, Guardian Life Insurance, American Can Co., Bank of New York.

*The Brookings Institution.* Today the foremost policy-planning group in domestic affairs is the Brookings Institution. Since the 1960s, it has overshadowed the CED, the American Assembly, the Twentieth Century Fund, the Urban Institute, and all other policy-planning groups. Brookings has been extremely influential in planning the War on Poverty, welfare reform, national health care, and tax reform.

The Brookings Institution directors today are as impressive a group of top elites as assembled anywhere:

*Robert V. Roosa.* Chairman of board of trustees of the Brookings Institution; senior partner, Brown Brothers, Harriman & Co. (New York investment firm). He is a director of American Express Co., Anaconda Copper, Owens-Corning Fiberglass Co., and Texaco. He is a former Under-Secretary of the Treasury and a director of the Council on Foreign Relations. Roosa has an earned Ph.D. in economics from the University of Michigan and was a Rhodes scholar. A trustee of the Rockefeller Foundation.

*Louis W. Cabot* (of the original Boston Cabots, whose ancestors explored America). Chairman of the board of the Cabot Corporation. A director of Owens-Corning Fiberglass Co. and New England Telephone, and chairman of the Federal Reserve Bank of Boston. A trustee of the Carnegie Corporation, M.I.T., and Northeastern University, and Member of the Council on Foreign Relations.

*Robert S. McNamara.* President of the World Bank. Former Secretary of Defense, 1961–67. Former president, Ford Motor Company.

*William McChesney Martin, Jr.* Former chairman of the Federal Reserve Board. Former chairman of the Export-Import Bank, governor of the New York Stock Exchange, and partner in the investment firm of A. G. Edwards & Sons. He is a director of IBM, Caterpillar Tractor, and General Foods. He is also a trustee of the American Red Cross, Johns Hopkins University, and Yale University.

*Douglas Dillon.* Chairman of board of the New York investment firm of Dillon, Reed, and Co., member of New York Stock Exchange. A director of U.S. Foreign Securities Corp. and U.S. International Securities Corp., Rockefeller Foundation, Brookings Institution, New York Hospital, and Metropolitan Museum of Art. He was Secretary of the Treasury, 1961–63.

*Eugene R. Black.* Former president, Chase Manhattan Bank. A director of Chase Manhattan, American Express Co., Equitable Life Assurance Society, IT&T, New York Times Company, Electric Bond & Share Co., Cummins Engine, F. W. Woolworth Co., Royal Dutch Shell, Trust Company of Georgia. A trustee of the J. P. Morgan Library, Harvard University, Johns Hopkins University, Population Council, Planned Parenthood, Project Hope, and the Girls' Club of America.

*Luther G. Holbrook.* Former president, T. Mellon & Sons, and trustee of the Mellon Foundation.

*Arjay Miller.* Former president, Ford Motor Company; dean of the Graduate School of Business at Stanford University.

*Herbert P. Patterson.* President, Chase Manhattan Bank. A director of American Machine & Foundry and the Urban Coalition.

*Edward W. Carter.* President of Broadway Hale Stores. A director of AT&T, Southern California Edison, Del Monte Corporation, Western BanCorporation, and Pacific Mutual Life Insurance Company.

Two women are listed among the 21 trustees and 10 honorary trustees of the Brookings Institution: Barbara W. Newell, president of Wellesley College, and Lucy Wilson Benson, former national president of the League of Women Voters; secretary for human services, Commonwealth of Massachusetts; and a director of the Dreyfus Fund, Continental Can, and Federated Department Stores.

If the names are growing repetitious by now, it is for good reason.

Those who occupy top posts in the leading corporate, governmental, and mass media institutions are frequently the same individuals who direct the leading foundations, civic associations, and cultural organizations. In the next few pages, we shall see many of their names again, when we examine the trustees of the nation's leading universities. The purpose of "naming names," even when they become repetitive, is to suggest frequent interlocking of top elites in different institutional sectors. In Chapter 6, we will examine interlocking in greater detail.

## THE UNIVERSITIES

The growth of public higher education since World War II—the creation of vast state university, state college, and community college systems in every state in the nation—has diminished the influence of the prestigious private universities. There are now over 2500 separate institutions of higher education in America, enrolling over nine million students— about half of all high school graduates; however, only about a quarter of these students are enrolled in *private* colleges and universities. Moreover, some leading public universities, for example, the University of California at Berkeley, the University of Wisconsin, and the University of Michigan, are consistently ranked with the well-known private universities in terms of the quality of higher education offered. Thus, the leading private universities in the nation no longer exercise the dominant influence over higher education that they did before World War II.

Nonetheless, among private colleges and universities it is possible to identify those few top institutions which control over half of the resources available to *private* higher education. The twelve universities listed in Table 5–3 control 54 percent of all private endowment funds in higher education; this was the formal basis for their selection. Moreover, they are consistently ranked among the "best" educational institutions in the nation. Finally, as we will see, a disproportionate number of the nation's top leaders attended one or another of these institutions.

The presidents and trustees of these twelve institutions, then, can exercise significant influence over higher education and thus over the quality of life in America. A brief look at the careers of some of these people who head our institutions of higher education tells us a great deal about the educational elite. Note how their careers involve two or more similar positions, and their close ties with other fields, notably business, culture, politics, and public interest. We will list some names of trustees for the nation's top three private universities—Harvard, Yale, and the University of Chicago.

**TABLE 5-3    The Top Privately Endowed Colleges and Universities**

| Rank | | Endowment (in billions of dollars) | Cumulative Percent |
|------|---|---|---|
| 1 | Harvard | 1,013 | 18.5 |
| 2 | Yale | 358 | 25.0 |
| 3 | Chicago | 275 | 30.0 |
| 4 | Stanford | 223 | 34.1 |
| 5 | Columbia | 201 | 37.7 |
| 6 | Massachusetts Institute of Technology | 184 | 41.1 |
| 7 | Cornell | 163 | 44.0 |
| 8 | Northwestern | 135 | 46.5 |
| 9 | Princeton | 134 | 48.9 |
| 10 | Johns Hopkins | 112 | 51.0 |
| 11 | Pennsylvania | 95 | 52.7 |
| 12 | Dartmouth | 91 | 54.4 |
| | | 2,984 | |

Number of Institutions = 107
Total private endowments funds, U.S. = 5,488 billion dollars

*Harvard University*

*Osborn Elliott.* Editor of *Newsweek* and a director of Washington Post Co.

*C. Douglas Dillon.* Former Secretary of the Treasury, and a director of defense.

*Gardiner Cowles.* Chairman of board of Cowles Publications (largest U.S. newspaper chain).

*Francis Keppel.* Former U.S. commissioner of education and Assistant Secretary of HEW.

*Robert C. Seamoris, Jr.* Former Secretary of the Air Force, and deputy director of NASA.

*Louis W. Cabot.* Chairman of the board of the Cabot Corporation.

*Yale University*

*John Hay Whitney.* Centimillionaire, former publisher of *New York Herald Tribune* and ambassador to Great Britain.

*William McChesney Martin, Jr.* Former chairman of the Federal Reserve Board, former governor of New York Stock Exchange.

*William P. Bundy.* Senior partner, Covington and Burling. Former Assistant Secretary of State for the Far East; former Assistant Secretary of Defense.

*William W. Scranton.* Former Governor of Pennsylvania.

*Cyrus R. Vance.* Secretary of State; senior partner, Simpson, Thachter & Bartlett; former Secretary of the Army.

*Arthur K. Watson.* Former chairman of the board, IBM.

*University of Chicago*

*David Rockefeller.* Chairman of the board, Chase Manhattan.

*Cyrus S. Eaton.* Former director Republic Steel Corp., Inland Steel Corp., Kingstown Sheet & Tube, Sherman-Williams Co.

*Albert Pick, Jr.* President of Albert Pick Hotels.

*Robert O. Anderson.* Chairman of the board, Atlantic Richfield Co.; a director of Smith Kline & French (pharmaceuticals).

*Katherine Graham.* Publisher *Washington Post–Newsweek.*

*Robert S. Ingersoll.* Chairman of board, Borg-Warner Corp.

*David M. Kennedy.* Former Secretary of the Treasury; chairman of the board of Continental Illinois National Bank & Trust.

*John D. Rockefeller IV.* Son of John D. Rockefeller III. Former Appalachian area poverty worker, and later Secretary of State for West Virginia, and former President of W. Virginia Wesleyan College. Now Governor of West Virginia.

*Charles H. Percy.* U.S. Senator from Illinois.

We have already acknowledged the growing importance in higher education of the nation's leading *state* universities. Is there any reason to believe that their rise to prominence since World War II has distributed power in education more widely and opened positions of authority to men whose elite credentials are not necessarily as impressive as the ones we have seen again and again in our lists of top leaders? Our answer is a very qualified "yes": State boards of regents for state universities are on the whole composed of individuals who would probably *not* be among the top institutional elites according to our definition in Chapter 1. Many of these regents hold directorships in smaller corporations (ranked below the top 100), smaller banks (ranked below the top 50), and smaller communications, transportation and utility companies (ranked below the top 33); they frequently have held state rather than national political office; their legal, civic, cultural, and foundation affiliations are with institutions of state rather than national prestige and power.

Nonetheless, it is interesting to see, for example, who controls the University of California's multi-campus, billion-dollar educational enterprise. Four of the 24 regents are elected state officials—the Governor, Lieutenant Governor, state assembly speaker, and superintendent of education. The other 20 appointed regents, serving 16-year appointments, sit on a total of 60 corporate boards. According to David N. Smith, these corporations include Western Bancorporation, Croker-Citizens National Bank, United California Bank, AT&T, Pacific Telephone and Telegraph, Broadway Hale Stores (including Neiman Marcus), Western Airlines, Pacific Lighting Corporation, Southern California Edison, Pacific Mutual Life Insurance, Northern Pacific Railway, Lockheed Aircraft and the

Los Angeles Rams and California Angels.[10] Catherine Hearst (wife of publisher Randolph Hearst and mother of Patty Hearst), was a regent, as well as Norton Simon, whose firm Norton Simon, Inc., is the 120th largest industrial corporation in the nation. Thus the most prestigious of our state universities do seem to be acquiring some share of power within the educational elite, as measured by the clout of their trustees and their ties with the financial elite.

University presidents, particularly the presidents of the nation's top institutions, are frequently called upon to serve as trustees or directors of other institutions and to serve in high government posts. Most university presidents today have come up through the ranks of academic administration, suggesting that universities themselves may offer channels for upward mobility into the nation's elite. We must keep in mind, however, that presidents are hired and fired by the trustees, not the students or faculty.

## THE INTELLECTUAL ELITE

The intellectual "community" is not sufficiently organized or institutionalized to provide its leadership with formal control over any significant portion of society's resources. Indeed, "intellectuals" do not even have much control over universities, the institutions that house the largest group of the nation's intellectuals. Some intellectuals of course have "influence" because directors of large institutions read their books and listen to their lectures and are persuaded by them. But intellectuals per se have no direct control over the institutional structure of society, *unless they are recruited into top institutional positions.* Our formal definition of elites as individuals in positions of control over institutional resources, then, means that we can count as intellectual elites only those who have been recruited to high institutional positions—particularly in government, the foundations, and the civic and cultural organizations. The prototype of the intellectual in power, of course, is Henry Kissinger.

Historian Richard Hofstadter has categorized intellectuals in a fashion that reflects our own notion about treating those in power differently from those not in power. Hofstadter expressed the hope that "the intellectual community will not become hopelessly polarized into two parts, one part the technicians concerned with power and accepting the terms of power put to them, and the other of willfully alienated intellectuals more concerned with maintaining their own sense of purity than with making their ideas effective." [11]

[10] David N. Smith, *Who Rules the Universities?* (New York: Monthly Review Press, 1974), pp. 30–33.

[11] Richard Hofstadter, *Anti-Intellectualism in American Life* (New York: Knopf, 1963), p. 429.

Actually, it is difficult to define precisely who is an intellectual. Seymour Martin Lipset defines intellectuals as

> all of those who create, distribute, and apply culture, that is, the symbolic world of man, including art, science, and religion. Within this group there are two main levels; the hard core of creators of culture—scholars, artists, philosophers, authors, some editors and some journalists; and the distributors—performers in the various arts, most teachers, and most reporters.[12]

Such a broad definition includes millions of individuals with a wide range of institutional affiliations.

Perhaps the most systematic attempt to identify an intellectual *elite* is found in the work of Charles Kadushin and his associates at Columbia University.[13] According to Kadushin, "An elite intellectual may be defined roughly as one who is an expert in dealing with general ideas on questions of values and esthetics and who communicates his judgments on these matters to a fairly general audience." (Note that Kadushin excludes many specialists, particularly in the physical and biological sciences, who deal with specific scientific questions and communicate to a very specialized audience; this may be the greatest weakness in his definition.) To operationalize this definition, Kadushin employed a reputational approach to select 20 leading intellectual journals of general interest, excluding specialized or technical ones. A sample of professors, writers, and editors selected the following publications:

| | |
|---|---|
| *New York Review of Books* | *Daedalus* |
| *New Republic* | *Ramparts* |
| *Commentary* | *Yale Review* |
| *New York Times Book Review* | *Dissent* |
| *New Yorker* | *American Scholar* |
| *Saturday Review* | *Hudson Review* |
| *Partisan Review* | *Village Voice* |
| *Harpers* | *The Progressive* |
| *The Nation* | *Foreign Affairs* |
| *Atlantic* | *The Public Interest* |

It turns out that nearly 8000 persons had contributed articles to these intellectual journals in a four-year period. A second sample was then asked to identify those intellectuals "who influenced them on cultural

---

[12] Seymour Martin Lipset, *Political Man* (New York: Doubleday, 1960), p. 310.

[13] Charles Kadushin, Julie Hover, and Monique Richy, "How and Where to Find an Intellectual Elite in the United States," *Public Opinion Quarterly*, 35 (Spring 1971), 1–18; see also Charles Kadushin, "Who Are the Elite Intellectuals?" *The Public Interest* (Summer 1972), pp. 109–125.

**TABLE 5–4    The Most Prestigious Contemporary American Intellectuals**

---

*Ranks 1 to 10 (2 tied for 10th place)*

| | |
|---|---|
| Daniel Bell | Norman Mailer |
| Noam Chomsky | Robert Silvers |
| John Kenneth Galbraith | Susan Sontag |
| Irving Howe | Lionel Trilling |
| Dwight MacDonald | Edmund Wilson |
| Mary McCarthy | |

*Ranks 11 to 20*

| | |
|---|---|
| Hannah Arendt | Herbert Marcuse |
| Saul Bellow | Daniel Patrick Moynihan |
| Paul Goodman | Norman Podhoretz |
| Richard Hofstadter | David Riesman |
| Irving Kristol | Arthur Schlesinger, Jr. |

*Ranks 21 to 25 (numerous ties)*

| | |
|---|---|
| W. H. Auden | Pauline Kael |
| Norman O. Brown | Alfred Kazin |
| Theodore Draper | Murray Kempton |
| Jason Epstein | George Lichtheim |
| Leslie Fiedler | Walter Lippmann |
| Edgar Friedenberg | Marshall McLuhan |
| John Gardner | Hans Morgenthau |
| Eugene Genovese | I. F. Stone |
| Richard Goodwin | C. Vann Woodward |
| Michael Harrington | |

*Ranks 26 and 27 (numerous ties)*

| | |
|---|---|
| Edward Banfield | Willie Morris |
| Isaiah Berlin | Lewis Mumford |
| Barbara Epstein | Reinhold Niebuhr |
| R. Buckminster Fuller | Robert Nisbet |
| Nathan Glazer | Phillip Rahv |
| Elizabeth Hardwick | James Reston |
| Robert Heilbroner | Harold Rosenberg |
| Sidney Hook | Philip Roth |
| Ada Louise Huxtable | Richard Rovere |
| George F. Kennan | Bayard Rustin |
| Christopher Lasch | Franz Schurman |
| Seymour Martin Lipset | John Simon |
| Robert Lowell | George Steiner |
| Robert K. Merton | Diana Trilling |
| Barrington Moore | James Q. Wilson |

---

Source: Charles Kadushin, "Who Are the Elite Intellectuals?" *The Public Interest,* Number 29 (Fall 1972), p. 123. Copyright © 1972 by National Affairs, Inc.

or social-political issues, or who they believed had high prestige in the intellectual community." The result was the listing that constitutes Table 5–4.

We can now make some observations about the nation's intellectual elite. A few have occupied high places in government—Galbraith, Moynihan, Schlesinger, Gardner—but most have remained on the sidelines, perhaps exercising "influence" from time to time, but not "power" in terms of institutional authority. About half of America's intellectuals are Jewish (less than three percent of the nation's total population is Jewish). One-third are under 50 years old; one-third is between 50 and 60; and one-third is over 60. Their median income in 1969 was only $35,000, considerably less than the other elites identified in this book. There are very few women among the nation's *top* intellectuals, and only one black—Bayard Rustin.

The American intellectual elite is far more liberal than any other segment of the nation's elite. Richard Hofstadter writes:

> If there is anything that could be called an intellectual establishment in America, this establishment has been, though not profoundly radical (which would be unbecoming in an establishment), on the left side of center.[14]

Kadushin confirms this judgment; his intellectuals are left-liberal and generally critical of the government and the economic system. But only about 20 percent could be classified as "radical"—that is, convinced that the overthrow of capitalism is essential to improvement in the quality of life in America. Kadushin found that the few elite intellectuals who rose from working-class backgrounds are somewhat more *conservative* than the majority of intellectuals who came from middle-, upper-middle-, and upper-class families. But he adds, "The elite intellectuals have so long been involved in the culture of intellectuals that their past backgrounds have become almost irrelevant." [15]

## SUMMARY

Using the term *civic establishment,* we refer collectively to the nation's top law firms, its major foundations, its national cultural institutions, influential civic organizations, and powerful universities. At the top of the legal profession, the senior partners of the nation's largest and best known New York and Washington law firms exercise great power as

[14] Hofstadter, *Anti-Intellectualism.*
[15] *Ibid.,* p. 120.

legal representatives of the nation's largest corporations. These "super-lawyers" generally reflect the same liberalism and concern for public welfare that prevail among other segments of the nation's elites. Super-lawyers are frequently called upon for governmental leadership, particularly when high-level, delicate negotiations are required. Many superlawyers have been educated at Ivy League law schools and serve apprenticeships in governmental agencies before entering law firms.

The power of the nation's large foundations rests in their ability to channel corporate and personal wealth into the policy-making process. They do this by providing financial support and direction over university research and the activities of policy-oriented, civic associations. There is great concentration of foundation assets: Twelve of the nation's 6,803 foundations control 40 percent of all foundation assets. There is also a great deal of overlapping among the directorates of the leading foundations and corporate and financial institutions, the mass media, universities, policy-planning groups, and government.

A small number of cultural organizations exercise great power over the nation's art, music, theater, and ballet. A brief glance at the directors of these institutions confirms that they are the same group of people identified earlier as influential in business, finance, government, and the mass media.

The civic associations, particularly the leading policy-planning groups—the Council on Foreign Relations, Committee on Economic Development, and the Brookings Institution—play key roles in national policy making. They bring together men at the top of various institutional sectors of society to formulate recommendations on major policy innovations. More will be said about the important role of policy-planning groups in Chapter 9. But we have noted here that the directors of these groups are top leaders in industry, finance, government, the mass media, law, and the universities.

There may not be as much concentration of power in higher education as in other sectors of American life. The development of state universities since World War II has diminished the influence of the private, Ivy League-type universities. However, among *private* universities, only 12 institutions control over half of all private endowment funds. A glance at the trustees of three of these institutions—Harvard, Yale, and Chicago—suggests heavy overlapping of those in power in corporations, government, the mass media, the foundations and civic organizations. The intellectual "community" does not exercise any formal control over any significant portion of the nation's resources. Only when an intellectual is recruited to high position, as in the case of Henry Kissinger or Zbigniew Brzezinski, can he be said to have power.

# THE STRUCTURE
# OF
# INSTITUTIONAL
# ELITES

part III

# interlocking
# and specialization
# at the top

▶▶▶▶▶▶▶▶▶▶▶▶▶▶▶▶▶▶▶▶▶▶▶▶▶▶▶▶▶▶▶▶▶▶▶▶▶▶▶▶▶▶▶▶▶▶▶▶▶▶▶▶▶▶▶▶▶▶

# 6

## CONVERGENCE OR SPECIALIZATION AT THE TOP?

Is there a convergence of power at the top of an institutional structure in America, with a single group of individuals, recruited primarily from industry and finance, who occupy top positions in corporations, education, government, foundations, civic and cultural affairs, and the military? Or are there separate institutional structures, with elites in each sector of society having little or no overlap in authority and many separate channels of recruitment? In short, is the structure of power in America a pyramid or a polyarchy?

Social scientists have differed over this important question, and at least two varieties of leadership models can be identified in the literature on power.[1] A *hierarchical model* implies that a relatively small group of individuals exercises authority in a wide variety of institutions— forming what has been called a "power elite." In contrast, a *polyarchical model* implies that different groups of individuals exercise power in various sectors of society, and acquire power in separate ways.

The hierarchical model derives from the familiar "elitist" literature on power. Mills argues that "the leading men in each of the three

---

[1] This literature is voluminous, and any characterization of positions results in some oversimplification. For good summary statements of positions, see the works of Mills, Hunter, Berle, Kolko, and Dahl, cited elsewhere in chapter notes. See also Arnold M. Rose, *The Power Structure* (New York: Oxford University Press, 1967); Suzanne Keller, *Beyond the Ruling Class* (New York: Random House, 1963); G. William Domhoff, *Who Rules America?* (Englewood Cliffs, N.J.: Prentice-Hall, Inc., 1967); Nelson Polsby, *Community Power and Political Theory* (New Haven: Yale University Press, 1963); and David Ricci, *Community Power and Democratic Theory* (New York: Random House, 1971).

domains of power—the warlords, the corporation chieftains, and the political directorate—tend to come together to form the power elite of America." [2] According to Mills, leadership in America constitutes "an intricate set of overlapping cliques." And Hunter, in his study *Top Leadership, U.S.A.*, concludes: "Out of several hundred persons named from all sources, between one hundred and two hundred were consistently chosen as top leaders and considered by all informants to be of national policy-making stature." [3] The notion of interlocking directorates has widespread currency in the power elite literature. Kolko writes that "interlocking directorates, whereby a director of one corporation also sits on the board of one or more other corporations, are a key device for concentrating corporate power. . . ." [4] The hierarchical model also implies that top leaders in all sectors of society—including government, education, civic and cultural affairs, and politics—are recruited primarily from business and finance.

In contrast, "pluralist" writers have implied a polyarchical leadership structure, with different sets of leaders in different sectors of society and little or no overlap, except perhaps by elected officials responsible to the general public. According to this view, leadership is exercised in large measure by "specialists" who limit their participation to a narrow range of societal decisions. These specialists are felt to be recruited through separate channels—they are not drawn exclusively from business and finance. Generally, pluralists have praised the dispersion of authority in American society. Dahl writes: "The theory and practice of American pluralism tends to assume, as I see it, that the existence of multiple centers of power, none of which is wholly sovereign, will help (may indeed be necessary) to tame power, to secure the consent of all, and to settle conflicts peacefully." [5] But despite the theoretical (and ideological) importance of the question of convergence versus specialization in the leadership structure, there have been very little *systematic* research on the concentration of authority or the extent of interlocking among top institutional elites.

### "INTERLOCKERS" AND "SPECIALISTS"

Earlier we identified over *5000* top institutional positions in 12 different sectors of society which we defined as the nation's elite (see Chapter 1). Individuals in these positions control half of the nation's industrial and

[2] C. Wright Mills, *The Power Elite* (New York: Oxford University Press, 1956), p. 9.

[3] Floyd Hunter, *Top Leadership, U.S.A.* (Chapel Hill: University of North Carolina Press, 1959), p. 176.

[4] Gabriel Kolko, *Wealth and Power in America* (New York: Praeger, 1962), p. 57.

[5] Robert A. Dahl, *Pluralist Democracy in the United States* (Chicago: Rand McNally, 1967), p. 24.

financial assets and nearly half of all the assets of private foundations and universities; they control the television networks, the news services, and leading newspapers; they control the most prestigious civic and cultural organizations; and they direct the activities of the executive, legislative, and judicial branches of the national government.

These 5000 top positions were occupied by roughly 4000 individuals. In other words, there were fewer top individuals than top positions—indicating multiple holding of top positions by some individuals. Table 6–1 presents specific data on this phenomenon which we shall call *interlocking*.

Approximately 20 percent of those we identified as the nation's elite held more than one top position at a time. These are our "interlockers." Most of them held only two top positions, but some held six, seven, eight, or more! Eighty percent of the people at the top are "specialists"—individuals who hold only one top position. Many of these specialists hold other corporate directorships, governmental posts, or civic, cultural, or university positions, but not *top* positions as we have defined them. Thus our "specialists" may assume a wide variety of lesser positions: directorships in corporations below the top hundred; positions on governmental boards and commissions; trusteeships of less well-known colleges and foundations; and directorships of less influential civic and cultural organizations. We will also observe that over a lifetime many of our specialists tend to hold a number of top positions, serially, rather than concurrently.

About 40 percent of all top *positions* are interlocked with other top positions. The reason that 40 percent of the top positions are interlocked, but only 20 percent of the top individuals hold more than one position,

**TABLE 6–1    Interlocking and Specialization in Top Institutional Positions**

| | Number Top Institutional Positions | Percent of Total Positions | Number of Individuals in Top Positions | Percent of Total Individuals |
|---|---|---|---|---|
| Total | 5,416 | 100.0 | 4,101 | 100.0 |
| Specialized | 3,284 | 60.6 | 3,297 | 80.4 |
| Interlocked | 2,132 | 39.4 | 804 | 19.6 |
| Number of Interlocks: | | | | |
| Two | 1,026 | 18.9 | 513 | 12.5 |
| Three | 552 | 10.2 | 184 | 4.5 |
| Four | 260 | 4.8 | 65 | 1.6 |
| Five | 105 | 1.9 | 21 | 0.5 |
| Six | 48 | 0.9 | 8 | 0.2 |
| Seven or more | 147 | 2.7 | 13 | 0.3 |

is that some individuals are "multiple interlockers"—they hold three or more positions.

The multiple interlockers turned out to be individuals of considerable stature, as the listing in Table 6–2 indicates.[6] This list was compiled from extensive data collected and analyzed in the early 1970s; but it is unlikely that there has been any change in the character of the multiple interlockers, despite the addition or subtraction of some particular names.

These individuals comprised our top group of "multiple interlockers" in 1970—individuals occupying *six or more* top positions concurrently. By any criteria whatsoever, these individuals must be judged important figures in America. The fact that our investigation of positional overlap revealed the existence of such a coterie lends some face validity to the assertion that interlocking is a source of authority and power in society. However, despite the impressive concentration of interlocking authority in this top group, it should be remembered that most of the remaining 80 percent of top position-holders were "specialists."

**TABLE 6–2    Multiple Interlockers in Top Institutional Positions, 1970**

---

*Lloyd DeWitt Brace.* Former chairman of the board and now a director of First National Boston Corp. Also a director of General Motors, AT&T, and John Hancock Life Insurance Co.

*Ralph Manning Brown, Jr.* Chairman of the board of New York Life Insurance Co. A director of Union Carbide, Morgan Guaranty Trust Co., Union Camp Corp., A & P, and Avon Products. Is also a trustee of the Sloan Foundation, Princeton University, and a director of the Metropolitan Museum of Art.

*Arthur H. Dean.* Senior partner, Sullivan & Cromwell; chairman of the U.S. delegation on Nuclear Test Ban Treaty, chief U.S. negotiator of the Korean Armistice Agreement; a director of American Metal Climax, American Bank Note Co., National Union Electric Corp., El Paso Natural Gas Company, Crown Zellerbach Corp., Campbell Soup Co., Northwest Production Corp., Lazard Fund, Inc., and the Bank of New York; a trustee of New York Hospital, Cornell Medical Center, Cornell Medical College, Cornell University, the Carnegie Foundation, and the Council on Foreign Relations.

*C. Douglas Dillon.* Chairman of the board of Dillon, Reed & Company and member of the New York Stock Exchange. He was formerly Secretary of the Treasury and Undersecretary of State. He is presently a director of the Chase Manhattan Bank, the Rockefeller Foundation, the Metropolitan Museum of Art, the Brookings

---

[6] In addition to these *individuals,* it is important to know that several *family groups* whose members together hold a large number of authoritive positions also have positions of power in institutions. The Rockefeller family accounted for 18 top positions in 1970. The duPonts accounted for 11, the Houghtons for eight, and the Fords and Mellons for seven each. No *systematic* attempt was made to examine these or other family groupings. Interlocking here is treated only as an attribute of individuals. See Ferdinand Lundberg, *America's Sixty Families* (New York: Vanguard Press, 1937) and his *The Rich and The Super-Rich* (New (York: Lyle Stuart, 1968) for an extended discussion of the importance of kinship ties and family groupings.

TABLE 6–2    (cont.)

general in the Reserves, a trustee of the Carnegie Institute of Technology, the Mellon Institute, and the University of Pittsburgh.

*Ellmore C. Patterson.* President, J. P. Morgan & Co. He is a director of Atlantic Richfield Co., Canadian Life Assurance Co., International Nickel, Atcheson, Topeka and Santa Fe Railroad, Warner Patterson Co. He is a trustee of the Alfred P. Sloan Foundation, the Carnegie Endowment for International Peace, and the University of Chicago.

*Richard S. Perkins.* President and chairman of the board of Perkins-Elmer Corp. A director of Ford Motor Co., IT&T, New York Life Insurance Co., Consolidated Edison, Southern Pacific Railroad, Aetna Life Insurance Co., New England Telephone Co., U.S. Trust Co. of New York. A trustee of Metropolitan Museum of Art, American Museum of Natural History, and Pratt Institute.

*David Rockefeller.* Chairman and chief executive officer, Chase Manhattan Bank. He is a director and trustee of the Rockefeller Foundation, Museum of Modern Art, Harvard University, University of Chicago, Council on Foreign Relations. He is also a director of Chase International Investment Corporation, Morningside Heights, Inc., Rockefeller Center, Inc., Downtown Lower Manhattan Association. He is a centimillionaire and a heavy political contributor.

*James Stillman Rockefeller.* Former chairman and current director of First National City Bank of New York (now Citicorp). A director of the International Banking Corp., National City Foundation, First New York Corp., First National City Trust Co., Mercantile Bank of Canada, National City Realty Corp., Kimberly-Clark Corp., Northern Pacific Railway Co., National Cash Register Co., Pan-American World Airways, and Monsanto Co.

*Haakon Ingolf Romnes.* Former chairman and chief executive officer of American Telephone and Telegraph. He is a director of United States Steel, Chemical Bank of New York, Colgate-Palmolive Co., Cities Service Oil Co., and Mutual Life Insurance Co. He is a trustee of M.I.T., the National Safety Council, and the Committee for Economic Development; he is also active in the United Negro College Fund, the Urban League, and the Salvation Army.

*Robert V. Roosa.* Partner, Brown Brothers, Harriman & Co. (investments). Chairman of the Board of the Brookings Institution, and a director of American Express Co., Anaconda Copper Co., and Texaco. He is a trustee of the Rockefeller Foundation, The Rye County Day School, and a member of the Council on Foreign Relations and the National Bureau of Economic Research. He was formerly Under-Secretary of the Treasury. He holds an earned Ph.D. from the University of Michigan.

*Robert Baylor Semple.* President of Wyandotte Chemical Corp. He is a director of Michigan Consolidated Gas Co., American Natural Gas Co., National Bank of Detroit, Atlantic Mutual Insurance Co., Centennial Insurance Co., and the Chrysler Corp. He is also on the board of the Committee on Economic Development, the National Industrial Conference Board, M.I.T., Harper Hospital, and is the president of the Detroit Symphony Orchestra.

*Cyrus R. Vance.* Secretary of state and senior partner of Simpson Thacher & Bartlett. He is a director of Pan-American World Airways, Aetna Life Insurance Co., IBM, Council on Foreign Relations, the American Red Cross, the Rockefeller Foundation, and a trustee of the University of Chicago. He was the chief U.S. negotiator at the Paris Peace Talks on Vietnam under President Lyndon Johnson.

*Albert L. Williams.* Former chairman of the board of directors of Citicorp, and IBM. A director of General Motors Corp., Mobil Oil Corp., General Foods Corp. He is a trustee of the Alfred P. Sloan Foundation.

*Leslie B. Worthington.* Former president, United States Steel Corporation, and a current director. Also a director of Mellon National Bank and Trust Co., TRW, Inc., American Standard, Greyhound Corp., Westinghouse Air Brake Co., and the Pittsburgh Pirates. A trustee of the University of Illinois and the University of Pittsburgh.

Let us turn now to an examination of the pattern of interlocking among the various sectors of society. The vast majority (84.6 percent) of top *governmental* position-holders are "specialists"—individuals who occupy only one top position at a given time (see Table 6–3). Moreover, an examination of the pattern of interlocking reveals that governmental leadership is *not* interlocked with the corporate world. To the extent that governmental leadership is interlocked at all, it is interlocked with the public interest sector. High government officials and military officers ordinarily do not hold top positions in anything other than civic, cultural, or educational institutions. If there is convergence between the corporate and governmental sectors of society, then, it is not by means of "interlocking directorates." Of course, convergence may result from patterns of *interaction* among specialized governmental and corporate elites, but the notion of formal interlocking directorates can be put to rest.

Interlocking *within the corporate sector* is widespread. Approximately 44 percent of all top corporate positions were found to be interlocked with other top positions, most of which were in the corporate sphere. Yet a majority of top corporate elites were "specialists." The notion of interlocking directorates has widespread currency in the power elite literature. But our figures confirm those of the Temporary National Economic Committee, which reported in 1939 that within the top 200 corporations there were 3,511 directorships held by 2,500 persons, an overlap of less than one-third of all positions.[7] Of course, it must be noted that we are examining overlap among the *top* positions in all sectors of society. It is, after all, more likely that individuals with top positions in the leading institutions would also hold positions in smaller, less influential organizations. But the figures shown in Table 6–3 deal only with the concurrent occupancy of multiple positions in top-ranked institutions.

Leadership in the *public interest* sector is only moderately interlocked. Nearly two-thirds of top elites in law, education, the foundations, the mass media, and civic and cultural affairs were "specialists." (Again, these "specialists" may hold other positions in the corporate or governmental sectors, but not *top* positions, according to the definition set forth earlier.) Interlocking in the public interest sector was more common in the foundations, education, and civic and cultural associations than in law. Interlocking in this sector was primarily with the corporate sector; few top public interest positions are interlocked with governmental positions.

[7] Temporary National Economic Committee, U.S. Senate, 76th Congress, *Investigation of Concentration of Economic Power* (Washington, D.C.: Government Printing Office, 1941).

TABLE 6-3  Specialization and Interlocking among Corporate, Governmental, and Public Interest Elites

| | Corporate | Public Interest | | | | Media | Governmental | |
|---|---|---|---|---|---|---|---|---|
| | All | Law | Found. | Educ. | Civic | | Domestic | Military |
| Number of positions | 3,562 | 176 | 121 | 656 | 392 | 213 | 227 | 59 |
| Positions "interlocked" | | | | | | | | |
|   Number | 1,560 | 26 | 64 | 216 | 168 | | 44 | 0 |
|   Percent | 43.8 | 14.8 | 52.9 | 32.9 | 42.9 | | 80.6 | 0 |
| Positions "specialized" | | | | | | | | |
|   Number | 2,002 | 150 | 57 | 440 | 224 | | 183 | 59 |
|   Percent | 56.2 | 84.2 | 47.1 | 67.1 | 57.1 | | 19.4 | 100.0 |
| Pattern of interlocking: | | | | | | | | |
| Percent of interlocking with | | | | | | | | |
|   Corporate positions | 72.7 | | | 58.8 | | | 6.6 | |
|   Public interest positions | 25.9 | | | 60.4 | | | 91.2 | |
|   Governmental positions | 0.2 | | | 4.7 | | | 2.2 | |
| | 100.0 | | | 100.0 | | | 100.0 | |

Let us pursue the notion of "vertical" overlap a bit further. How many positions of authority in all types of institutions have top leaders *ever held* in a lifetime? We carefully reviewed the biographies of our top position-holders to see how many authoritative positions—president, director, trustee, and so on—were ever held by these men. The record of leadership of an average top official turned out to be truly impressive. The average corporate elite held 11.1 authoritative positions in his lifetime; the average public interest elite, 10.7; and the average governmental elite, 7.0 (see Table 6–4).

These are not merely previous posts, offices, or occupations, but top positions as presidents or directors of corporations, banks, or insurance companies; trustees or directors of colleges, universities, foundations, museums, civic and cultural organizations; partnerships in law firms or investment firms; and so forth. Of course, these positions are not all in *top-ranked* institutions. But it is clear that top leaders occupy a number of authoritative positions in their lifetime.

This impressive record of position holding is found among leaders in all sectors of society. Table 6–4 shows the average number of authoritative positions ever held by top leaders in each sector of society. Leaders in government have held somewhat fewer top positions in their lifetime than leaders in the corporate world, but nonetheless their record of leadership experience is impressive. However, governmental leaders tended to gain their experience in *governmental* or *public interest* positions—over 80 percent of governmental leaders had held previous governmental posts and over half had held posts in the public interest sector. Only about one-quarter of top governmental elites had previously held any top positions in the corporate world.

The tradition of public service is very much alive among top institutional leaders in every sector. Both corporate and governmental elites reported one or more public appointments during their lifetime. Nearly 40 percent of corporate elites held at least one government post at some time during their careers.

As we might expect, corporate directorships are common among top leaders in industry, communications, utilities, and banking. It is common for these individuals to have held four or more directorships in a lifetime. In contrast, top government officials have *not* held many corporate directorships. Their experience in authoritative positions is derived mainly from public service, and to a lesser extent from education, law, and civic organizations.

**TABLE 6–4** Previous Experience of Corporate, Governmental, and Public Interest Elites

| | Corporate | Public Interest | | | | | Governmental | |
|---|---|---|---|---|---|---|---|---|
| | All | Law | Found. | Educ. | Civic | Media | Domestic | Military |
| Average number of authoritative positions ever held by elites: | | | | | | | | |
| Total | 11.1 | 9.0 | 11.1 | 10.9 | 11.7 | 9.1 | 7.0 | 0.9 |
| Corporate | 6.2 | 2.4 | 5.2 | 3.6 | 4.4 | 2.0 | 1.0 | 0.3 |
| Public interest | 3.9 | 5.3 | 4.2 | 5.6 | 4.7 | 5.1 | 2.9 | 0.4 |
| Governmental | 1.0 | 1.3 | 1.7 | 1.7 | 2.6 | 2.0 | 3.1 | 0.2 |
| Percent of elites having held authoritative positions in: | | | | | | | | |
| Corporate | 99.9 | | | 87.5 | | | 26.7 | |
| Public interest | 82.5 | | | 92.0 | | | 62.0 | |
| Governmental | 39.6 | | | 48.5 | | | 83.5 | |

Our aggregate data indicate that a majority of the people at the top are specialists, that corporate and governmental elites are not interlocked, and that there appear to be multiple, differentiated structures of power in America. Earlier we suggested that many corporate, governmental, and public interest leaders were self-made managerial elites rather than "inheritors" who started at the top. All of these findings tend to undermine confidence in the hierarchical model, at least as it is represented in the traditional power elite literature.

Nonetheless, there are important concentrations of combined corporate, governmental, and social power in America. And these concentrations center about great, wealthy, entrepreneurial families—the Rockefellers, Mellons, duPonts, Fords, and the J. P. Morgan group. Doubtlessly the most important of these concentrations is the "Rockefeller Empire." Certainly no better illustration of convergence of power can be found than the Rockefeller network of industrial, financial, political, civic, and cultural institutions, headed by David Rockefeller of the Chase Manhattan Bank.

The Rockefeller family fortune was founded by John D. Rockefeller, originator of the Standard Oil Company. With his partners, H. M. Flagler and S. V. Harkness, Rockefeller created the company that controlled 90 percent of the nation's oil production by the 1880s. A series of antitrust cases, culminating in the Supreme Court in *U.S.* v. *Standard Oil* (1911), resulted in the forced dissolution of the company into several separate corporations: Exxon, formerly Standard Oil of New Jersey (the nation's number-one-ranked industrial corporation in 1976), Standard Oil of California (ranked number 7), Standard Oil of Indiana (ranked number 10), Standard Oil of Ohio (ranked number 20), Atlantic Richfield (ranked number 13), Mobil Oil (ranked number 3), and the Marathon Oil Company (ranked number 47).[8] The best available evidence suggests that the Rockefeller family continues to hold large blocks of stock in each of these companies.[9] But the key to Rockefeller power today is no longer the oil industry, however impressive the holdings in this industry may be. The center of Rockefeller power is banking and finance.

The core financial institutions of the Rockefeller Empire consist of four large banks and three insurance companies. Three of the four banks are in New York—Citicorp (the nation's number-two-ranked bank

---

[8] See Table 2–1 for rankings.

[9] House of Representatives, Banking and Currency Committee, *Tax-Exempt Foundations* (Washington, D.C.: Government Printing Office, 1968).

in 1976), Chase Manhattan (number three), and the Chemical Bank of New York (number six); the out-of-town bank is the First Chicago Corp. (number nine). The three insurance companies are Metropolitan (the nation's number-two-ranked insurance company in 1976), Equitable (ranked number three), and New York Life (number four). These institutions *alone* control 12 percent of all banking assets in the nation, and 26 percent of all insurance assets. These Rockefeller financial institutions are tied together in a close pattern of interlocking directorates, a pattern that is revealed in Figure 6–1, where each solid line represents multiple position-holding by family members.

The Rockefeller banks influence corporate decision making in several ways—by giving or withholding loans to corporations, by placing representatives on corporate boards of directors, and by owning or controlling blocks of common stock of corporations. The Federal Reserve Board estimates that 90 percent of the lending of large banks is made to large corporations. These corporations are dependent upon bank loans for capital expansion. Often the banks dictate specific aspects of corporate policy as a condition of granting a loan (in the same fashion that federal agencies often dictate policies of state and local governments as a condition of receiving federal grants-in-aid). Frequently, banks will also require corporations that borrow money to appoint bank officers or directors to the boards of the corporation. This gives the bank continuous oversight of the activities of the debtor corporation. Finally, the trust departments of major banks hold large blocks of common stock of industrial corporations on behalf of individuals, pension funds, and investment companies. Generally the banks vote the shares held in trust in corporate elections. The rules of the Securities and Exchange Commission presume that the ownership of 5 percent of a corporation's stock can give the holder a position of influence over its affairs.

Interlocking among the five core Rockefeller group institutions and large industrial corporations is extensive. Table 6–5 reveals interlocking of Chase Manhattan directors only; the list of interlocking corporations for all five institutions would have over 150 names. Consolidated Edison and Anaconda are generally regarded as Rockefeller-influenced, as well as Eastern Airlines, TWA, Pan-American World Airlines, and Boeing. (The airlines, including Howard Hughes' TWA, fell into Rockefeller hands when they required large loans to purchase jet aircraft in the late 1950s).

The Rockefeller interest in foreign affairs is particularly strong. The oil companies, which have long been the industrial core of Rockefeller holdings, require constant attention to foreign sources of supply. In addition, Rockefeller banks are deeply involved in overseas banking and investment activities. Chase Manhattan has over 40 branches scattered throughout the world, and Citicorp boasts offices in 60 countries.

A. Individual Interlocks
1. Black, Eugene (CM) (E)
2. Eaton, Frederick (C) (NYL)
3. Fitzhugh, Gilbert (CM) (M)
4. Funston, G. Keith (CB) (M)
5. Heineman, Ben (FCC) (M)
6. Helm, Harold (CB) (E)
7. Houghton, Amory (C) (M)
8. Jenkins, George P. (C) (M)
9. Kappel, Frederick (CB) (M)
10. Keehn, Grant (CB) (E)
11. Long, Augustus (CB) (E)
12. Metcalf, Gordon (C) (FCC)
13. Miller, J. Irwin (CB) (E)
14. Oates, James (E) (FCC)
15. Oates, James (E) (CM)
16. Oates, James (CM) (FCC)
17. Paynter, Richard K. (CB) (NYL)
18. Perkins, Richard S. (C) (NYL)
19. Renchard, William (CB) (NYL)
20. Saunders, Stuart (CM) (E)
21. Seiler, Lewis (CB) (E)
22. Sivage, Gerald (FCC) (M)
23. Swearingen, John (CM) (FCC)

B. Family Interlocks
24. David Rockefeller (CM) – James
    Stillman Rockefeller (C)
25. Hulbert S. Aldrich (CB) –
    Malcolm Aldrich (E)
26. Amory Houghton (C) – Arthur
    K. Houghton, Jr. (NYL)
27. Amory Houghton, Jr. (C) –
    Arthur K. Houghton, Jr. (NYL)
28. Amory Houghton (M) – Arthur K.
    Houghton, Jr. (NYL)

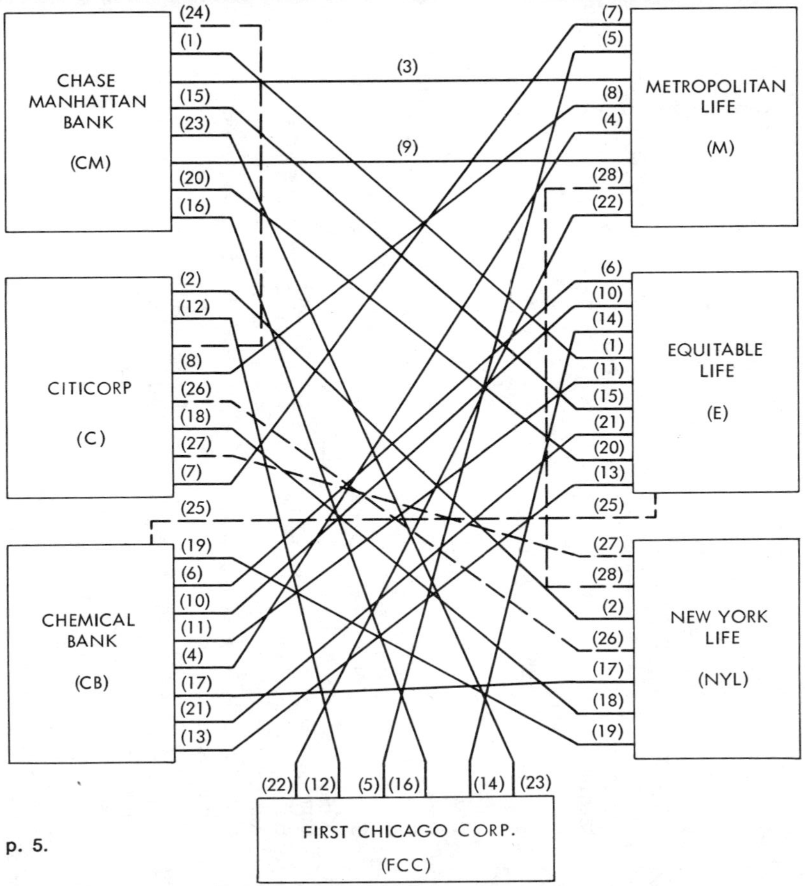

Source: James C. Knowles,
"The Rockefeller Financial Group"
(Warner Modular Publications, Module 343, 1973), p. 5.

FIGURE 6-1    Interlocking Directorates Among the Core Financial Institutions in the Rockefeller Group. (Numbers in parentheses link each director interlock to a particular individual.

155

**TABLE 6-5    Chase Manhattan's Influence in Industrial Corporations**

| Interlocking Directors with Chase Manhattan | Common Stock Ownership of over 5%* |
|---|---|
| Allegheny Ludlum Steel | Eastern Airlines |
| Youngstown Sheet & Tube | Pan-American World Airlines |
| United States Steel | Western Airlines |
| Metropolitan Life | Safeway Stores |
| Equitable Life | Reynolds Metal |
| Travelers Insurance | J. C. Penney |
| American Machine | Northwest Airlines |
| Bucyrus-Erie | TWA |
| Otis Elevator | Ryder System |
| General Foods | Universal Oil |
| Chrysler Corporation | North Carolina Natural Gas |
| Standard Oil of Indiana | Armstrong Rubber |
| Standard Oil of New Jersey (Exxon) | Texas Instruments |
| New York Tire Co. | Beckman Instruments |
| Cummins Engine | Sperry Rand |
| Burlington Industries | Boeing |
| American Broadcasting Co. | Columbia Broadcasting System |
| R. J. Reynolds Tobacco | American Broadcasting System |
| Scott Paper | Aetna Life |
| International Paper | National Steel |
| United Aircraft | Addressograph |
| Singer Co. | Mobil Oil |
| ITT | |
| Goodyear Tire & Rubber | |
| Great Southwest Corp. | |
| Anaconda Copper | |
| American Smelting & Refining | |
| F. W. Woolworth | |
| Allied Stores | |
| Federated Department Stores | |
| R. H. Macy | |
| Penn Central | |
| Piedmont Aviation | |
| Wabash Railroad | |
| Celanese Corp. | |
| Colgate-Palmolive | |
| General Aniline & Film | |
| Consolidated Edison | |
| AT&T | |

* Data on stock ownership from Report of House Banking Committee, Chairman Representative Wright Patman, reported in *New York Times*, August 9, 1968.

The Rockefeller group has supplied the top foreign affairs personnel for the nation, including Secretaries of State John Foster Dulles, Dean Rusk, and Henry Kissinger. Dulles, Secretary of State under President Eisenhower, was a senior partner in the Wall Street law firm of Sullivan & Cromwell, whose principal client for many years was Standard Oil Company (Exxon). Dulles was also chairman of the trustees of the Rockefeller Foundation. Dean Rusk, secretary of state under Presidents Kennedy and Johnson, served seven years as president of the Rockefeller Foundation. Henry Kissinger was director of the Rockefeller Brothers Special Studies Project and personal adviser on foreign policy to Nelson Rockefeller before becoming special assistant for national security affairs and later Secretary of State under President Richard Nixon. Zbigniew Brzezinski, President Carter's National Security Advisor, was director of the Trilateral Commission—David Rockefeller's influential group of top leaders from industrialized nations of the world.

Other Rockefeller group associates have played key roles in the nation's foreign involvements. John J. McCloy, a Chase Manhattan director, served as U.S. High Commissioner for Germany during the postwar occupation; he later became special adviser to the president on disarmament (1961–63) and chairman of the Coordinating Committee on the Cuban Crisis in 1962. Cyrus Vance, a director of the Rockefeller Foundation as well as Pan-American World Airlines, Aetna Life Insurance, and IBM, was the chief U.S. negotiator at the Paris peace talks on Vietnam. Arthur Dean, another senior partner in the firm of Sullivan & Cromwell, was chairman of the U.S. delegation on the Nuclear Test Ban Treaty and chief U.S. negotiator of the Korean Armistice Agreement. Thus, Rockefeller representatives played a key role in such major national and world events as the Vietnam and Korean peace agreements and the Cuban situation. It was David Rockefeller himself who provided the major stimulus to the re-opening of U.S. relations with Communist China and the spectacular Nixon visit to China in 1972. Shortly after the president's visit, Chase Manhattan announced the opening of its own offices in Peking. Today David Rockefeller himself serves as chairman of the influential Council on Foreign Relations, which is responsible for many of the nation's most important foreign policy initiatives. (See Chapter 9 on "The Policy Planning Establishment.")

## DAVID ROCKEFELLER:
## THE VIEW FROM CHASE MANHATTAN

The single most powerful private citizen in America today is David Rockefeller, chairman of the board of Chase Manhattan Bank and director of the vast Rockefeller empire. The extent of that empire—from banking and insurance to oil, airlines, computers, steel, machinery, and utilities—and the extension of Rockefeller influence to government, international relations, education, law, foundations, and civic, cultural, and charitable affairs has already been described. Our interest for the moment is in the man who stands at the apex of financial and political power in America—"the only man for whom the presidency of the United States would be a step down."

David Rockefeller is the youngest of five sons of John D. Rockefeller, Jr., himself the only son of the founder of the Rockefeller empire, John D. Rockefeller. Despite the seniority of his brothers,[10] it was recognized that David was the serious and scholarly one. And it was to David that the family wisely entrusted most of its wealth; this is the really convincing evidence of his recognized leadership.

David was raised with his brothers at the Rockefeller's 3500-acre Pocantico Hills estate, east of Tarrytown, New York. He attended nearby Lincoln School. His early interest in art continues today. As a child, he traveled about to Rockefeller holdings—the Seal Harbor, Maine retreat, the Virgin Islands estate, the Venezuela ranch, the Grand Teton Mountains ranch—and collected beetles as a hobby. It soon became clear to David's father and grandfather that Nelson, Lawrence, and Winthrop were more interested in politics and pleasure than hard work, and that John D. III was content to pursue cultural interests. The elder Rockefellers wanted a businessman to care for the family fortune, and they were successful in motivating David in this direction.

David's undergraduate career at Harvard was undistinguished. But later he spent a year at the Harvard Graduate School of Business and a year at the London School of Economics. He married Margaret "Peggy" McGrath, whose father was a senior partner in the esteemed Wall Street law firm of Cadwalader, Wickersham & Taft. He enrolled at the Rockefeller-funded University of Chicago and *earned* a Ph.D. in economics in 1940. He returned to New York for a short stint in public service as an unpaid assistant to Mayor Fiorello La Guardia. In 1942 he enlisted in the Army as a private, went through Officers Training School, and served in North Africa and Europe as an intelligence officer. He speaks French, Spanish, and German.

After the war he began his banking career in his uncle Winthrop W. Aldrich's bank, the Chase Manhattan. His first post was assistant manager of the foreign department; three years later he became vice-

---

[10] John D. III, chairman of the Rockefeller Foundation and the Lincoln Center for the Performing Arts; Nelson A., former vice-president of the United States and four-term governor of New York; Lawrence, family dilettante in "venture capitalism"; and Winthrop, former governor of Arkansas and cattle rancher (now deceased).

president and director of the bank's business in Latin America. When his uncle became ambassador to England in 1952, David became successively executive vice-president, vice-chairman of the board, and finally, president and chairman of the board.

Of course, David Rockefeller is active in civic and cultural affairs. He is, or has been, chairman of the Museum of Modern Art, president of the Board of Overseas Study of Harvard University, a director of the Council on Foreign Relations, a trustee of the Carnegie Endowment for International Peace, a trustee of the University of Chicago, a trustee of the John F. Kennedy Library, and so forth.

Above all, Rockefeller is an internationalist. His active intervention in American foreign policy has produced remarkable results. As has been mentioned, he was personally involved in Nixon's arrangement of détente with the USSR, the Strategic Arms Limitations Talks (SALT), and Nixon's spectacular trip to China. He is chairman of the board of the Council on Foreign Relations, and he formed the Trilateral Commission in 1972.

Under David Rockefeller's direction, Chase Manhattan has developed a reputation in the business world for "social responsibility"—which included the active recruitment and promotion of blacks, women, and other minorities; granting a large number of loans to minority-owned business enterprises; and active involvement in a variety of social projects. Indeed, this may be one reason that Chase Manhattan has fallen behind Citicorp as the leading banking institution in New York. (Not only does Citicorp lead in assets but also in return on investment: in recent years Chase has shown 12.5 percent profit, compared to 15.1 percent for Citicorp.) Another reason for Chase's performance may be that David Rockefeller is so deeply involved in national and international affairs that he cannot devote full attention to banking matters.

Rockefeller himself believes that his own power, and the power of business and financial institutions is limited by public opinion.

> I don't believe a bank such as ours, for example, could long fly in the face of welfare consideration—welfare in the broader sense—without having major problems with Congress and with all kinds of groups in our society who would resent us and would do their best to take steps to force us to act differently.[11]

But Rockefeller's liberal concern for "doing good" is constrained by his institutional responsibilities in a capitalist system, and he recognizes this fact:

[11] "The Dilemma of Corporate Responsibility and Maximum Profits: An Interview with David Rockefeller," *Business and Society Review* (Spring 1974), p. 10.

I don't think one has to go to extremes. We don't feel that we can do everything for the community that we'd like to, nor do we feel it's wise to go all out 100 percent for the highest profits disregarding the best interests of the community. We have to find some kind of middle ground. We're very much bottom-line conscience,[12] but we also feel we have responsibilities to the community.[13]

David Rockefeller exercises great power, with *modesty*, of course, as one would expect of a man who has no reason to try to impress anyone. Indeed, he consistently understates his own power:

I feel uncomfortable when you ask how I exert power. We accomplish things through cooperative action, which is quite different than exerting power in some mysterious and presumably evil way. I have no power in the sense that I can call anybody in the government and tell them what to do. Because of my position, I'm more apt to get through on the telephone than somebody else, but what happens to what I suggest depends on whether they feel this makes sense in terms of what they are already doing.[14]

David Rockefeller's own views on power tend to reinforce the importance of achieving consensus among separate groups of leaders. In commenting on the redevelopment of downtown New York City—Rockefeller Plaza and the World Trade Center—Rockefeller characteristically sees himself as a *catalyst* rather than as a *chieftain*:

If you are interested in the analysis of power [says Rockefeller], I would think this is somewhat relevant: I'm not sure it is the power of an individual or even an institution, but more the power of cooperation and ideas. . . .

. . . We got the community and government working together in the development of a plan that was of common interest to all parties involved. This isn't so much power; it is organization, coordination, cooperation. The reason we could do this is this group exists. The city couldn't have pulled this thing off by itself. Certainly neither could we. But working together, we could.

I didn't do this thing myself; this is a joint undertaking where I have been to some extent the catalyst in the sense of bringing others together, and I certainly served as chairman of the committee, but the strength of it is the unity and sense of cooperation.[15]

[12] A businessman's phrase meaning concern with whether the last line on a quarterly or annual financial account shows a profit or loss. [Footnote added.]
[13] "The Dilemma of Corporate Responsibility," p. 11.
[14] "Beyond Wealth, What?" *Forbes* (May 15, 1972), pp. 250–252.
[15] *Ibid.*, pp. 251–252.

Of course, what Rockefeller is really saying is that when David Rockefeller is calling, people answer their phone; when he asks them to serve on a committee, they are flattered to be asked; when he suggests that they do something, they do it.

## EVIDENCE OF POLYARCHY:
## INTERLOCKING CORPORATE GROUPS

The "Rockefeller Empire" is suggestive of concentration of industrial, financial, governmental, and social power. Yet there is also considerable evidence of "polyarchy"—multiple, differentiated groupings of corporate power. This evidence can be gleaned from close observation of the network of interlocking directorates in corporate America. Recent advances in the application of statistical methods allow us to observe some interesting groupings of corporate interlocks.[16] These groupings suggest the existence of a series of corporate groupings—industries, banks, utilities, and insurance companies—centered around distinct *geographic* areas.

Ten major interlocking groupings are identified in Table 6–6. These groupings, systematically described by sociologist Michael Patrick Allen,[17] indicate the most heavily interlocked groupings, the location of each corporation, the total number of interlocks each corporation maintains with other corporations, and the number of interlocks it maintains with corporations within its own grouping.

There is an obvious tendency for corporations to maintain interlocks with other corporations in the same geographic area, even though many New York based corporations occur across the board. Five interlocking groups involve corporations based primarily in Chicago, Pittsburgh, Los Angeles, Philadelphia, and Detroit. Four others are based primarily in New York. This finding, generally supportive of the polyarchial model of corporate power, suggests that geography rather than financial or family interests plays a major role in creating concentrations of corporate power.

However, another way of identifying the interlocking corporate

---

16 A variation of factor analysis applied to sociometric data permits the extraction of matrix of relationships based on interlocking among corporations. The matrix systematically identifies relatively independent and cohesive cliques. See Duncan MacRae, Jr., "Direct Factor Analysis of Sociometric Data," *Sociometry*, 23 (1960), 360–371; also Philip M. Lankforth, "Comparative Analysis of Clique Identification Methods," *Sociometry*, 37 (1974), 287–305.

17 Michael Patrick Allen, "Economic Interest Groups and the Corporate Elite Structure," *Social Science Quarterly* (forthcoming).

**TABLE 6–6    Ten Principal Interlock Groups in 1970**

| GN | Corporation | IC | Location | PCS | TI | GI |
|----|-------------|----|----------|-----|----|----|
| 1 | Chemical New York | B | New York | 5.3 | 47 | 12 |
|   | New York Life | L | New York | 5.0 | 32 | 8 |
|   | Consolidated Edison | U | New York | 5.0 | 22 | 11 |
|   | Southern Pacific | T | San Fran | 2.8 | 24 | 4 |
|   | Equitable Life Assurance | L | New York | 2.7 | 41 | 6 |
|   | Borden | I | New York | 2.5 | 12 | 5 |
| 2 | Continental Illinois | B | Chicago | 5.2 | 29 | 15 |
|   | International Harvester | I | Chicago | 4.8 | 22 | 11 |
|   | Commonwealth Edison | U | Chicago | 4.0 | 12 | 10 |
|   | First Chicago Corp. | B | Chicago | 3.5 | 25 | 11 |
|   | Sears Roebuck | R | Chicago | 2.8 | 18 | 5 |
|   | Standard Oil (Indiana) | I | Chicago | 2.6 | 11 | 6 |
|   | Inland Steel | I | Chicago | 2.6 | 10 | 6 |
|   | Illinois Central, Inc. | I | Chicago | 2.6 | 18 | 5 |
|   | Borg-Warner | I | Chicago | 2.1 | 10 | 5 |
| 3 | Mellon National Bank | B | Pittsburgh | 5.6 | 30 | 14 |
|   | Gulf Oil | I | Pittsburgh | 5.4 | 11 | 10 |
|   | Aluminum Co. of America | I | Pittsburgh | 4.3 | 10 | 6 |
|   | Pittsburgh Plate Glass, Inc. | I | Pittsburgh | 3.4 | 7 | 6 |
|   | Westinghouse Electric | I | Pittsburgh | 2.5 | 19 | 4 |
| 4 | Morgan Guaranty Bank | B | New York | 5.1 | 38 | 11 |
|   | General Electric | I | New York | 3.2 | 26 | 7 |
|   | General Motors | I | Detroit | 2.8 | 27 | 5 |
|   | Continental Oil | I | New York | 2.5 | 20 | 4 |
|   | Scott Paper | I | Philadelphia | 2.5 | 12 | 4 |
|   | U.S. Steel | I | New York | 2.0 | 27 | 3 |
|   | Procter & Gamble | I | Cincinnati | 2.0 | 18 | 4 |
| 5 | Citicorp | B | New York | 4.6 | 51 | 11 |
|   | Monsanto | I | St. Louis | 2.6 | 13 | 6 |
|   | National Cash Register | I | Cleveland | 2.6 | 17 | 5 |
|   | Westinghouse Electric | I | Pittsburgh | 2.4 | 19 | 3 |
|   | Kimberly-Clark | I | Milwaukee | 2.2 | 7 | 5 |
|   | Pan-American World Airways | T | New York | 2.1 | 22 | 4 |
|   | AT&T | U | New York | 2.0 | 33 | 2 |
| 6 | Republic Steel | I | Cleveland | 5.2 | 21 | 13 |
|   | Avco | I | Greenwich | 4.1 | 13 | 10 |
|   | Metropolitan Life | L | New York | 2.8 | 39 | 7 |
|   | Standard Oil (Ohio) | I | Cleveland | 2.7 | 9 | 4 |
|   | Chemical New York | B | New York | 2.6 | 47 | 7 |
|   | International Business Machines | I | Armonk | 2.2 | 25 | 7 |
|   | Illinois Central, Inc. | I | Chicago | 2.1 | 18 | 6 |
|   | Olin | I | Stamford | 2.0 | 9 | 6 |
| 7 | Chase Manhattan | B | New York | 4.8 | 37 | 9 |
|   | General Foods | I | New York | 2.8 | 20 | 5 |
|   | Metropolitan Life | L | New York | 2.6 | 39 | 5 |
|   | International Paper | I | New York | 2.1 | 15 | 5 |
|   | AT&T | U | New York | 2.0 | 33 | 4 |
| 8 | Western Bancorporation | B | Los Angeles | 4.1 | 19 | 6 |
|   | Southern California Edison | U | Los Angeles | 3.4 | 11 | 9 |

**TABLE 6–6    (cont.)**

| GN | Corporation | IC | Location | PCS | TI | GI |
|----|-------------|----|----------|-----|----|----|
|    | Union Oil of California | I | Los Angeles | 3.2 | 18 | 6 |
|    | BankAmerica | B | San Francisco | 2.8 | 17 | 5 |
|    | North American Rockwell | I | Los Angeles | 2.7 | 13 | 6 |
|    | Security Pacific National Bank | B | Los Angeles | 2.5 | 13 | 5 |
|    | Getty Oil | I | Los Angeles | 2.0 | 14 | 5 |
| 9  | Pennsylvania Mutual | L | Philadelphia | 5.1 | 21 | 12 |
|    | First Pennsylvania | B | Philadelphia | 4.1 | 11 | 7 |
|    | Girard | B | Philadelphia | 3.2 | 8 | 6 |
|    | Philadelphia Electric | U | Philadelphia | 3.2 | 10 | 8 |
|    | Philadelphia National Bank | B | Philadelphia | 2.6 | 7 | 5 |
|    | Atlantic Richfield | I | New York | 2.4 | 15 | 4 |
| 10 | National Bank of Detroit | B | Detroit | 4.7 | 21 | 10 |
|    | Burroughs | I | Detroit | 2.8 | 8 | 6 |
|    | Detroit Edison | U | Detroit | 2.8 | 10 | 4 |
|    | National Steel | I | Detroit | 2.5 | 10 | 4 |
|    | Bendix | I | Detroit | 2.2 | 7 | 4 |
|    | S. S. Kresge | R | Detroit | 2.2 | 7 | 4 |

| Legend | GN | = Group Number | U | = Utility |
|--------|-----|----|-----|-----|
| | IC | = Industry Code | T | = Transportation |
| | PCS | = Principal Component Score | R | = Retailing |
| | TI | = Total Interlocks | B | = Banking |
| | GI | = Group Interlocks | L | = Life Insurance |
| | I | = Industrial | | |

Source: Michael Patrick Allen, "Economic Interest Groups and the Corporate Elite Structure," *Social Science Quarterly.*

groups in Table 6–6 would be by the major banks which provide the largest number of interlocking directors within each group. The banks which appear to lead corporate groupings include Citicorp, Chase Manhattan, Mellon, Morgan Guaranty, Chemical New York, Continental Illinois, Western Bancorp, and the National Bank of Detroit. This finding lends support to the notion that banks are acquiring increasing control of corporate America.

Thus, the systematic analysis of corporate interlocking suggests (1) multiple concentrations of financial and industrial power, (2) based in part upon geographic proximity, and (3) dominated by large commercial banks.

### SUMMARY

The question of hierarchy versus polyarchy in America's elite structure is a familiar one in the literature on power. The "elitist" literature describes a convergence of power at the top, with a single group of leaders, recruited primarily from industry and finance, exercising power in many different sectors of society. The "pluralist" literature describes many separate structures of power in different sectors of society with little or no overlap in authority and many separate channels of recruitment.

Our findings cannot be subsumed by either the elitist or the pluralist leadership model. The fact that roughly 4000 persons in 5000 positions exercise formal authority over institutions that control roughly half of the nation's resources is itself an indication of a great concentration of power. But despite institutional concentration of authority, there is considerable specialization among these 4000 leaders. Eighty percent of them have held only one "top" position. Only 20 percent are "interlockers"—holders of two or more top positions. However, because of "multiple interlockers," about 40 percent of all top positions were found interlocked with another top position. Moreover, the top multiple interlockers (those people with seven or more top positions) turned out to be impressive figures in America, lending some support to the notion that interlocking itself is a source of power in society.

There is very little overlap among people at the top of the corporate, governmental, and military sectors of society. To the extent that high government officials are interlocked at all, it is with civic and cultural and educational institutions. It is *within* the corporate sector that interlocking is most prevalent. If there is a "coming together" of corporate, governmental, and military elites as C. Wright Mills contends, it does not appear to be by means of interlocking directorates.

The notion of hierarchy is strengthened, however, if we examine the record of leadership experience of top institutional elites *over a lifetime*. Most top leaders have held more than one top position in their career. Governmental leaders, however, have generally gained their leadership experience in governmental positions or in the law; only one-quarter of top governmental leaders have ever held high positions in the corporate world.

These aggregate figures suggest specialization rather than convergence at the top of the nation's institutional structure. However, we agree that there are special cases of concentrated corporate, governmental, and social power. These concentrations center about the great entrepreneurial families—Rockefellers, Mellons, duPonts, Fords. We believe the most important concentration of power in America today centers in the Rockefeller family group. Nonetheless, there is also evidence of polyarchy in identifiable groupings of corporations with extensive interlocking directorates. These groupings each appear to be headed by banks.

# elite recruitment:
# getting to the top

▶▶▶▶▶▶▶▶▶▶▶▶▶▶▶▶▶▶▶▶▶▶▶▶▶▶▶▶▶▶▶▶▶▶▶▶▶▶▶▶▶▶▶▶▶▶▶▶▶▶▶▶▶▶▶▶▶▶

# 7

## A RULING CLASS OR AN OPEN LEADERSHIP SYSTEM?

Are there opportunities to rise to the top of the institutional structure of America for individuals from all classes, races, religions, and ethnic groups, through multiple career paths in different sectors of society? Or are opportunities for entry into top circles limited to white, Anglo-Saxon Protestant, upper- and upper-middle-class individuals whose careers are based primarily in industry and finance?

Social scientists have studied data on the social backgrounds of corporate and governmental leaders for many years. But there is still disagreement on the interpretation of the data. A "ruling class" school of thought stresses the fact that elites in America are drawn disproportionately from among wealthy, educated, "well-employed," socially prominent, "WASP" groups in society. These "ruling class" social scientists are impressed with the fact that leadership in industry, finance, government, education, the law, the mass media, and other institutional sectors is recruited primarily from society's upper social classes. Many of the elite have been educated at a few esteemed private prep schools and gone to Ivy League colleges and universities. They have joined the same private clubs, and their families have intermarried. Moreover, a disproportionate share of the top leadership in all sectors of society has made its career mark in industry and finance. "Ruling class" social scientists infer that these similarities contribute to cohesion and consensus among the institutional leaders in America.

By contrast, "pluralists" describe an open leadership system that enables a significant number of individuals from the middle and lower classes to rise to the top. High social background, or wealth, or WASP-ishness *itself* does not provide access to top leadership positions. Instead, top institutional posts go to individuals who possess outstanding skills of leadership, information, and knowledge, and the ability to communicate and organize. Admittedly, opportunities to acquire such qualities for top leadership are unequally distributed among classes. But lower-class origin, the "pluralists" believe, is not an insurmountable barrier to high position.

Classical elitist writers such as Mosca acknowledge that some "circulation of elites" is essential for the stability of a political system. The very opportunity for the brightest among the lower classes to rise to the top siphons off potentially revolutionary leadership, and the elite system is actually strengthened when talented and ambitious individuals enter top positions. The fact that only a minority of top leaders are drawn from the lower classes is not really important. It is the availability of a modicum of opportunity that encourages talented people to believe they can rise to the top and strengthens support for the system throughout all social classes.

Defenders of the pluralist theory also argue that social background, educational experience, and social group membership are poor predictors of decision-making behavior. Members of the social elite often hold very different views about policy questions, differences that can be attributed to a variety of factors, all of which are more influential than social background. Among these are the nature of the top position occupied; the individual's perception of his own role; the institutional constraints placed upon him; systems of public accountability; interest-group pressures; public opinion; and so forth. Thus, pluralists argue that the class homogeneity among top leaders that is reported in many socal background studies is meaningless, since the class background–decision-making behavior linkage is weak.

In contrast, the evidence of social class influence on behavior is truly impressive.[1] Social scientists have shown that social background affects whether or not you shoplift[2] or use LSD.[3] It has an important influence on whom you date and marry,[4] how happy your marriage is likely to be,[5]

---

[1] The following evidence was compiled from the numerous sources cited by psychologist Richard L. Zweigenhart, "Who Represents America?" *The Insurgent Socialist*, 5 (No. 3), 119.

[2] George Won and George Yamamoto, "Social Structure and Deviant Behavior: A Study of Shoplifting," *Sociology and Social Research*, 53, No. 1 (1968), 44–55.

[3] Reginald G. Smart and Dianne Fejer, "Illicit LSD Users: Their Social Backgrounds, Drug Use and Psychopathology," *Journal of Health and Social Behavior*, 10, No. 4 (1969), 297–308.

[4] A. B. Hollingshead, *Elmtown's Youth: The Impact of Social Classes on Adolescents* (New York: John Wiley & Sons, Inc., 1949).

[5] William J. Goode, "Marital Satisfaction and Instability: A Cross-Cultural Class Analysis of Divorce Rates," *International Social Science Journal*, 14, No. 3 (1962), 507–526.

how you vote,[6] how many children you have,[7] and how you go about raising them.[8] It largely determines your values,[9] how happy you are,[10] and how long you're likely to live.[11] It can even influence how large you think the circumference of a quarter is! [12] In our opinion, it would be most unlikely that social class membership could affect all these varied attitudes and behaviors and *not* affect decision-making behavior.

The recruitment of some non-upper-class individuals to elite positions may be essential to society, because these individuals bring new and different perspectives to societal problems. Sociologist Suzanne Keller speaks of "two irreconcilable tendencies in social life—the need for order and the need for change":

> If the social leadership becomes so conservative as to be immune to new ideas and social developments, the pressure for unfulfilled needs mounts until that leadership declines, resigns, or is violently displaced. If it is so receptive to the new as to neglect established traditions, social continuity is endangered.[13]

Thus, we would expect to find some recruitment of non-upper-class individuals to elite positions even in an essentially hierarchical society. The question remains, *how much* opportunity exists in America for middle- and lower-class individuals to climb to the top?

## GETTING AHEAD IN THE SYSTEM

The American ideal is not a classless society, but rather a society in which individuals are free to get ahead on the basis of merit, talent, hard work, and good luck. Upward mobility is valued very highly in

[6] P. F. Lazarsfeld, B. Berelson, and H. Caudit, *The People's Choice* (New York: Columbia University Press, 1948). Also G. J. Selznick and Stephen Steinberg, "Social Class, Ideology, and Voting Preferences: An Analysis of the 1964 Presidential Election," in *Structural Social Inequality: A Reader in Comparative Social Stratification,* ed. Celia S. Heller (New York: Macmillan, 1969).

[7] Dennis H. Wrong, "Trends in Class Fertility in Western Nations," *The Canadian Journal of Economics and Political Science,* 24, No. 2 (May 1958), 216–229.

[8] R. R. Scars, E. MacCoby, and H. Levin, *Patterns of Child Rearing* (New York: Harper & Row, 1957).

[9] Herbert H. Hyman, "The Value Systems of Different Classes: A Social Psychological Contribution to the Analysis of Stratification," in *Readings on Social Stratification,* ed. Melvin M. Tumin (Englewood Cliffs, N.J.: Prentice-Hall, Inc., 1970), pp. 186–203.

[10] Alex Inkeles, "Class and Happiness," in Tumin, *Readings on Social Stratification,* pp. 180–186.

[11] I. M. Moriyama and L. Guralnick, "Occupational and Social Class Differences in Mortality," in Tumin, *Readings on Social Stratification,* pp. 170–178.

[12] J. S. Bruner and L. Postman, "Symbolic Value as an Organizing Factor in Perception," *Journal of Social Psychology,* 27, (1948), 203–208.

[13] Suzanne Keller, *Beyond the Ruling Class: Strategic Elites in Modern Society* (New York: Random House, 1968), p. 172.

TABLE 7-1    Social Mobility: Occupational Mobility of Sons in
Relation to Fathers by Educational Level

|  | Upward | Stable | Downward |
|---|---|---|---|
| Total | 54% | 11% | 35% |
| College | 69 | 17 | 14 |
| High School | 49 | 6 | 45 |
| Some High School | 52 | 12 | 36 |
| Grade School | 48 | 11 | 41 |

Source: Derived from Chicago Labor Mobility Sample figures reported by Otis Dudley Duncan and Robert W. Hodge, "Education and
Occupational Mobility," *American Journal of Sociology*, 79 (May 1963),
629–644.

American culture. The nation is portrayed in its own literature as a
"land of opportunity" where individuals can better themselves if they
work at it.

And, indeed, there is a great deal of upward social mobility in
America. Research on social mobility reveals that every major occupational category contains a majority of individuals whose fathers followed
other occupations. The results of a typical study of social mobility are
shown in Table 7–1. These figures suggest that very few sons have occupations with the same prestige as their fathers. Table 7–1 shows that
on average 54 percent of sons have jobs with higher prestige than their
fathers, while only 35 percent have jobs with lower prestige. There is
more upward mobility than downward mobility in the American system,
a phenomenon that can be attributed to an economic growth that has
in reality permitted upward mobility for successive generations of
Americans.

Does this evidence of general social mobility tell us much about
opportunities for getting to the *top?* Not really. There are several important reservations concerning this generally rosy picture of opportunity and mobility in America.

Most social mobility occurs within a very narrow range of occupations. Few individuals start life on the bottom rung of the social ladder
and climb all the way to the top in their lifetime. Most upward mobility
occurs step by step—from unskilled to skilled labor, from clerk to manager, from small businessman to professional, and so forth.

In summary, although there is a great deal of social mobility in
America, we can expect a majority of the individuals at the top to be
recruited from the upper social classes. Even those who have experienced
considerable upward mobility are likely to have risen from middle- or
upper-middle-class families rather than working-class families.

What are the social class origins of the nation's elite? Determining this from biographical information is a subjective task—there are no hard-and-fast rules. Sociologist G. William Domhoff suggests the following major indicators of "upper-class" origin:

1. Parents or wife's parents listed in the Social Register
2. Attendance at a private prestigious prep school
3. Membership in an upper-class club

Domhoff emphasizes the social-psychological, symbolic indicators of upper social class. Our own bias toward the institutional basis of power suggests additional indicators of "upper-class" origin:

4. Parent an officer or director of a major industrial corporation, bank, insurance company, or public utility
5. Parent a high government official or general in military service
6. Parent an attorney in a top law firm; a newspaper owner or director; or a president or trustee of a university, foundation, major civic or cultural association

Note that this is a very restricted definition of "upper-class"—one that would include less than 1 percent of the total population of the United States.

"Upper-middle-class" origin is indicated by a person's private school education, or college or university attendance. Today about 21 percent of the nation's population is "upper-middle-class" by this definition. (An even smaller percentage of the general population was "upper middle class" at the time present-day elites were of college age). Lower-middle- or lower-class origin according to our definition is indicated by the absence of any college or university education.[14] About 79 percent of the nation's population fits this definition of lower-middle and lower class. Our biographical information did not permit us to make any distinction between lower middle class and lower class.

The results of our investigations into the social backgrounds of our elite are shown in Table 7–2. By our estimate, 30 percent of the *corporate* elite are "upper-class" in origin as we have defined it. Approximately 59 percent are "upper-middle-class"; 3 percent are lower-middle or lower-class; and 8 percent are not classifiable. Note that governmental elites are somewhat less "upper-class" in social origin than corporate elites. Military elites were distinctly *not* "upper-class" in origin.

[14] U.S. Bureau of the Census, *Statistical Abstract of the United States,* 1974 (Washington, D.C.: Government Printing Office, 1975), p. 116.

TABLE 7–2   Social Origins of the People at the Top

| Social Origin | Corporate | Public Interest | | | | | Governmental | |
| | All | Law | Found. | Educ. | Civic | Media | Domestic | Military |
|---|---|---|---|---|---|---|---|---|
| Upper Class | 30 | 35 | 42 | 25 | 40 | 30 | 25 | 10 |
| Middle Class | 59 | 53 | 52 | 66 | 53 | 59 | 61 | 70 |
| Lower Class | 3 | 2 | 0 | 1 | 0 | 3 | 5 | 15 |
| Not Classified | 8 | 9 | 6 | 8 | 7 | 8 | 9 | 5 |

(Indeed, if we dropped the criterion of "parent a general," in our definition of upper class, none of our military elites would be "upper class.")

Combining all of our elites, and using the definitions of "upper class" and "upper middle class" suggested above, produces the recruitment picture shown in Figure 7–1.

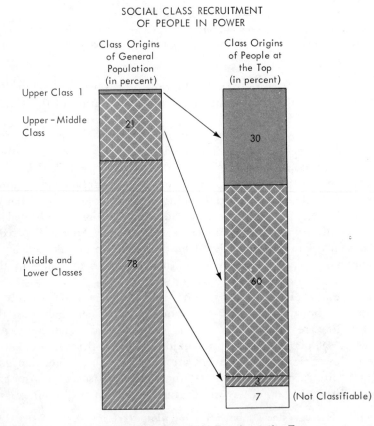

SOCIAL CLASS RECRUITMENT
OF PEOPLE IN POWER

FIGURE 7–1   Social-Class Recruitment of People at the Top

## SOCIAL CHARACTERISTICS OF INSTITUTIONAL LEADERS

What do we know about the people who occupy authoritative positions in American society? There are a number of excellent studies of the social backgrounds of political decision makers,[15] federal government executives,[16] military officers,[17] and corporate executives.[18] These studies consistently show that top institutional leaders are *atypical* of the American public. They are recruited from the well-educated, prestigiously employed, older, affluent, urban, white, Anglo-Saxon, upper- and upper-middle-class male populations of the nation. We expected our top institutional elites to conform to the pattern, and we were not at all disappointed (see Table 7–3).

*Age.* The average age of all the corporate leaders identified in our study is 61. Leaders in foundations, law, education, and civic and cultural organizations are slightly older—average age 64. Top positions in the governmental sector are filled by slightly younger people. A new presidential administration will bring in somewhat younger leaders in its first year. But these same individuals will grow older, of course, in office, so that an average age of 58 is representative of governmental elites.

*Sex.* The feminine sector of the population is seriously underrepresented at the top of America's institutional structure. Male dominance in top positions is nearly complete in the corporate world. The same is true in government; one woman served in the Ford cabinet and two women serve in the Carter cabinet. No women serve as chairpersons of any of the standing committees of the House or Senate; none serve as members of the Supreme Court, the Council of Economic Advisers, or the Federal Reserve Board. Only in civic and cultural affairs, education, and foundations are women found in significant numbers among the top position-holders.

*Education.* Nearly all our top leaders are college-educated, and more than half hold advanced degrees. Some 25.8 percent hold law degrees and 23.8 percent advanced academic or professional degrees. (These are earned degrees only; there are a host of honorary degrees that were

[15] Donald R. Matthews, *The Social Background of Political Decision-makers* (New York: Doubleday & Co., 1954).

[16] David T. Stanley, Dean E. Mann, and Jameson W. Doig, *Men Who Govern* (Washington: The Brookings Institution, 1967).

[17] Morris Janowitz, *The Professional Soldier* (New York: Free Press, 1960).

[18] Lloyd Warner and James C. Abegglen, *Big Business Leaders in America* (New York: Harper & Row, 1955).

**TABLE 7-3  Social Characteristics of Corporate, Governmental, and Public Interest Elites**

| | Corporate | Public Interest | | | | | Governmental | |
| | All | Law | Found. | Educ. | Civic | Media | Domestic | Military |
|---|---|---|---|---|---|---|---|---|
| Average age | 61.0 | 65 | 64 | 66 | 64 | | 58 | 56 |
| Female percentage | 0.3 | 0 | 6.2 | 8.5 | 10.5 | 0.5 | 0.4 | 0 |
| Schools | | | | | | | | |
| Public | 81.8 | 70.2 | 76.8 | 68.5 | 73.2 | 70.9 | 90.9 | 92.0 |
| Private | 7.0 | 8.8 | 7.1 | 13.2 | 8.8 | 12.8 | 3.0 | 3.0 |
| Prestigious * | 11.2 | 21.0 | 16.1 | 18.3 | 18.0 | 16.2 | 6.1 | 5.0 |
| Colleges | | | | | | | | |
| Public | 31.8 | 10.5 | 24.6 | 4.0 | 17.5 | 36.5 | 35.5 | 30.0 ‡ |
| Private | 13.3 | 5.6 | 6.7 | 0 | 16.5 | 15.7 | 21.0 | 2.0 |
| Prestigious † | 55.0 | 83.9 | 68.6 | 96.0 | 66.0 | 47.8 | 43.5 | 22.0 |
| Education | | | | | | | | |
| College educated | 90.1 | 100.0 | 88.0 | 96.5 | 90.2 | 85.5 | 88.3 | 96.0 |
| Advanced degree | 49.2 | 100.0 | 62.0 | 62.5 | 55.8 | 56.5 | 70.5 | 38.0 |
| Urban percent | 89.0 | 88.5 | 87.9 | 84.9 | 84.8 | | 69.7 | 52.8 |

* Andover, Buckley, Cate, Catlin, Choate, Cranbrook, Country Day, Deerfield, Episcopal, Exeter, Gilman, Groton, Hill, Hotchkiss, Kingswood, Kent, Lakeside, Lawrenceville, Lincoln, Loomis, Middlesex, Milton, St. Andrew's, St. Christopher's, St. George's, St. Mark's, St. Paul's, Shattuck, Taft, Thatcher, Webb, Westminister, Woodbury Forest.

† Harvard, Yale, Chicago, Stanford, Columbia, M.I.T., Cornell, Northwestern, Princeton, Johns Hopkins, Pennsylvania, and Dartmouth.

‡ U.S. Military Academy (West Point) and U.S. Naval Academy (Annapolis) account for an additional 46.0 percent.

not counted.) Governmental leaders were found to be somewhat more likely to hold advanced degrees than were corporate leaders.

A glance at the pre-collegiate education of our top elites reveals that about 18 percent of the corporate leaders and 10 percent of the governmental leaders attended private school. Perhaps the more surprising fact is that 11 percent of corporate leaders and 6 percent of the governmental leaders attended one of the 30 "name" prep schools in America. When these individuals were attending school, only 6 or 7 percent of the population of the nation attended private school at all. Needless to say, only an infinitesimal proportion of the population had the benefit of education at a prestigious "name" prep school. What is even more impressive is the fact that 55 percent of the corporate leaders and 44 percent of the governmental leaders are graduates of 12 heavily endowed "name" private universities—Harvard, Yale, Chicago, Stanford, Columbia,, M.I.T., Cornell, Northwestern, Princeton, Johns Hopkins, Pennsylvania, and Dartmouth. Elites in America are notably Ivy League.

*Urban.* Most of our top leaders were urban dwellers. Governmental leaders (notably congressmen) are somewhat more likely to be drawn from rural areas than are leaders in business, finance, and law, but fewer than one-third of the key government posts in our study were found to be filled by individuals from rural areas.

These social background characteristics suggest again a slight tendency for corporate elites to be more "upper-class" in origin than government elites. Among governmental leaders, a somewhat lower proportion attended private schools, and there were fewer Ivy Leaguers. The study showed a slight tendency for governmental leaders to have had more advanced professional education, however, and more governmental leaders were seen to come from rural backgrounds.

### BLACKS AT THE TOP

There are very few blacks in positions of power in America. In 1970, we were able to identify only two blacks in 5000 positions of authority in top-ranked institutions. Both were in government: one was Thurgood Marshall, associate justice of the Supreme Court, former solicitor general of the United States, and former director of the Legal Defense and Educational Fund of the NAACP; the other was James Farmer, assistant secretary of HEW and former national director of the Congress of Racial Equality. We were unable to identify any blacks in top institutional positions in industry, banking, communications and utilities, insurance, or law, although it is possible that some may have escaped identification in our biographical search.

However, the new movement toward "corporate responsibility" has resulted in some recent appointments of blacks to top corporate boards. Illustrative of blacks who have recently won positions at the top of the corporate structure are:

*Vernon Jordan.* Executive director of the National Urban League. A graduate of DePauw University and Howard University Law School. He began his career in civil rights affairs as the Georgia field secretary of the NAACP in the early 1960s, and later became director of the Voter Education Project of the Southern Regional Council, leading black voter registration drives in the South. He served briefly as executive director of the United Negro College Fund before becoming head of the National Urban League in 1972. In recent years he has accepted directorships of Bankers Trust of New York, Celanese Corporation, J. C. Penney Co., and the Xerox Corporation. He is also a director of the Rockefeller Foundation.

*Vivian W. Henderson.* President of Clark College, Atlanta. A graduate of predominantly black North Carolina Central University who earned a Ph. D in economics at the University of Iowa. He became chairman of the department of economics at Fisk University and later (1965) president of predominantly black Clark College. He served on the Southern Regional Council in the 1960s. In recent years he has been appointed a director of Citizen and Southern Bank and the Bendix Corporation, and a trustee of the Ford Foundation.

*Franklin A. Thomas.* President of the Bedford Stuyvesant Restoration Corporation in New York. He received his B.A. and law degree from Columbia University, and served as Deputy Police Commissioner under New York's mayor John Lindsay. He is now a director of Citicorp, Columbia Broadcasting System, New York Telephone, Cummins Engine, and New York Life Insurance. He is also a director of the Carnegie Corporation, Lincoln Center for the Performing Arts, and the Urban Institute.

Yet in spite of these recent appointments, it remains true that very few blacks have acquired high positions in industry, finance, the mass media, the foundations, or leading civic and cultural organizations. In 1976, we estimate that there were no more than 15 blacks in the 5,000 top positions studied. No blacks have ever been *presidents* of any of the organizations studied—the industrial corporations, banks, utilities, communication networks, foundations, prestigious universities, or top civic and cultural organizations. Black leadership has been confined to a small number of board members.

One black served in the Ford cabinet (Secretary of Transportation William Coleman), and one black serves in the Carter cabinet:

*Patricia Roberts Harris.* Secretary of Housing and Urban Development. Ms. Harris is the daughter of a railroad dining car waiter and a graduate of Howard University (B.A., 1945). She received a law degree from George Washington University in 1960. She began her career as a YWCA director in Chicago and later as executive director of Delta Sigma Theta, a national black sorority. She was a delegate to the Democratic National Convention in 1964, and seconded the nomination of Lyndon Johnson; President Johnson appointed her Ambassador to Luxembourg (1965–67). She returned to a brief, troubled tenure as dean of Howard University Law School and resigned during student protests. She became a law partner of Sargent Shriver (Kennedy brother-in-law) and a prominent Washington attorney. She was appointed a director of IBM, Chase Manhattan, and Scott Paper Co. She is a member of the Council on Foreign Relations and the NAACP Legal Defense Fund.

President Carter's appointment of Georgia representative Andrew Young as Ambassador to the United Nations was widely heralded as a major breakthrough for blacks in high office. Young was an early member of Martin Luther King, Jr.'s Southern Christian Leadership Conference; Young was beaten and jailed in Birmingham in 1963 with King. Young helped to bring King's father and widow into Carter's camp during the campaign, and helped Carter survive the "ethnic purity" remark which might have alienated his black political support. But the U.N. ambassadorship is a traditional dumping ground for political figures who are too important to be ignored but who carry little influence with the president (for example, Adlai Stevenson, Daniel Patrick Moynihan, William Scranton). The surprise is that the handsome, articulate Young accepted this largely ceremonial position.

The first black four-star general in the armed forces of the United States was appointed in 1975—Air Force General Daniel "Chappie" James, Jr. General James, the highest ranking black man in American military history, graduated from Tuskegee Institute in Alabama and joined the Army Air Corps in 1943. He flew 101 combat missions in Korea and 87 in Vietnam. In his public statements he emphasizes the opportunities that have opened for blacks in recent years, particularly in the armed forces.

## WOMEN AT THE TOP

Women now comprise about 40 percent of the labor force.[19] But most of these women are secretaries (12 percent), cooks and household domestics (6 percent), clerks in stores (5 percent), bookkeepers (4 percent), teachers (4 percent), and waitresses (3 percent). Only 3 percent of the female labor force are listed as "managers and administrators." Men outnumber women in these jobs by more than five to one. Few women are in the ranks of top leadership in corporations, banks, government, television networks, or Wall Street or Washington law firms.

[19] U.S. Bureau of the Census, *Statistical Abstract of the United States, 1974* (Washington, D.C.: Government Printing Office, 1975), pp. 354–355.

In 1972, *Fortune* magazine surveyed the 1000 largest industrial corporations and the 300 largest nonindustrial businesses and acquired lists of names of officers and directors who earned $30,000 or more. Of some 6,500 names received, *only 11 were women!* [20] To add further to this portrait of male dominance, *Fortune's* investigations of these women revealed that three were co-founders of corporations with their husbands, and four others inherited large blocks of stock in their corporations. Only two moved up the corporate hierarchy without family sponsorship. [21]

The few women at the top deserve closer observation. Our own list of top institutional leaders includes:

*Katherine Graham.* Owner of the *Washington Post* and *Newsweek* magazine. (See Chapter 4, pp. 102–3, "Katherine Graham: The Most Powerful Woman in America.")

*Patricia Roberts Harris.* Secretary of Housing and Urban Development. (See pp. 173–75, "Blacks at the Top.")

*Catherine B. Cleary.* President and director of First Wisconsin Trust. Cleary is a single, up-the-organization manager; she received her B.A. from the University of Chicago in 1937, and a law degree from the University of Wisconsin. Her career centered on First Wisconsin Trust (ranked number 32 in the nation). She served as Assistant Treasurer of the United States in the Eisenhower Administration. In recent years she has accepted directorships of General Motors, AT&T, Kraft Co., and Northwestern Mutual Life Insurance. She has appointed women to top posts at First Wisconsin, but she reportedly has little interest in "women's liberation." "We've gone beyond the point where we're looking for women just because they are women."

*Juanita Morris Kreps.* Secretary of Commerce. Ms. Kreps worked her way through tiny Berea College, Kentucky, in the late 1930s and later earned a Ph.D in economics from Duke University. She taught at a number of universities before returning to Duke as a professor of economics. She authored several books in economics (including *Sex in the Marketplace: American Women at Work*) and became vice-president of Duke in 1973. When leading corporations decided to add some women to their boards in the early 1970s, Ms. Kreps' work as an economist and educator brought her to the attention of the top elites. She was appointed to the boards of

[20] Catherine Cleary, First Wisconsin Trust; Dorothy Chandler, Times Mirror Co.; Stella Russell, Norton Simon Co.; Ruth Handler, Mattel Toys (inventor of Barbie Dolls); Olive Ann Beech, Beech Aircraft (wife of company president and founder); Katherine Graham, *Washington Post* and *Newsweek*; Bernice Lavin, Alberto Culver (wife of company president and founder); Vera Neuman, Vera Co.; Tillie Lewis, Ogden Corp.; Mala Rubinstein, Helena Rubinstein, Inc. (niece of deceased founder); Rose Cook Sunall, Bluebird, Inc. See Wyndham Robertson, "The Highest Ranking Women in Big Business," *Fortune* (April 1973), pp. 81–89.

[21] Catherine Cleary and Stella Russell.